St. Thomas Aquinas

JACQUES MARITAIN

ST.

THOMAS AQUINAS

Meridian Books, Inc.
New York

ACKNOWLEDGMENT

The translation of the encyclical *Aeterni Patris* of Leo XIII, as well as the Introduction, Summary, and Variant Readings to the encyclical, are reprinted from *The Church Speaks to the Modern World* by Etienne Gilson, published by Doubleday & Company, Inc. (Image Books), copyright 1954 by Doubleday & Company, Inc. Reprinted by permission of the publishers.

The translation of the encyclical *Humani Generis* of Leo XIII is reprinted by permission of the National Catholic Welfare Conference.

First edition of Saint Thomas Aquinas, *translated by J. F. Scanlan, published by Sheed & Ward, 1931*

Meridian Edition newly translated and revised by Joseph W. Evans and Peter O'Reilly

First published October 1958
First printing September 1958

Library of Congress Catalog Card Number: 57-10837

Manufactured in the United States of America

JACQUES MARITAIN

Jacques Maritain was born in Paris in 1882. One of the major Christian thinkers in the world today, Maritain seeks, through the reconsideration of the philosophy of Saint Thomas Aquinas, to interpret anew the bases of modern thought. Since the war, Maritain has lived with his wife, the poet Raïssa Maritain, at their home in Princeton.

His works in English include: *The Degrees of Knowledge; True Humanism; Art and Scholasticism; Existence and the Existent; Creative Intuition in Art and Poetry; On the Philosophy of History;* and *Reflections on America.*

CONTENTS

CONTENTS

FOREWORD

The first edition of this book appeared in 1930. It was a kind of Thomist manifesto, especially directed to the French Catholic public. In those years following the First World War, a great effort—rendered possible by the work of some eminent thinkers in the previous generation—was undertaken by a group of philosophers and theologians to rediscover the basic insights and doctrine through which Thomas Aquinas brought perennial philosophy to a peak, and to make them emerge, from a school tradition restricted to the intellectual preparation of clerics, into the open and global compass of contemporary thought; in other words, to make them enter the general realm of culture. I do not say to make them *re-enter* this realm, for, to tell the truth, the decadent Middle Ages were unable to be true to the greatest medieval Doctor; and Thomas Aquinas' thought, while illumining the Church, had no opportunity, either in the last medieval centuries or in the baroque age, to manifest its potentialities in the general movement of culture. If it is to do so in our time, this, far from being a return to the past, will be a great historic novelty, and a genuinely modern achievement. Hence the urgency with which, in those years when it was a question of removing powerful obstacles that blocked the road, we endeavored to deliver the message of the Angelic Doctor to the modern mind.

To come back to the present book, I am aware of the fact that, by reason of my particular purpose and perspective in writing it, it departs from the general rule according to which a philosopher directs his words to any reader interested in the works of reason, and not especially to those who share in his religious faith. I am only too aware, also, of the youthful emphasis and rhetoric which I could not completely eliminate in revising my text, and which appear now and then in the expression of certain basic verities. These verities, to which I cling more than ever, and which are as valid today as they were a quarter of a century ago, are all that matters, and I hope that for their sake I shall be forgiven the defects in form and style which were just mentioned. Thus it is that when Mr. Arthur Cohen kindly proposed to reprint *Saint Thomas Aquinas* in Meridian Books, I was happy to avail myself of the opportunity of having a new, up-to-date edition and revised translation of *Le Docteur Angélique* appear. I thank him cordially, too, for the final touch he and Mrs. Tommye Murphy gave to the translation.

This new edition would not have been possible without the scholarly cooperation and the affectionate devotion of my friends the Reverend Father Peter O'Reilly and Professor Joseph W. Evans. I am deeply indebted to them both for their new translation and for their complete recasting of the Appendices. These Appendices (which are now four in number) have particular importance in the volume, on the one hand as regards the testimonials which the Popes, especially since the famous encyclical of Leo XIII, have given to the doctrine and philosophy of Thomas Aquinas, and, on the other hand, as regards the controversial question, which the labor of scholars is constantly elucidating, of the list and chronology of the works of Saint Thomas. The way in which Father O'Reilly, with the assistance of Dr. Evans, has made these Appendices complete and up-to-date, has vastly improved this new edition of my book.

As a small tribute of my gratitude I am happy to dedicate it to them.

JACQUES MARITAIN

Princeton
April 1958

PREFACE TO THE FIRST
FRENCH EDITION

This work is not an exposition of Thomist doctrine. Rather, it is an attempt to bring to light certain essential aspects of the personality and work of the Angelic Doctor. As much as of his past work, indeed even more than of it, I am speaking of his present and forever efficacious work. For it is not of a *medieval* Thomism, but of a lasting and *present* Thomism that I speak.

I wrote in the preface to *Antimoderne:* "It would be exceedingly naive to enter upon modern thought and to sympathize with all the good that there is in it without first attempting to discern its spiritual principles. . . . On the contrary, once this scrutiny has been completed, once the foundation-work which protects the specific character of our intellectual life has been assured, then—but only then—*can* we and *ought* we give free play to the *universalist* tendency, so admirably manifested in one like Saint Thomas Aquinas, which benevolently and peaceably draws Catholic thought to seek everywhere agreements rather than oppositions, fragments of truth rather than privations and deviations, to save and assume rather than destroy, to build up rather than break down. Assuredly work is not lacking for Catholics, and there is in such work something to try their spirit of initiative. For they are obliged to face a task of universal integration. . . ."

It is above all to this task of integration that contemporary Thomist philosophy will henceforth, we hope, apply its effort. It was necessary to begin by renewing the vital bonds which permit wisdom to *continue* among men, and by undoing the great errors which impeded this continuity. This critique of past error ought truly never cease; but it is toward the future that we are turned.

We have no illusions about the fact that such an enterprise has to be continued amid an environment of general frivolity. As regards Catholics, if it is true that too great a number have not been willing, even after fifty years, to comprehend the lessons of the Holy Spirit and of Rome, which asked them not to diminish a divine religion by imposing on it too human standards, how can one be surprised that too often also, in the face of that most difficult of all tasks—which however is theirs—of thinking the present world and moment in the light of eternal truths, they have refused to acquire, as Leo XIII exhorted them to do, the doctrinal equipment they needed from the Common Doctor of the Church. Thus it is not surprising that from the midst of an intelligentsia at once pious and shallow, the most insidious and the most lively opposition to Saint Thomas has appeared.

As to those regions where one believes himself to be free from the First Truth, what would be extraordinary is if Thomism were not there the object of strong aversion.

These enmities, however, can but encourage us to persevere the more. They show how much the Thomist renaissance inconveniences both a certain eclectic complacency, as well as all those who contemn

Christian culture. Already it has triumphed over many obstacles; one can no longer ignore it, one can no longer stifle it, and all over the world it attracts minds to its study. We know that the wisdom of Saint Thomas traverses the paths of the earth before the footsteps of God. The more the powers of illusion increase, the more those who love truth will feel themselves drawn toward the vast light of this wisdom: *ibi congregabuntur et aquilae.*[1] Our task is to pave a way toward it. This is why we have said and say again: *Vae mihi, si non thomistizavero.*[2]

If those who are scandalized by this sentence had done me the honor of reading with some attention, instead of indulging in convenient simplifications, they would perhaps have understood that it is not "for the tranquillity of my soul" but rather for the love of their souls that I thomistize; they would not allege that I am interested only in "declaring illegitimate" and "doing away with" the aspirations of our time, and they would not hold against me the very thing that I too am thinking, to wit, that "it is a matter of putting in order the abundance of those desires which the modern world engenders, and in order to accomplish this it is necessary to reckon with them." Finally they would realize my aim is not to "proclaim order" but rather, as long as my strength and voice hold out, to summon workers who under the direction of the Angelic Doctor will consecrate themselves to "making order" according to the truth. In the domain of philosophy this work was begun a long time ago; yet it was hardly begun, so vast is the work and so difficult to conduct. As for me, I feel I have as yet done nothing.

It is simply nonsense to interpret, as do other critics, "neo-Thomism" as a "panacea" proposed in order to dispense with intellectual effort and encourage immobility, or destined, in the words of yet another, to assure a feeling of social security; to pretend that for Thomists the *Summa Theologiae* is a "massive and even exclusive revelation" of all truth, etc. I confess some satisfaction in seeing the adversaries of a philosophy I love reduced to such obvious untruths.

Nonetheless, I am taking advantage of the occasion they furnish to declare again:

There is a Thomist philosophy; there is no neo-Thomist philosophy. I am not trying to include the past in the present, but to maintain in the *now* the presence of the eternal.

Thomism does not want to return to the Middle Ages. As I wrote in the preface to *Antimoderne*, "If I am anti-modern, it is not by personal taste, certainly, but because modern self-complacency, the offspring of the anti-Christian revolution, obliges me to be so by its spirit; because it itself makes opposition to the human patrimony its own distinctive characteristic, hates and despises the past and adores itself, and because I hate and despise this very hating and despising and this spiritual impurity; but if it is a matter of saving and assimilating all the riches of being which are accumulated in modern times, of desiring renewals, and of loving the effort of those who continue to pioneer and break new ground, then I wish nothing so much as to be ultra-modern. And in truth do not Christians beseech the Holy Spirit to renew the face of the earth? Are they not awaiting the life of the world to come? It is there that there will be something new, and for everyone. I love the art of the cathedrals, Giotto and Angelico. But I detest neo-Gothic and pre-Raphaelism. I know that the course of time is irreversible; much as I admire the era of Saint Louis, I do not therefore wish, according to the absurd desire that certain penetrating critics generously claim for me, to return to the Middle Ages. I hope to see restored, in a new world, and for the informing of a new matter, the spiritual principles and the eternal norms of which medieval civilization, in its better periods, presents us with but a particular historic realization, superior in quality, despite its enormous deficiencies, but definitely past."

Thomism claims to use reason to distinguish the true from the false; it does not wish to destroy but to purify modern thought, and to integrate everything true that has been discovered since the time of Saint Thomas. It is an essentially assimilative and unifying philosophy, the only one which attempts, across the centuries and continents, a work of continuity and universality. It is also the only one which, while rising to knowledge of the supra-sensible, first demands of experience a full adherence to the sensible real. It is its task to draw forth from the immense contributions of the experimental sciences, accumulated after four centuries, an authentic philosophy of nature—as, in quite another domain, to join the artistic treasure of modern times to a philosophy of art and beauty that is truly universal and at the same time comprehensive of the efforts of the present moment.[3]

Thomism is neither of the right nor of the left; it is not situated in space, but in the spirit.

Thomism is a wisdom. Between it and the particular forms of culture incessant vital exchanges ought to prevail, but it is in its essence rigorously independent of these particular forms. Thus Thomist philosophy possesses the most universal principles of esthetics, and yet one could not—this is very clear—speak of a specifically "Thomist" literary school, painting, novel, or poem. Thomist theology, also, incorporates the great principles of Christian politics—and yet one could not speak of a "Thomist" political party. The wisdom of Saint Thomas transcends every particularization. And in this it shares something of Catholicism itself. *Nolite tangere*. Catholicism is a religion, both universal and universalist, the true religion. Thomism is a philosophy and a theology. "Catholic" applied to something other than this religion, "Thomist" to something other than this philosophy and this theology, are no more than material designations, referring not to what derives essentially from Catholicism or from Thomism, but to the activity actually exercised, in a particular domain, by some Catholic or Thomist "subject." There is nothing we ought to dread more than having the truth, divine or human, judged according to our limitations and our errors.

To imagine Thomism as a garment which was worn in the thirteenth century and is worn no longer, as though the value of a metaphysics were a matter of time, is simply an illiterate way of thinking. Intelligence demands that we hold one philosophic system out of all others—if it is true—as alone valid. This need not obscure one's awareness that philosophic research is indefinitely progressive. (This progress is brought about in a different way for the experimental sciences; for the sciences are constantly controlled and rectified by empirical verifications. The price of the superiority of philosophy over science is that it can be developed in error. It is necessary, therefore, to distinguish two ledgers of its progress, according as it progresses *of itself* by virtue of the increases of truth due to the continuity of a constantly maintained effort in the line of the true, or according as it progresses *accidentally* by virtue of the increases of truth procured in fact by the endless multiplicity of devious attempts, which can advance in error only by draining from the true.)

It is no less childish to regard the value of a metaphysics as dependent on a social structure to be preserved or to be destroyed. Wisdom has other standards. The interpretations of history inspired by Marx or by Sorel, by the very fact that they consider material causality to be effectively at work in the human order, can indeed account for the success or failure of a philosophy in a certain social environment: they can say nothing of what is *formal* (genuinely distinctive and typical) in this philosophy. And when it is a question of a doctrine more or less outlined or prepared in the most ancient philosophic traditions of humanity, formed in the Hellenic society of the time of Aristotle, taken up and systematized in the feudal society of the days of Thomas Aquinas, and whose spirituality passes intact over the most divers ages, it is a particularly striking absurdity to see in it a "defense reaction" of the bourgeois society of our time, a society, moreover, based upon supreme principles which are the very opposite of the principles of Saint Thomas.

The philosophy of Saint Thomas is independent in itself of the data of faith: its principles and structure depend upon experience and reason alone.

While remaining, however, completely distinct from such data of faith, this philosophy is still in vital communication with the superior wisdoms of theology and contemplation. It is through its contact with these superior wisdoms, as with the intellectual life of the Church, that it receives the strength to maintain among men the purity and the universality which characterize it.

The truths which I have just recalled are, I admit, most elementary. Whatever use I may have made of italics, in lieu of billboard letters or illuminated signs, is, I think, insufficient to hold the attention of certain minds who are set against understanding. As for myself, when I explain to my contemporaries the necessity of enrolling in the school of Saint Thomas Aquinas, I know that I am there merely to say it to them, not to persuade them in spite of themselves. "He that heareth, let him hear: and he that forbeareth, let him forbear." [4]

There is, in the depths of the opposition to the present renaissance of the philosophy of Saint Thomas, a unique prejudice: one of my critics ingenuously allowed it to appear, when he spoke of that "author of the thirteenth century" whom one "is pleased to raise above history." The question is to know whether or not one is right in admitting that there is something *above history,* and that there can be supra-historical values. No! reply my critics. They are quite prepared to recognize that Thomas Aquinas was a great luminary, as great as one wishes, sublime, immense: but on condition that his light *was* and no longer is; on condition that nothing of Saint Thomas remains but what of him was able to pass, from wave to wave, into the flux of what succeeded him. What offends them, shocks and scandalizes them, is that one thinks that he persists always, that he, Thomas Aquinas, dominates history, that his light because it is spiritual, that his thought because it is true, remain, with their essential grandeur and their essential efficacy, today as in the time of Saint Louis. Immersing every reality, even the spiritual, in the flux of time, regarding the very substance of wisdom as essentially temporal and historical, they think that to admit any immutability compelling recognition is to obstruct time, to halt history, to solidify the very flux of succession; they do not see that the immutability of what wisdom has once acquired is not in time, but above it, and far from stopping history, accelerates its course and the progress of knowledge. Their philosophy, beneath its lively manner, is poverty itself, devoid of intellectuality, a basic materialism. What I affirm against it is that truth does not pass, does not flow away with history; that the spirit does not run out, that there are stabilities not of inertia, but of spirituality and of life; non-temporal values; eternal acquisitions; that time is in the eternal as a piece of gold clasped in a hand; and that the intellect is above time.

January 1930

chapelle, accustom us to observe time. To individuals, in reality the very fact of succession they
not and that the immobility of what a datum has
acquired is not to cling, but above it, and far from
stopping history, accelerate its course and the progress
of knowledge. Their philosophy beneath its livery
appears, is where itself, devoid of intellectuality, a
pure materialism. What I admit against it is that I do
not deny that, does not flow away, with their cry that
that spirit does not run, that there are no abolition
not of inertia, but of spirituality and of time itself;
temporal values eternal acquisitions; that time is to
the eternal as a phenomenon placed to a head, and
that the problem is above time.

January 1890.

THE SAINT

> *"Friar Giacomo di Viterbo, Arch-*
> *bishop of Naples, often said to me*
> *that he believed, in accordance*
> *with the Faith and the Holy Spirit,*
> *that our Savior had sent, as doctor*
> *of truth to illuminate the world and*
> *the universal Church, first the apos-*
> *tle Paul, then Augustine, and finally*
> *in these latest days Friar Thomas,*
> *whom, he believed, no one would*
> *succeed till the end of the world."*
> (Testimony of Bartolommeo di
> Capua at the hearing of the case
> for the canonization of Saint
> Thomas, August 8, 1319.)

Early in the year 1225 (the most probable date),[1]
Thomas, the seventh and last son of Count Landulf
of Aquino and Theodora of Theate, was born in a
castle at Roccasecca, near Naples. His father belonged
to the Lombard nobility; his paternal grandmother,
Francesca di Suabia, was a sister of Frederick Bar-
barossa; his mother was descended from Norman
nobility. The complementary gifts of the North and the
South, transmitted through a double lineage of nobility, met in this infant to compose a marvelously
tempered body, chosen to become the instrument of
a preeminent intelligence and of wisdom the maker of

unity. He came into the world at the beginning of
a century in which Christian civilization—already
threatened and on the verge of collapse—was in the
process of recovering itself in order to bring forth its
best fruits. The thirteenth century was marked by
immense agitations, dominated in spite of everything
by the flame of the spirit—war, politics, poetry,
religion, the struggle between Pope and Emperor,
the power of feudalism and the power of the Church,
the arrogance of the strong, the virtues of the saints.
He was born at the most vigorously and most violently
human moment of medieval humanity. His mother,
who was to do everything to prevent him from following the will of God, was a woman of great virtue and
self-denial. And while his brothers, rather than see him
a mendicant religious, would not hesitate to provoke
him to mortal sin, his sister Theodora, Countess of
San Severino, was to spend her life in works of mercy
and penance, and leave behind her a memory of
sanctity.

One day, as his nurse was going to bathe him, the
little Tommaso grasped a piece of parchment which no
amount of pleading would convince him to give up.
He wept so copiously that it was necessary to bathe
him with his hand closed. His mother came and,
despite his crying and screaming, opened the hand
by force: on the piece of parchment the *Hail Mary*
was written.

At the age of five he was placed as an oblate in the
abbey of Monte Cassino. There he had but one question on his lips: WHAT IS GOD?

This silent child thought only of study and piety;
he desired only to give himself to God. What could be

simpler? He would be a Benedictine. Providence itself intervened to confirm the wise decision of his parents. By offering him in 1230 to the abbey which he had besieged and ravaged the year before with the armies of Frederick II, the Count of Aquino sealed his peace with the monks and contrived for the future an alliance with them advantageous to all concerned— even to the material interests of the Count, for the powerful monastery had rich benefices; and Thomas would be Abbot. He was bound to be, for this Benedictine vocation was a sort of state affair, wherein God, the Emperor, and the family were all benefited.

"No," said Thomas. "I will be a Preacher."

He was fifteen or sixteen years old. At fourteen, political events had obliged his father to withdraw him from Monte Cassino, which had once again been ruined by Frederick II. The child therefore put aside his oblate's habit and was sent to Naples to complete his studies at its Faculty of Arts, where he quickly won the admiration of all. The Dominicans, founded some twenty years before, had in 1231 established in the town a public school of theology, incorporated into the University. Thomas became acquainted with them there. Although he was to retain throughout his life great love for the observance of Saint Benedict and the stamp of Benedictine spirituality was not to be obliterated from his heart, it became a matter of obeying the secret voice which calls each one by name—and this silent one was listening to God. An indomitable strength of soul is at the root of his sanctity.

Vocation is a supernatural mystery. All the human explanations that one can bring forth deal only with its accessory aspects, which are insignificant in their bearing on its essential motive. Was it in order to have a teaching position, or in order to devote himself to a more active life, that Thomas wanted to become a Dominican? or to escape the worldly cares and ambitions of grandeur which his family would have tried still to heap upon him, had he taken the habit of Saint Benedict? Was it even out of love for the poverty of the mendicant Friars, or out of pity for the souls to whom the word of the Lord had not been preached, or in reaction against the abuses which earthly possessions had spread amongst the black monks, or from an attraction to a new Order whose conquering youth and extremely bold ideal (religious life informing intellectual activity itself, so as to make of each an apostolic person, transmitting to others what he himself had contemplated) responded exactly to the needs of the time? All this remains secondary. He had asked: What is God? He had to find the answer, to gather together the principles of wisdom in the unity of a doctrine destined ever to grow.

A privileged moment of history rendered possible such a synthesis. Yesterday Christian thought was not yet ripe, tomorrow it will begin to decay. Before the grace of Christ and the Cross, and the burden of nature and the world, were to share divided man for centuries, there was yet time for the baptized intelligence to assume and reconcile all in the light of Him who is. This work of strength, which from a fleeting point of duration—a measure of man, a work of twenty-three years—will govern all time to come, this was to be accomplished by Thomas Aquinas. He is sent for the salvation of the intellect; it is for this that he must embrace the apostolic life. There is his mission; woe to him if he fails it. The vast future hidden in the will of God pressed upon his soul, reached him under the form of a very simple, irresistibly effective command.

Later his family, severely tried after their split with the Emperor, whom Innocent IV had deposed,[2] would in vain call him to their aid, and the Pope offer him (with permission to keep the habit of his Order) the abbacy of Monte Cassino—later the see of Naples. He would not yield. It was at the time a question of ignoring the will of his father and mother, of braving the wrath of his own people, who were not persons of slight vigor or easily placated. As he was to write later, "When parents are not in such want that they have a great need of the services of their children, the children can enter into religious life without the consent of their parents and even against their expressed will, because, after having passed the age of puberty, any free man has the right to dispose of himself in the choice of a state of life, above all if it is a matter of the service of God; it is better to obey the Father of spirits, in order that we may live, than the parents of our flesh." [3]

Guided and confirmed in his vocation by the old Friar Giovanni di San Giuliano, Thomas received the habit in the spring of the year 1244, in all likelihood from the hands of the Master General, John the Teuton, who was then visiting Naples. He was almost twenty years old. His father had died some months before. But the Countess Theodora had to show that the store of family authority, transmitted to her charge, would be maintained without fail.

As soon as she had been informed of the event, she dispatched a special messenger to those of her sons who were with the Emperor at the camp at Acquapendente, in Tuscany; and enjoined them, in the name of her maternal blessing, to take in hand and send back to her under secure guard their young brother, whom the Preachers were having flee the realm. Indeed, in order to remove him from the resentment of his people, as well as to assure the theological development of this arts student who now knew as much as his masters, John the Teuton had decided to take him away at once to the *studium generale* at Paris, where he himself was going. The Master General, the novice and three other Friars were making their way on foot; they had passed through Rome, and had reached Tuscany. As they sat there near a fountain, armed men assailed them; Thomas' brothers grabbed hold of him and pulled him away from those other brothers whom he had chosen for himself. And he wrapped himself so tightly in his habit that it was impossible to strip him of it; they forced him onto a horse[4] and brought him to Roccasecca, where the Countess Theodora awaited her son.

One of Thomas' brothers, Raynaldo, the poet—a favorite of the Emperor up to the time the Emperor was to have him put to death—was in command of the little troop. After some days of travel they stopped at the fortress of Monte San Giovanni; this fief of the Aquinas family was two or three hours from Roccasecca. Is it there, or at Roccasecca itself, that the famous incident of the temptation ought to be placed, from which Thomas came forth girded with a cincture by the angels? Raynaldo, an upright and honorable man in the eyes of the world, but one who lived according to the world, had concocted this supreme attack on what he considered the misguided enthusiasm of his younger brother. One knows the story: the "pretty young girl, with all the charms of the temptress," introduced into the room where he was sleeping; and how he leapt up, grabbed hold of a flaming firebrand, chased her out, and traced the sign of the cross on the door with the brand. And from that time on, by an angelic grace, he was never to experience any impulse of the flesh.

For a little more than a year he was held captive at Roccasecca, where despite scenes and remonstrances he kept the habit and the observances of his Order, read the Bible and the Master of the Sentences,[5] instructed his sisters in sacred letters, and converted his eldest sister, Marotta, to Saint Benedict, when she tried to turn him away from Saint Dominic. Tommaso did so well that in the end his mother herself aided him, it is said, to get around the surveillance of his brothers and escape. The chroniclers relate that he fled through a window, like Saint Paul of old. Actually, it seems likely that his liberation had been decided upon by his family, whose political fortune was in danger, and against whom the Master General John the Teuton had filed a complaint before Innocent IV.

From Naples he was again sent to Paris, to the convent of Saint-Jacques, where he made his novitiate and remained nearly three years. Albert the Great was teaching there at the time; when the time came for him to be sent to Cologne, Friar Thomas accompanied him there; it was at Cologne, under the direction of that tremendous genius, that the "big dumb ox of Sicily" completed his studies and became a theologian.

At the end of four years, he left Cologne, assigned, on the recommendation of Master Albert, to the convent of Saint-Jacques, to teach there as *biblical bachelor* (1252-1254) and *sententiary bachelor* (1254-1256). The commentary on the four books of the Sentences was composed in this period, as also the *De ente et essentia*, and probably the commentary on the *Divine Names* of the pseudo-Dionysius.[6] At the age of thirty-one—four years earlier than the limit fixed by university legislation, and thanks to a dispensation granted by the Pope—he was promoted to the mastership in theology, at the same time as his friend Friar Bonaventure.

The modern world is blasé; in it all values are made equal, jaded by use. The term master in theology evokes in us only a degree of some sort, and the usual image of the persons who have worn the doctor's cap with more or less success. Through the fault of the doctors, a civilization that has known them to excess holds the doctorate, if not doctrine, as a paltry thing. The very wise simplicity of the thirteenth century saw in the mastership all that such a charge signified *de jure*, and according to its essential form; the gaze of a Saint Thomas penetrated to the depths the spiritual reality of the mastership. Master in theology, he has in the name of the Church the mission of engendering sacred wisdom in the intellects of those who hear him; from then on he is entirely at their service to cooperate with the living work which is going on in them; he has power over the truth in souls, terrible power for which he will be held accountable, for "to raise a doubt and not resolve it is the same as to concede it; it is to open a cistern and not cover it again."[7] Were it not for the grace of God, there would have been cause to faint for fear. Friar Thomas beseeched God, with tears, to grant him the gifts required to bear the responsibility of Master. "Lord," he prayed, "save me, for truths are disappearing from amongst the children of men." He prayed and wept for a long time; finally he fell asleep.—Friar Thomas, why these prayers and these tears?—Because I am being compelled to assume the task of Master, and I am lacking the necessary knowledge. I do not even know what theme to develop for my reception.—Accept in peace the charge of Master; God is with you. And for your inaugural lecture, develop only these words: "He watereth the hills from his lofty dwelling: the earth shall be filled with the fruit of thy works." [8] The text of that lecture of Saint Thomas has been found. In it he describes the grandeur of the teaching office, and the economy of the communication of wisdom. "God communicates it by his own power; it is with his own wisdom that He watereth the hills. Doctors, on the contrary, communicate it only by a ministerial power, so that the fruit of the hills is to be attributed not to the hills but to the works of God."

Friar Thomas taught every day on the mountain Sainte-Geneviève, at the convent of Saint-Jacques, in one of the two chairs of theology reserved for the Preachers, and which were incorporated into the University of Paris. Seated before him on the straw listening to his lectures were all the religious present in the convent—for no one was excused from the theology course—and a great number of students from outside: men trained in dialectic, a number of whom had already taught in the Faculty of Arts. On the days on which solemn disputations were held, the dignitaries of the University and the bishop himself attended the debate.

Immediately he became famous. Everyone rushed to his lectures. Moreover, he arrived in full battle array, for error was multiplying. He had to confront it on all sides, and first in the attack of Guillaume de Saint-Amour and the seculars, who denied the mendicant Friars the right to teach and presented these

"false apostles" ever on the move, these "uncommis-
sioned adventurers," as the precursors of Antichrist.
There was a first debate on academic freedom, one of
extreme importance, one in which the very existence
of the two new Orders, Preachers and Minors, was at
stake, and in which was already noticeable the vanity
of that University of Paris which was soon to pass itself off as the light of the world, before dishonoring
itself by condemning Joan of Arc. For a moment Rome
seemed won over to the cause of the seculars; she
abolished the privileges of the religious, then thought
the better of it. Guillaume de Saint-Amour and the
secular Masters, furious at this reversal, wrote their
collective pamphlet, *On the Dangers of the Present
Time*. Friar Thomas refuted them with his treatise
Contra impugnantes (1257). Guillaume's book was
condemned and burnt in the court of Rome, and he
himself was banished from France by Saint Louis.

After three years of theological teaching at Paris
as Master (at this time he wrote the commentaries
on the *De Trinitate* and on the *De Hebdomadibus* of
Boethius, on *Isaias* and on *St. Matthew*, the disputed
questions *De Veritate*, the first *Quaestiones Quodlibetales*, and the greater part of the *Summa Contra
Gentiles*), Friar Thomas returned to Italy in 1259, for
the summer vacation (June 29). He was to remain
there nine years, first at the papal court in Anagni and
in Orvieto, then at Rome in the convent of Santa
Sabina, then again at the Curia in Viterbo. The popes
never ceased to encourage him. Immediately Alexander
IV sensed his genius. Urban IV and Clement IV were
likewise to show their predilection for him. With
the splendor, the clarity of an extraordinary privilege

of predestination, the mission received from the visible head thus sanctioned immediately the spirit invisibly received—and the spirit was equal to the mission. Thomas Aquinas conducted his work as commissioned by the Church, and from the very beginning of this work the Church made it her own.

The Master worked incessantly, manifesting a tremendous power of understanding, and a tenacious and calm activity (witnesses report that he not only dictated to three or even four secretaries at a time on different subjects,[9] but also managed when he lay down to rest in the midst of the dictation to continue to dictate while sleeping). He spent himself without counting the cost; he knew well that while contemplation is beyond time, action, which takes place in time, ought to move with speed and do violence to the malice of the moment; this work, which dominates the flow of the ages like some huge peaceful pyramid, was produced in haste, but without a trace of haste in it, because it overflowed purely from the contemplative fullness of a heart joined to eternity.

The commentaries on Aristotle—the fundamental work undertaken at the instigation of the popes which were to cleanse the Philosopher of pagan and Averroistic errors, and render him assimilable by Catholic thought—were for the most part composed during that sojourn in Italy[10] (commentaries on the *Physics,* the *Metaphysics,* the *Nicomachean Ethics,* the *De sensu et sensato,* the *De memoria et reminiscentia,* the *Posterior Analytics,* and the first four books of the *Politics*). The completion of the *Summa Contra Gentiles,* the first commentary on the epistles of Saint Paul, the commentaries on the Canticle of Canticles, on the Lamentations, on Jeremias, the *Catena aurea,* the treatise *De Regno,* and part of the *Disputed Ques-*

tions (the *De Potentia* and *De Malo* notably) also belong to these years. And the *Summa Theologiae* was begun.

In November of 1268, Friar Thomas was suddenly sent to Paris, where the situation was becoming serious, and where Siger of Brabant, a rash and seductive intellect, threatened to bring about in the Faculty of Arts the triumph of Averroes under the colors of Aristotle, and thus jeopardize the whole Peripatetic movement. Four more years of battle at its pitch and unheard-of activity, during which time the treatises *On the Perfection of the Spiritual Life* against the adversaries of the religious state, *On the Unity of the Intellect* against the Averroists, *On the Eternity of the World* against Aristotle's detractors, the commentaries on the *De Causis*, on the *Meteorology*, on the *Perihermeneias* and on the treatise *On the Soul*, on Job and on Saint John, the last *Disputed Questions*, and the second part of the *Summa Theologiae* were composed; and, finally, the greater part of the *Quaestiones Quodlibetales*, which are related to a method of teaching largely developed, it seems, and perhaps created, by Saint Thomas himself during his two stays in Paris, and occasioned by his conflict with the secular doctors. Perpetual vagabonds, the religious, according to the seculars, could not make serious, truly competent professors. And so, in the great discussions held twice a year, at Christmas and at Easter, of which the *Quaestiones Quodlibetales* are the written rendition, Friar Thomas showed that a religious knows how to reply to any question at all that anyone at all happens to pose. . . .

After Easter of 1272, he was called back by his

superiors to Italy to establish a *studium generale* of theology there. The choice of the site was left to him; he decided on Naples. It was there that he worked on the third part of the *Summa Theologiae,* composed the valuable *Compendium Theologiae,*[11] commented on the *Psalms,* the *Epistle to the Romans,* and the treatises of Aristotle *On Heaven and Earth* and *On Generation and Corruption.*

When he went for a walk in the fields with his companions, the peasants turned to gaze in astonishment at his lofty stature. He was big, dark, quite portly, and erect. He was tanned the color of wheat, his head large and a bit bald. The Viterbo portrait, more or less well copied and restored, shows a countenance stamped with an admirable power, peaceful and pure; under the raised and open arches of the brows, the tranquil eyes of a child; the features regular, a bit heavy with fat, but strengthened by intelligence; the witty mouth with fine precise curves, one that never told a lie. He had, William of Tocco tells us, that delicate and tender flesh which is, according to Aristotle, characteristic of great intellectuals. His very keen sensibility made the least scratch on his body quite painful to him. But if he had to undergo a bleeding (bleedings were frequent in those hardy days, and even imposed by the constitutions of the Order) or a cauterization, he had but to begin to meditate, and straightway he entered into such abstraction of spirit that one could do as one pleased with him; he felt nothing more. In the refectory, he always had his eyes on things from above, and one could take his bowl from him and return it to him many times without his noticing it. His *socius* (companion), Reginald of Piperno, was obliged to assume the role of foster-brother, placing before him the dishes he ought to eat, and setting aside what could harm him.

This faculty of being elsewhere, extraordinarily developed in him, sometimes played tricks on him. At the table of Saint Louis (to whose invitation he had to yield by order of the Prior, tearing himself away from the *Summa Theologiae*, which he was then dictating), he suddenly pounded on the table and cried: "There is the clinching argument against the heresy of the Manichaeans!"—"Master," said the Prior to him, "pay attention, you are now at the table of the King of France," and he tugged him vigorously by the cape to bring him out of his state of abstraction. The King had a secretary quickly summoned, and writing materials brought. Another day, in Italy, a Cardinal asked to see him. Friar Thomas came down from his work, saw no one, and continued to meditate; then cried with great joy: "Now I have what I was looking for!" It was again necessary to tug him by the cape to get him to notice the Lord Cardinal, who, receiving no sign of reverence, was beginning to grow indignant.

He lived secluded in his spirit and advanced in a density of silence along a path which never deviated, surrounded solely by the murmur of his prayer and of his thought. Throughout the course of his studies and his years of preparation, he applied all his energy to an extraordinary effort of concentration, heaping into his prodigious memory all the knowledge of his masters and of his books, leaving nothing that was not penetrated and brought to life by the intellect. (And he was always to maintain this intellectual discipline, never leaving a doubt without clearing it up, nor a

true observation, coming from whomever it might,
without putting it in reserve, in short, exercising the
greatest vigilance, and keeping himself free from all
else.) When at last the time came for him to speak
—*in medio Ecclesiae aperuit os ejus*[12]—he concentrated all his energy on remaining invincibly
attached to his sole object: First Truth, to be seen and
pointed out.

All exterior goods were certainly flimsy in comparison with the universe in which he was living. (The
dialogue between the Master and his students, return-
ing together from a visit to Saint-Denis, is well known:
"Master, how beautiful is that city of Paris!—Yes,
indeed, it is beautiful.—Please God that it would be
yours!—And what should I do with it?—You would
sell it to the King of France, and with the money you
would build all the convents for the Friar Preachers.—
In truth, I would prefer to have at this moment the
homilies of Chrysostom on St. Matthew.") But consider the interior use he made of his gifts, and of a
genius capable of unbalancing the most vigorous soul;
a heroic will was there, which, stabilized in a charity
without measure, kept everything within bounds, and
assured the perfect rightness of moral life amid the
violence and the diversity of intellectual attractions.
All his knowledge was employed for the service of
others. His immense work was conducted not according to his choice, but according to the commands of
Providence. He was at the mercy of one after another,
and they did not hesitate to overburden him with
questions and consultations; at Paris the King of
France came to take counsel with him; he told him in
the evening what difficulties were bothering him and
received the answer the following day. In this Friar
Thomas once more performed his duty as theologian,

for sacred doctrine is at once speculative and practical. And he would never perform any duty but this. He had but one thing to do and he did it well. All the more or less parasitical curiosities in which his reason could have excelled, and which were promising him so many discoveries, he curtailed. That temptation to leave the intellectual life in order to settle down to practical activity, which all intellectuals well know, even masters in theology, he was not touched by, because he drank at a certain secret source much superior to the intellectual life itself, which rendered him detached from everything, both from himself and from his own knowledge. Thus, superabound as he might in spiritual riches, he was truly poor in spirit. Look for him, Thomas, the son of Landulf and Theodora, where is he? Effaced, lost in the light. A sign so pure that it disappears before that which it makes known—in looking at him, you see only the object that he points out, and the splendor of the visage of God.

To be sure, he had received too many graces of illumination, and knew too well what a creature is, to be able to consider himself as anything before God. But also what would he have received had he not possessed this very humility? He confessed to his students that he had never consciously experienced a feeling of vainglory. One day, at Bologna, a Friar of another convent, who did not know him, and whom the Prior had permitted to go into town accompanied by the first Friar whom he met, found him meditating in the cloister: "My good Friar, the Prior said that you are to come with me." Master Thomas Aquinas followed this Friar at once, and accompanied him on his way, not without being reprimanded for not going fast enough, being less inclined to walking than to obedience, "in which," he said, "the whole religious life is summed up, because therein man submits himself to man for God, as God has for man obeyed man."

Inflexible as he was in the defense of truth, his students were often astonished that he would bear personal attacks so placidly. A considerable magnanimity enabled him to regard many things as trifles. Of keen sensibilities, his nature would have inclined him to irony; he conquered this by meekness. He never meddled in the affairs of others, hated rash judgment, and preferred to appear naive rather than readily believe evil—the perfection of the speculative intellect, we know, being unharmed by an error in a contingent matter. One day a Friar in a jovial mood cries out: "Friar Thomas, come see the flying ox!" Friar Thomas goes over to the window. The other laughs. "It is better," the Saint says to him, "to believe that an ox can fly than to think that a religious can lie."

Tocco and the witnesses at the process of canonization portrayed him as "soft-spoken, affable, cheerful and agreeable of countenance, good in soul, generous in his acts; very patient, very prudent; all radiant with charity and tender piety; marvelously compassionate towards the poor"; filled with love for the Sacrament of the Altar, devoted to the saints, to the Virgin Mary, to the apostle Paul, and to blessed Dominic. He carried on his person some relics of St. Agnes, which one day cured Reginald of a fever; after which he promised to treat the brethren and students of the Naples convent to a good meal each year on the feast of the Saint. Close to death himself, he was able to fulfill his promise but once.

It was commonly thought, the same witnesses tell us, that he remained as pure as he was when he left his mother's womb. His life was spent entirely in praying, studying, writing or dictating, teaching or preaching, so that there was not a wasted moment. (He preached, either in Latin before the Roman Curia or the University or at Paris, or in Neapolitan in his native land—he never had the time to learn another vernacular language. In a Lenten series preached at Naples, he touched hearts so deeply that he had to break off in order to let the congregation weep.) He was always the first to rise at night for prayer, and as soon as he knew at a given signal that the other brethren were coming he would withdraw to his room. After his Mass, which he celebrated early in the morning, he attended a second Mass out of devotion, then mounted the rostrum for his lecture. After this he wrote and dictated. Then he took his meal and went back to his room, where he devoted himself to divine things until the time came to rest. As soon as he awoke he began again to write. When the brethren would fetch him into the garden for recreation, he would soon withdraw and return to his room. When he wanted exercise he walked alone in the cloister, head erect.

He was full of simplicity, of ingenuousness; he had great love for his brethren. He wept for the faults of another as though they were his own. The purity of his heart was such that, on the testimony of his confessor, Reginald, his general confession, before dying, was like that of a child of five.

From the first day of his teaching, from the time when he commented in Paris on the Master of the Sentences, he was seen to rise like a sign in the heavens. Some were indignant, the majority marveled at such freshness and youth. "A new method, new reasons, new points of doctrine, a new order of questions, a new light," he was a great innovator, because he was not looking for the new but simply and solely for the true; he took the rust off scholasticism.

The novelty *par excellence*, prepared by some of his elders, above all by Albert the Great, but whose accomplishment was reserved for him, was the integration of Aristotle into Catholic thought. Aristotle, having arrived successively and by pieces, was after a half century exerting a terrible pressure on Christendom. Not only did he make his appearance escorted by Jews and Arabs with their dangerous commentaries; but also, though he himself brought the most noble treasure of natural wisdom, pagan poisons nonetheless circulated there; and the mere dazzle of the promises of pure reason was enough to unbalance an ingenuous and inquiring world. Prudent, the Church at first treated the Philosopher as suspect, allowing only Masters to study him in private. He gained ground nonetheless each day. Were the gods of antiquity going to triumph over the Christian heart? What the fifteenth and sixteenth centuries failed to achieve in the order of art and the allurements of the senses, the thirteenth, thanks to Thomas Aquinas, achieved in the order of metaphysics and theology. It did not excommunicate Aristotle and the whole effort of reason; it did not yield nor apostatize before them; it converted them. Saint Thomas transfigured Aristotle without deforming him, not contenting himself with restoring his true meaning against the alterations of commentators, with completing and correcting him wherever he makes a mistake or hesitates, but working the miracle of disengaging from the historic Aristotle —*such as into himself at last Theology changes him*[13] —a pure Aristotelian form much more purely Aristote-

lian than Aristotle himself had known. Aristotle, moreover, is above all for Thomas the treasurer of natural
reason; with Aristotle it is the whole of antiquity that
he assumes, not without also retaining all the good that
the Jews and Arabs were able to discern. He likewise
gathered all the testimonies of Scripture and the
Fathers, the whole of Christian thought, in such a way
that "for having profoundly venerated" the Fathers and
holy Doctors who preceded him, "he in a way inherited
the intellect of all." [14] His newness is thus a newness
not of destruction but of accomplishment. His originality consists of having himself taught by all. He is not
only the disciple of uncreated Wisdom, of the wisdom
of the saints and of the wisdom of the philosophers.
Formerly, at Cologne, did he not let himself be instructed by an ignorant comrade? He is also the
disciple of the human race.

The universal heritage grasped completely, and completely redone, born anew in the intellect: this is quite
the contrary of eclecticism or a mosaic of opinions. An
immaterial word, endlessly complex in its structure
and perfectly one in its being, is vitally engendered in
the womb of the spirit. Nothing loftier than such a
synthesis, nothing that demands a greater independence and a purer personal strength of thought. But
neither is there any work more impersonal in itself.
The doctrine of Saint Thomas is not the property of
Saint Thomas. It is the common property of the
Church and of men. Alone among all other doctrines,
its proper character is to be no one's property, strictly
impersonal, absolutely universal. Giacomo di Viterbo,
even in his day, spoke of it to Bartolommeo di Capua
as: "Common truth, common clarity, common illumination, common order, and doctrine that leads quickly
to perfect understanding." That is why "it is not

Catholicism which is Thomist, it is Thomism which is Catholic; and it is Catholic because it is universalist." [15] For the real in its entirety finds itself at home there. If Friar Thomas was living secluded in the depths of his thought, the eyes of his thought were open wide on things. But with what simplicity! He never does violence to things, never covers them over, never with him do you have those arrangements of lighting, those exaggerations of relief, in which all the philosophers, save Aristotle, secretly indulge. His great artistic gifts he employs only for exactness of judgment and of expression. He knows no compromise with the truth; he proposes it in all its grandeur. That men say "A hard doctrine!" matters little. This pacific wisdom brings the investigations of reason—entirely human in philosophy, superelevated by faith in theology—to bear on the whole expanse of the created and of the uncreated; but everywhere it measures the mind by that which is, making it respect both the twilight from below due to the obscurity of matter, and the night from above due to the too pure transparency of divine things. Fundamentally opposed to agnosticism and to rationalism, contrasting devices both of which separate intelligence and mystery, Thomist realism weds intelligence and mystery at the heart of being.

Theology makes use of philosophy, illuminates it as it judges it in its own light. It is by this means that Saint Thomas transplanted Aristotelian concepts to a new climate—the supernatural—where faith impels them to yield in our mind some understanding of the mysteries of God. There is—based upon the evidences of reason alone—a Thomist philosophy; Saint Thomas produced great philosophical works, he had an extraordinary metaphysical genius. But he is not only, nor principally, a philosopher; essentially he is a theologian. It is as theologian, from the peak of architectonic knowledge *par excellence,* that he definitively secures the order of the Christian economy.

Against the old scholasticism which was not able to recognize in him the true heir of Augustine, he defends the rights of the truth of the natural order, and the value of reason; against the Averroists, who were unable to recognize in him the true interpreter of Aristotle, he defends the rights of revealed truth, and the value of faith. Affirming at once the essential *naturality* of metaphysics and the essential *supernaturality* of infused virtues, and the essential subordination of the natural to the supernatural, proclaiming at once that grace perfects and does not destroy nature, and that the properly divine life it implants in us can alone heal nature and ought to take hold of it thoroughly, his proper work was to lead all the energies of the intellect into the service of Jesus Christ. It was the whole problem of culture and of humanism that was posed in him. His solution is: *sanctity.* Man has his perfection only if it is supernatural, he develops only on the cross. A humanism is possible, but on condition that it have for its end union with God through the humanity of the Redeemer, and that it proportion its means to the essentially supernatural end;—a humanism of the Incarnation: on condition that it order itself completely to love and contemplation, that it perfectly subordinate, as did the saintly soul of Thomas Aquinas itself, science to wisdom, and metaphysical wisdom to theological wisdom, and theological wisdom to the wisdom of the saints; and that it understand that the form of reason can conquer the world only if it itself submits to the supra-rational and supra-human order of the Holy Spirit and His gifts. Otherwise humanism,

even Christian humanism, inevitably slips toward the
destruction of man and universal ruin.

Friar Thomas, Tocco tells us, was a man marvelously contemplative, *vir miro modo contemplativus.*
If his sanctity was the sanctity of the intelligence, this
is because in him the life of the intelligence was
fortified and completely transilluminated by the fire
of infused contemplation and the gifts of the Holy
Spirit. He lived in a kind of rapture and perpetual
ecstasy. He prayed without ceasing, wept, fasted,
yearned. Each of his syllogisms is as a concretion of
his prayer and his tears; the kind of grace of lucid
calm which his words bring to us springs doubtless
from the fact that the least of his texts retains invisibly the impregnation of his longing and of the
pure strength of the most vehement love. While he
was living, did not the mere bodily sight of him
procure, according to his contemporaries, a grace of
spiritual consolation? The masterpiece of strict and
rigorous intellectuality, of intrepid logic, is thus brim-
ming over from a heart possessed by charity. On his
return to Naples after the death of Thomas, Reginald
was to exclaim: "As long as he was living my Master
prevented me from revealing the marvels that I witnessed. He owed his knowledge less to the effort of
his mind than to the power of his prayer. Every time
he wanted to study, discuss, teach, write or dictate,
he first had recourse to the privacy of prayer, weeping
before God in order to discover in the truth the divine
secrets, and, though he had been in uncertainty before
praying, as a result of his prayer he came back instructed." When doubtful points would arise, Bartolommeo di Capua likewise reports, he would go to

the altar and would stay there weeping many tears
and uttering great sobs, then return to his room and
continue his writings.

"His gift of prayer," writes Tocco, "exceeded every
measure; he elevated himself to God as freely as
though no burden of flesh held him down. Hardly a
day passed that he was not rapt out of his senses."
There were plenty of tears in his prayers. Never en-
tangling himself in the affairs of the world, having
from his youth the custom of quitting at once every
conversation which ceased to concern the things of
God, "no occupation changed the movement of his
heart," or diverted him from prayer, into which, once
what he was doing among men was finished, he would
quietly re-enter. Very often, during Mass, he burst into
tears. Sometimes the congregation witnessed it. Once,
on Passion Sunday, at the convent of Naples, as he was
saying Mass before a large congregation of soldiers,
they saw him so rapt in spirit and shedding such tears
that he seemed to be present on Calvary and to be
bowing beneath the weight of the sufferings of Christ.
The Friars kept coming up, urging him to continue the
Mass. Often also he wept at Compline when, during
Lent, one chanted the verse: "Do not reject me in my
old age when my strength shall fail." At night, after a
short sleep, he remained prostrate in prayer in his
room or at the church.

The extraordinary graces which he often received
take their place in the uninterrupted stream of a very
lofty mystical life. One day the Virgin Mary appeared
to him and gave him full assurance concerning his
life and his doctrine, and revealed to him that his
station, as he had so often requested it, would never
be changed (i.e., that he would never be elevated to
any prelacy). Another time it was the saints who came

to help him with his commentary on Isaias. An obscure passage stopped him; for a long time he fasted and prayed to obtain an understanding of it. And behold one night Reginald heard him speaking with someone in his room. When the sound of conversation had ceased, Friar Thomas called him, telling him to light the candle and take the manuscript *On Isaias*. Then he dictated for an hour, after which he sent Reginald back to bed. But Reginald fell upon his knees: "I will not rise from here until you have told me the name of him or of them with whom you have spoken for such a long time tonight." Finally Friar Thomas began to weep and, forbidding him in the name of God to reveal the thing during Thomas' life, confessed that the apostles Peter and Paul had come to instruct him. Several times he was elevated from the ground during his prayer. He had a revelation of a temptation which obsessed a brother, he had twice the vision of the soul of his sister Marotta, a Benedictine abbess, who first asked him for Masses to deliver her from Purgatory, then announced to him her deliverance, and informed him that Raynaldo, unjustly put to death by Frederick II, was in Heaven; an angel then showed him a book written in letters of azure and gold, in which the name of his brother appeared in the gold-lettered columns devoted to the martyrs, for he was killed for his fidelity to the Pope. Another day a friend of his, a master in theology, Friar Romano, who had just died, appeared before him and spoke with him about questions that they had discussed while he was living. At Paris, consulted by the Masters on the manner of teaching the mystery of the Eucharist, he went first to place his answer on the altar, imploring the crucifix; the brethren who were watching him suddenly saw Christ standing before him on the manuscript he had written, and they heard these words: "You have written well of the Sacrament of My Body and you have well and truthfully resolved the question which was proposed to you, to the extent that it is possible to have an understanding of it on earth and to ascertain it humanly." And, by the intensity of the rapture, the saint was raised a cubit into the air. A similar occurrence took place another time at Naples. Friar Thomas was writing the third part of the *Summa,* and was treating of the Passion and Resurrection of Christ. One day, before Matins, the sacristan saw him raised nearly two cubits from the ground. He stood gazing at him for a long while. Suddenly he heard a voice come forth from the image of the Crucified, towards whom the Doctor was turned, praying tearfully: "You have written well of Me, Thomas. What recompense for your work do you want from Me?—None other than You, Lord."

Concerning the mystical life of Saint Thomas we are thus informed by the testimonies of his brethren and by exterior signs. In his writings, many unmistakable expressions, and his very teaching on infused wisdom, betray also, in spite of himself, his experience of divine things; finally, his work is the proof *par excellence* of the superhuman illuminations in the midst of which it was produced. But he himself tells us nothing of it, having put into practice only too well that saying of Saint Anthony, the hermit, which he could have read in Cassian (he had some pages of Cassian read to him every day), that "there is no perfect prayer if the religious himself perceives that he is praying." All the more so, as he did not have the mission, as a Saint John of the Cross or a Saint Teresa, to expound the things of contemplation in a practical way, from the point of view of introspection and experience. The secret of this mystical life, of which we know only by extrinsic indications that it was one of the highest conceivable, thus remains well guarded. All that we can presume is that the task of teaching accepted for the benefit of the Church and of the world must have drawn into a particularly luminous zone the secret universe of the contemplative gifts, and must have there substituted, perhaps, for the ordinary passive purifications, the type of uninterrupted suffering sustained by the intellect nailed to its mission; it must have blended with the obscurity of negative theology and of the wisdom of love, in which the heart of the Master was dissolved for sweetness, the clarity of the charismata of prophecy (the penetration of things divine) and of the manifestation of wisdom (*sermo sapientiae*).

The prayers composed by Saint Thomas are not admissions, but are works still, of his profound life, works which, beautiful as they may be, do not confide to us the measure of that life: works limpid as the sky and ever pointing, with a sublime simplicity, to the object. There is no poem purer, in which so much love is concealed in so much light, than the office of the Blessed Sacrament. It is surely in obedience to a design of providential harmony that in 1264, nine years after the death of the Blessed Julienne du Mont-Cornillon,[16] Pope Urban was to ask the saint to compose the office of this new feast, requested by the Lord more than thirty years before. In the doctrine and in the Sacrament it is the same truth which incorporates the unity of the Church. Thomas Aquinas, who had the mission of teaching the doctrine, was commissioned to hymn the Sacrament.

What harder trial could there be for such a Master than to see his teaching held in suspicion in the Church? During the four years of heroic battles of his last stay in Paris, the shadow of this ordeal passed over him.

The Averroist philosophers, idolaters of Aristotle, and the self-styled Augustinian theologians who feared the intellect—a short-sighted crowd was pitched against him, and strained to rend the seamless garment of his too pure doctrine. It was necessary to defend the true Aristotle against the second of these, and to attack against the first the Aristotle "corrupted" by Averroes. Doubtless, even at Paris he had numerous and fervent disciples, especially in the Faculty of Arts, which was not entirely won over to Siger of Brabant and Boethius of Dacia, and was in raptures over his explanations of Aristotle, and which after his death would petition the Dominicans to give it his body and his writings. Doubtless he had behind him the authority of the Pope and the Curia, whose theologian he was; he could always, if need be, appeal to the Roman Church. But almost all the masters in theology of the University opposed him, the seculars and the Franciscans (for these quarrels of self-love were in full play as early as then) wanted to have no more of him, and the bishop of Paris supported them. And it was in the name of the interests of the faith that they claimed to overthrow him.

In 1270 his great controversy with Siger took place; Siger published the treatise *De anima intellectiva,* and Thomas answered [17] him with the *De unitate intellectus.* That same year it was necessary for him to reply also to the murmurings of his other adversaries, the pseudo-Augustinians of the Faculty of Theology, against whom he wrote the *De aeternitate mundi*. Just before Easter, in a solemn dispute on the point of his doctrine for which they reproached him most ardently (the theory of the intellective soul as the only substantial form in man), Friar John Peckham, regent of the Friars Minor, harassed him with violent and bombastic remarks; his own brethren abandoned him, some even argued against him, the Bishop and the Doctors awaited his downfall and did all that they could to procure it. But his words passed among them, peaceably; all was futile against his sweetness. The Bishop of Paris, Etienne Tempier, who wanted to include the thesis in question (and still another of Thomas Aquinas, on the simplicity of spiritual substances) in the condemnation he was preparing of certain propositions of Siger, was forced to give up his project, and to limit his condemnation to the Averroist propositions (December 12, 1270). But when on March 7, 1277—three years, to the day, after the death of the Doctor—he was to renew his condemnation of Averroism, he would add to the theses of Siger of Brabant and of Boethius of Dacia censured by him a score of Thomist propositions. Some days later, the Dominican Robert Kilwardby, Archbishop of Canterbury and Primate of England, would likewise reprove the doctrine of Thomas Aquinas, in particular the famous thesis of the oneness of the substantial form, which raised at that time in the schools of England "an almost infinite scandal." In 1284 his successor, John Peckham, was to make the censure worse. Gates open for the subtleties of Scotus and for the Nominalist disputers who would darken the fourteenth century!

> The Middle Ages in their decline were unable to listen to Rome and make use of the gift of God.

Having returned to Italy after Easter of 1272, Friar Thomas took part in the General Chapter of the Order, at Florence, and then he went to Naples again to continue his teaching there. One day, December 6, 1273, while he was celebrating Mass in the chapel of Saint Nicholas, a great change came over him. From that moment he ceased writing and dictating.[18] Was the *Summa* then, with its thirty-eight treatises, its three thousand articles and ten thousand objections, to remain unfinished? As Reginald was complaining about it, his master said to him, "I can do no more." But the other was insistent. "Reginald, I can do no more; such things have been revealed to me that all that I have written seems to me as so much straw. Now, I await the end of my life after that of my works."

At the touch of God the soul was taking leave of the body. A few days afterward, he desired to see his sister, the Countess of San Severino, whom he loved tenderly, and he journeyed, at the cost of great fatigue, to pay her a visit. But as he arrived, and she came forth to meet him, he scarcely spoke to her. Alarmed, she asked Reginald: "What ails my brother? He seems stupefied and does not answer me at all."—"Since the feast of St. Nicholas he has been in that state," said Reginald, "and has written nothing since."

In January Gregory X summoned him to the Council he had convoked at Lyons. Thomas started on the way with Reginald; they traveled mounted on mules. Reginald risked some words, trying to distract him: "You and Friar Bonaventure will be made Cardinals, and it will redound to the glory of your Orders." "I will never be anything in the Order or in the Church," replied Friar Thomas. "In no other station can I serve our Order better than in the station I'm in."

He stopped at the Maënza castle of his niece, the Countess Francesca, in Campania. But hardly had he arrived when he collapsed from weariness, and illness seized him. It is then that Providence made him a present of a bit of fish. He had lost his appetite and did not have a taste for anything but fresh herrings such as he had eaten in France. Reginald was disconsolate, for this product of the North was not to be found in Italy. But behold, on opening one of the baskets of a merchant who was passing with a load of sardines, he found it filled, miraculously, with fresh herrings, which everyone in the castle ate.

Thomas stayed only four days at Maënza. Feeling seriously ill, he asked with great devotion that someone bring him to the monastery of Santa Maria at Fossanova, which was nearby. On entering he leaned on the wall with his hand and said: "This is my rest for ever and ever: here will I dwell for I have chosen it." [19] It was a Cistercian monastery; he had come back to Saint Benedict to die. He was ill for a month, enduring it all with great patience and humility. The monks carried wood with their own hands from the forest to make a fire for him, judging it unfitting that beasts of burden should carry the wood for the use of so great a man. And he, each time he saw them come into the room where he was lying, raised himself humbly and with great veneration, saying: "How does it happen that holy men are bringing me wood?" At the request of some monks, he explained briefly the *Canticle of Canticles*; then he asked for Viaticum. The Abbot, attended by his monks, brought him the Body of the Lord. When he saw the Host, he threw himself on the floor, burst into tears, and greeted Him with words of admirable and prolonged adoration: "I receive Thee, Price of my redemption, Viaticum of my pilgrimage, for love of Whom I have studied and watched, toiled, preached, and taught. Never have I said anything against Thee; but if I have done so, it is through ignorance, and I do not persist in my opinions, and if I have done anything wrong, I leave all to the correction of the Roman Church. It is in this obedience to Her that I depart from this life." He died three days later on March 7, 1274. He was forty-nine.

The sub-Prior of the monastery, who had nearly gone blind, recovered his sight by putting his face against Thomas'. Many other miracles took place after this; and many, too, according to the testimony of Bartolommeo di Capua, were hidden by the monks, who were afraid that someone would take the holy body from them. Having exhumed it at the end of the seventh month, they found it intact, and exhaling such fragrances that one would have thought himself to be in a dispensary full of sweet-smelling herbs; the whole monastery was perfumed with them. A second exhumation took place fourteen years later and the same facts were verified.

It is reported that at Ratisbon, where he was bishop, Master Albert knew of the death of his great disciple through a revelation. He wept bitterly at the time. And each time afterwards that he heard the name of Thomas mentioned he would weep again, saying: "He was the flower and glory of the world." When the rumor spread that at Paris the writings of Friar Thomas were being attacked, the old Master journeyed to defend them. On his return he convoked a solemn assembly at which he declared that after the

work accomplished by Thomas others would thenceforth labor in vain.

Nevertheless, the opposition of the Paris and Ox-
ford theologians did not subside; nor that of the
Franciscan doctors: in 1282 a General Chapter of the
Friars Minor prohibited the reading of the *Summa* in
Franciscan schools. To each his grace, says Saint
Paul. Not all the orders have a theological mission. The
Dominicans, however, quickly realized that in giving
them Saint Thomas, God had manifested to them the
reason for their existence. As early as 1278, at the
General Chapter in Milan, they decided to defend his
doctrine energetically, which was soon to become the
doctrine of the Order, and from which Pope Clement
VI would enjoin them never to deviate. But it is for
the common good of the Church and of the world that
they are commissioned to maintain the integrity of this
doctrine. It is the common patrimony of us all. From
the beginning it was the universal Church, in the
person of the Pope, which recognized in Thomas its
Doctor. It was the papacy which, discerning in him
the common spirit of the whole human and divine
tradition, and the greatest and most assiduous force
for the conservation of all that transcends time in the
past, but also the movement of life and the most
active power of assimilation and salvation of all that
is worth more than the moment in the future—it was
the papacy which, seeing the dividing night approaching, and deciding to oppose it with the great rallying
in the spirit of all created beings under the accorded
lights of reason and faith, sided with Thomas Aquinas
against the routine narrowness of the schools and
against a dull conservatism which was destined immediately to fall into dissolution. But the resistance

of these particularisms was strong. It took fifty years of violent polemics to put an end to the calumnies leveled against the orthodoxy of Thomism. The canonization of Thomas, proclaimed Saint by John XXII on July 18, 1323, at Avignon, was the last act of this battle. "Thomas, alone, has illuminated the Church more than all the other doctors," the Pope declared. "His doctrine could proceed only from a miraculous action of God." This doctrine could henceforth shed its radiance in full liberty. And on the 14th of February, 1324, at the insistence of Rome, the Bishop of Paris, Etienne de Boretto, revoked the condemnation pronounced in 1277 against the Thomist theses by his predecessor Etienne Tempier. Yet, though the glory of Thomas Aquinas was great, the Christian world, which was already failing, had not the courage to ask him for its cure, and scholasticism was to exhaust itself in vain rivalries and decadent systems.

But a new story begins for Saint Thomas. It is to him from now on that the Church has recourse in her battle against all the errors and all the heresies; his doctrine grows in heaven, it is this doctrine that the Church of Christ uses in her own intellectual life, one and universal; the Popes render it innumerable testimonies, whose agreement and reiteration over the course of time have a singular force. And behold, Leo XIII in the encyclical *Aeterni Patris* (August 4, 1879) and, in incessantly renewed acts, Pius X, Benedict XV, Pius XI, and Pius XII,[20] clearly without imposing this doctrine as an article of faith (which could not be the case for any theological or philosophical system), urge Catholic masters to teach it, and beseech the world with tragic insistence to turn to it as to the salvation of the intelligence and of civilization.

He who was called with good reason the *Angelic Doctor* and the *Doctor of the Eucharist* is also and above all the *Common Doctor of the Church*, because he alone perfectly answers to the universal breadth of Catholic thought. It is highly remarkable that even in Byzantine theology, at the decline of the Middle Ages, he enjoyed high esteem.

Summaries and translations into Greek of his principal works, the two *Summae*, the Commentaries on the *De Anima* and on the *Physics* of Aristotle, and several *opuscula*, were written at that time, in particular by Demetrios Kidones, minister of the emperor John VI Cantacuzene, the translator of the *Summa Contra Gentiles* and refuter of Kabasilas, and by George Scholarios Gennadios, Patriarch of Constantinople. Now it is in Arabic, in Chinese and in Sanskrit, as in Latin, in Greek and in Russian, that he would teach the grandeurs of God. He is the veritable apostle of modern times; his principles are sufficiently elevated and integrated to embrace in a superior and true, not eclectic, unity—a unity of discrimination, of order, and of redemption, not of confusion and of death— the immense diversities of race, of culture and of spirituality which divide the world of East and West. Beneath the Latin disposition of his form, the substance which he brings to men transcends every particularity of time and place; he alone can give them back the divine good of unity of spirit, where alone it is possible to attain it, in the light of the Incarnate Word.

THE WISE ARCHITECT

> *For as the master builder of a new house must have care of the whole building.* II Macab., II, 30.
>
> *According to the grace of God that is given to me, as a wise architect I have laid the foundation.*
> St. Paul, I Cor., III, 10.

I

1. Leibniz, even in his day, lamented the lost unity of Christian culture. This unity has been breaking apart for four centuries now. As has often been remarked, in three great spiritual crises—the humanist Renaissance, the Protestant Reformation, and the rationalist Enlightenment—man accomplished a historic revolution of unparalleled importance, at the end of which he took himself to be the center of his history and the ultimate end of his action on earth, and arrogated to himself that properly divine privilege of absolute independence or all-sufficiency which theologians call *aseitas.* The immense deployment of brutal force over the surface of the globe to which, under the pretext of industrially subjugating matter, Europe delivered itself over in the nineteenth century, is but the expression in the sensible order of this spiritual usurpation. Under

the optimistic trappings of positivist pseudo-science, a kind of false unity of the human spirit then arose like a vast mirage, and men believed that they were approaching the goal, that they were becoming the masters and possessors of themselves, of the whole of nature and of history. They were approaching catastrophe. While matter, seemingly dominated and vanquished, imposed on human life its own rhythm and the demands, multiplied without end, of the satisfactions that it procures, man found himself more divided than ever, separated from others and separated from himself: matter, a principle of division, can engender only division. Nations against nations, classes against classes, passions against passions, in the end it is human personality itself that is dissolved: man searches for himself in vain in the disjointed (yet scrutinized with what perspicacity!) pieces of his unconscious wishes and of his inconsistent sincerities; a fever of despair takes possession of the world.

On what conditions can this lost unity be, not recovered such as it was, for time is irreversible, but fashioned anew under new forms? One truth seems to me to command the whole discussion: *man does not find his unity in himself; he finds it outside himself, above himself*. It was in willing to be self-sufficient that he lost himself. He will find himself by clinging to his first principle, and to an order which transcends him. Like pure materiality, pure subjectivity disperses. Nothing is more illusory than to ask immanentism to reconcile man with himself. Man becomes reconciled with himself only on the cross, which is hard and exterior to him: that cross to which he is nailed. Objectivity is the first condition of unity.

There are other conditions, which are of the material order and which must not be neglected. But objectivity is fundamental, for it concerns the two noblest activities in man: *intelligence,* insofar as it is faithful to the object, and therefore to First Being; and *love,* insofar as it unites us to our first principle and to our true Whole.

A resurrection of metaphysics and a new expansion of charity: before all else this is the prerequisite for the return to human unity, to that unity which was perfect only in the Garden of Eden and in the heart of Christ in Gethsemane, but the longing for which will never cease to haunt us.

2. At the different moments of history, especially at the moments of major transformation, we can find, if we cut into the tissue of human events, two very different elements. There is an element that is very important as to matter, as to volume, and which represents the massive result, the residue, as it were, of past effort: an element that we could call the static factor or the factor of resistance, and which signifies above all something done, concluded, finished.

And there is another element which is nothing as to volume and appearance, but which is a great deal more important as to energy: an element that we could call the dynamic factor or the factor of living energy, and which signifies above all something in the making or about to be made, something in active preparation, something having the formal part to play in the generation of the future.

As far as the first element, the static factor, is concerned, what strikes us in the contemporary world, dominated as it is by anti-theological and anti-metaphysical civilization, is this unfortunate product called modern man, this being cut off from all his ontological roots and from all his transcendent objects, who, for having sought his center in himself, is no longer, as Herman Hesse put it, anything but a wolf howling in despair towards eternity. But by this very fact, too, we see that the world has tried and is finished with the experiment of positivism, pseudo-scientific skepticism, subjectivist idealism, and that this experience has been sufficiently demonstrative. These things are dead: they will be able to encumber us for a long time still, like the products of dead bodies, but they are done.

If we consider the other historic element, the dynamic factor of the present world, what we perceive, on the contrary, is a profound, an immense need of metaphysics, a great *élan* towards metaphysics, towards the restoration of ontological values. The world which wishes to be, the world which wishes to emerge in the future, is not a world of positivism but a world of metaphysics.

It is not, alas! sufficient to say: a resurrection of metaphysics. This metaphysics must be true metaphysics. I do not wish to ignore all the services that the Bergsonian movement in France, the neo-Hegelian movement and then the pragmatist and pluralist movements in England and America, and the phenomenologist[1] movement in Germany have in fact been able to render. But in the last analysis it must be said that a metaphysics that would conclude either in pure change and a more or less monist evolutionism, or in a polytheist moralism, or in an atheistic ontology, would be no remedy for humanity. The resurrection of metaphysics means above all that we are about to enter an era of great metaphysical conflicts, of great battles of the spirit: and not only will systems issued from Western speculation enter the lists, but also Asiatic systems rejuvenated by very informed and very remarkable modern thinkers, such as are already to be found in Japan and India.

What guide can we ask to lead us through the maze of all these metaphysical conflicts? Thomas Aquinas teaches us to make in the intellectual order that discernment of the good and the bad, of the true and the false, which is, as it were, an operation of angelic sifting; to save all the *intentions* of truth contained in the diversity of systems, and to rectify the rest in a synthesis balanced on the real. For, as has often been observed, one of the characteristics peculiar to his thought is, not indeed a feeble eclecticism devoid of principles, but on the contrary such an elevation and such a rigor of principles that it reconciles in its eminence, the while it transcends them, the most opposed doctrines, which then appear to be merely the opposite slopes, so to speak, of the same mountain.

Saint Thomas, in his probing the intimate nature of knowledge and the peculiar life of the intellect, establishes better than any other thinker—against positivism, but respecting the full role played by experience, and against idealism, but respecting the full role played by the immanent and constructive activity of the mind—the objectivity of knowledge, the rights and the value of the science of being. But he establishes also—against the false systems of metaphysics which threaten to assail us, against the pantheistic immanentism which some would impose on us in the name of the Orient, against the pragmatism of the West, against the Hegelian divinization of becoming and against the diverse forms of radical atheism which have sprung up in the world since Feuerbach, Auguste Comte, and Karl Marx—he establishes, I say, the transcendence of Him Whom we know through His creatures but Who is without common measure with them; Who is being, intelligence, goodness, life, beatitude, but Who overflows and surpasses infinitely our ideas of being, goodness and all the other perfections: in short, Whom our concepts attain through analogy but do not circumscribe.

Thus metaphysics rises in his hands above agnosticism and rationalism; it starts with experience and mounts right up to Uncreated Being, and thus reestablishes in the human spirit the proper hierarchy of speculative values, and initiates in us the order of wisdom.

3. If it is a question now of ethical values, and of the conduct of human life, then it is only too easy to see to what an extent the contemporary world is, as a rule, a world of selfishness, meanness and coldness. And how could it be otherwise, from the moment that man undertook to be self-sufficient? In truth, love lives only on God or on that which it deifies; and when it realizes that what it has deified is but a bit of nothingness, it turns to hatred and scorn.

But as far as the second historic element referred to above, the dynamic element, is concerned, what the contemporary world reveals to us, precisely by reason of the kind of impossibility of living created by anthropocentric egoism, is the need and the presentiment of a vast effusion of love. But here again we must be on our guard against counterfeits; just as we must be on guard against false systems of metaphysics, so we must be on guard against false forms of love.

A false humanitarian mysticism, pseudo-Buddhist, theosophical, or anthroposophical; a false reign of the heart which would claim to establish itself at the expense of intelligence, and in defiance of the creating and forming Word and Its laws; a kind of quietist heresy which would reduce us to no longer being men, because we would have lost the very notion of truth, and which would dissolve us in an equivocal poetic sensuality, unworthy of the name of love—these are some of the evils which threaten us from this point of view. We are far from the materialism of the nineteenth century: it is from the side of a pseudo-spiritualism and a pseudo-mysticism that the greatest dangers of deviation will arise for our time.

The Angelic Doctor shows us the right road: he reminds us that order is at the heart of holy love, and that if, in God, Subsistent Love proceeds from the Father and the Uncreated Word, in us too love must proceed from truth, must pass through the lake of the Word; otherwise it spreads only to destroy.

He reminds us also that there is only one efficacious and authentic way to love our brothers, and this is to love them with that same charity which first makes us love God above all. Then—according to that admirable order of charity which is described in the second part of the *Summa Theologiae,* and which goes out to all without injuring the natural rights of anyone—the love which joins us, above being, to the first principle of being, pours out upon creatures with a divine force; it breaks down every obstacle and melts every coldness; it opens up a new world which reveals the divine attributes in a more profound, an unsuspected manner, a world in which beings not only know one another but recognize one another; it makes us will good to our enemies. Thus must we affirm, faced as we are with the deliquescences of sentimentality and the

naturalist cult of the human species, the true nature
of divine love.

And against the hardening due to the worship of
force, to the naturalist cult of the individual, of class,
of race, or of nation, it is the primacy of this very love
that we must affirm. *Caritas major omnium.* Is there
any need to remark here that the whole ethical theory
of Saint Thomas is based on this doctrine, which he
gets from the Gospel and from Saint Paul? He con-
structed on this Gospel teaching an unbreakable
theological synthesis, in which he shows how Love,
which makes us desire undeviatingly our last end, has
an absolute practical primacy over our whole individual and social life, and constitutes the very bond
of perfection; how it is better to love God than to
know Him; and how without this love no virtue is
truly virtue or attains its perfect form, not even
justice. And Saint Thomas knows that this love truly
becomes master of human life and is an efficacious
love of God above all things and of one's neighbor as
one's self, only if it is supernatural, rooted in faith,
and proceeding from the grace of Christ, which makes
us, in the image of the Crucified, the sons and heirs of
the God Who is Love. Let us follow the Angelic
Doctor and we shall understand that peace in man
and among men (the direct work of charity, *opus
caritatis,* "for love is a unitive force, and the efficient
cause of unity") descends from that super-essential
Peace, from that eternal Love Which resides at the
heart of the Trinity.

4. The disease of our time, we stated at the beginning
of this chapter, issues from the fact that culture, which
is a certain perfection of man, has taken itself for its

ultimate end. It began by ignoring, in its Cartesian and philosophical phase, everything that surpasses the level of reason; it ends by ignoring reason itself, and suffering at once the law of the flesh and the spiritual vertigo that irrationality inevitably entails in man. "The error of the modern world has been to claim to assure the reign of reason over nature by refusing the reign of super-nature over reason." [2] This is why, even in the order of knowledge, metaphysics, of which we were speaking above, remains an inadequate remedy. Another wisdom, higher and more divine, is born of love itself, thanks to the gifts of the Holy Ghost. It is above all for this mystical wisdom that our distress hungers and thirsts, because it alone satisfies hunger and quenches thirst, being experiential union with divine things and beatitude begun. And yet it still leaves us hungering and thirsting, because vision alone can fully saturate us with God.

Saint John of the Cross is the great "experimental" Doctor of this wisdom; Saint Thomas Aquinas is its great theologian. And because he determined better than any other Doctor the central truth which one cannot ignore without dealing a mortal blow to contemplation, and to Christianity itself—I mean the distinction between nature and grace, and their living compenetration, and the whole organism of the infused gifts—he explains better than any other the true nature of mystical wisdom, and defends it more effectively than any other against all the counterfeits.

This is the highest benefit we can expect of him from the point of view of the restoration of Christian culture: for in the last analysis it is on this wisdom and on this contemplation that the whole Christian order depends here on earth.

II

5. What determines the unity of a culture is first and above all a common philosophical structure, a certain metaphysical and moral attitude, a common scale of values—in short, a common idea of the universe, of man and of life, of which the social, linguistic, and juridical structures are, so to speak, the embodiment.

This metaphysical unity has long been broken—not completely destroyed, certainly, but broken and as it were effaced in the West. What constitutes the drama of Western culture is that its common metaphysical basis is reduced to an absolutely insufficient minimum, so that it holds together now primarily through matter, and matter is incapable of keeping anything together. This drama is all the more serious for us because everything at the moment has to be done over again, everything has to be put back in place in our European house. Just suppose that a common philosophy would succeed in gaining acceptance by an elite in the Western world! It would be the beginning of the cure for this world.

As Thomas Aquinas united in his marvelously balanced temperament the talents of men of the North and South, of Norman and Lombard; as he integrated in his Doctor's mission the Italy of the Popes, the Germany of Albert the Great, the France of Saint Louis and of the University of Paris; as he joined to the heritage of the Fathers and of Christian wisdom the treasures of the Greeks and the Latins, of the Arabs and the Jews, in short, the whole contribution of the known world of his time—so also his uniquely comprehensive and organic theology, open to all the aspects of the real, offers to the intellectual tendencies peculiar to the different nations the means of exercising themselves freely, not in mutual destruction but in mutual completion and consolidation.

The fact is that Saint Thomas succeeded in constructing a philosophical and theological wisdom so elevated in immateriality that it is truly delivered from every particularization of race or place. Alas! in the course of the last few centuries we have witnessed an utterly opposite phenomenon, a kind of racial lowering of philosophy. Descartes is one of the glories of France, but he hypostatizes certain deficiencies, certain temptations peculiar to the French intellectual temperament. Hegel does the same for Germany; William James and John Dewey, the pragmatists and the instrumentalists, for the New World. It is time to turn toward truth itself, which is neither of one country nor of another; it is time to turn toward the universality of human reason and of supernatural wisdom. This is all the more urgent now, as it seems that the advent of a new philosophical age is imminent.

Imagine for a moment that Catholics in the various countries understood their whole duty. Let us dream of this utopia. Imagine that they understood the fundamental importance of intellectual questions, of metaphysics and theology, that they renounced silly prejudices against Scholasticism, and that they saw in it, not a medieval mummy to be studied archaeologically, but an armor of the living intelligence and the necessary equipment for the boldest explorations; imagine that they realized in themselves the ardent desire of the Church, which is not to win over partisans as if Catholicism were a human enterprise, but to serve everywhere divine Truth in souls and in the universe; imagine that they surmounted internal divisions and the petty rivalries of the school, which everywhere render their activity sterile; and, finally, that they saw the necessity for a serious and continuous intellectual cooperation among Christians of all nations—a cooperation which, when it comes to our dissident brethren, is obviously much easier on the philosophical than on the theological plane.

The Common Doctor would then become in all truth their common master; under his guidance they could work efficaciously for the restoration of the West and its unity. Then there would be workers for the harvest. Then, in the speculative sphere, Thomist metaphysics could assimilate into a true intellectual order the immense body of the particular sciences, which at the moment are delivered over to chaos, and whose admirable advances are in danger of being exploited by aberrant philosophies. In the moral sphere, Thomist metaphysics and theology could preside architectonically over the elaboration of that new social order, that Christian economy, that Christian politics, which the present state of the world so urgently needs. Finally, to revert to the great initial symptoms and the great initial causes of the divisions afflicting us, Humanism, Protestantism, and Rationalism, having been able in the course of time to experience both the various ravages engendered by their initial delusion and the value of many of the realities which this delusion disregarded, would be astonished to find in the treasury of the Angelic Doctor the very truths which they coveted without seeing them clearly and of which they generally fell short.

I would add that Greek and Russian piety, which differs, it seems, from Catholic piety not so much by divergences of dogma as by certain attitudes of spirituality, is much less hostile, in my opinion, to

Thomist thought than might at first be supposed. It approaches the problems from another angle and the usual Scholastic presentation irritates and offends it. But these are merely questions of modality; and I am convinced that the Thomist synthesis, when well understood, would dispel innumerable misunderstandings and permit many unexpected meetings of minds. I also believe that when our dissident brethren are led, under the pressure of the errors of our age, to a more systematic and more developed defense of the Judaeo-Christian tradition, it is in the principles elaborated by Saint Thomas that they will be brought to seek trusty weapons against vain philosophy.

In all this Saint Thomas appears as the great intellectual renovator of the West.

Need it be added that we would be ignorant of human nature if we believed in our utopias? Nevertheless, if a serious effort were not made in the direction indicated above, one might proclaim that Western culture is doomed. One can hope, in spite of everything, that this effort will be made.

6. I have spoken of the West. Where does the West really begin? We should not form too restricted an idea of it: let us remember that we are always east of someone.

It is at Golgotha that the West begins. It is Calvary, the center of the world, that marks the dividing line between East and West, and there Christ extends His redeeming arms over East and West alike. If we want to form an adequate cultural idea of the Western world, let us say that it is a world whose axis stretches from Jerusalem to Athens and Rome, and which extends from the deserts of Egypt and the Berber lands to the Atlantic and Pacific shores of America, and to the northern seas, embracing in one same community the richest variety of national traditions, institutions and cultures.

Greek and Byzantine culture, oriental in relation to Latin culture, and to the heritage of the Western Empire as history has defined it in the narrower sense of the term, is nevertheless an integral part of Western culture. Constantinople's break with Rome caused her to be confined within herself (and yet not so completely as is commonly thought) in the bosom of that culture; it did not tear her from it.

And if Eurasians are right in considering Russia as a continent apart, in which Europe and Asia are but one, if today the Communist Revolution draws this continent to the side of Asia, nevertheless the fact remains that by all its cultural past it belongs to the spiritual community of the West.

And now I put the question: Is one entitled on any ground whatsoever to identify the Western world with the Christian religion? No! To do so would be a deadly and supremely impertinent error, which the words of some clumsy apologists would sometimes seem to countenance, but which is essentially repugnant to the character *par excellence*, to the *catholicity*, of the religion of Christ.

Is this to say that the West does not have a particular mission to fulfill in regard to this religion? To say this would be another error. Pope Leo XIII himself underlined the importance of this mission. If the West, which owes so much to the Church, served Christian culture so long as a kind of secular body, it is precisely because it had been chosen to evangelize the rest of the world—not to enslave the universe to its military or commercial interests, but to serve the universe by bringing to it the message of Redemption.

Whatever may have been and whatever may still be the heroic effort of its saints, its missionaries and its martyrs, Western civilization has too long failed in this its duty. This duty is now imposed upon it under pain of death: it can now save itself only by serving the universe.

To attach oneself to the particularities of a country, to its language, its customs and its liberties, and thus to prolong a little more the beauty of perishable things, the works and the days with which the privilege of the place is charged, is the business of poets.[3] The statesman, too, is, in a way, particularist: for he is entrusted with the common good of a country, which must be his first aim, yet in such a way that while loving his country more than others, he does not therefore cease to love the others and to will them good, and does not injure the rights of the human person nor the interests of the human race.

But in the order of intelligence, of thought, of culture, one must be resolutely *universalist*. All the barriers of intellectual protectionism are now things of the past. Every book, every newspaper article (and Catholic writers ought to realize this) has readers on the banks of the Ganges and the Yellow River no less than the Rhine and the Thames. All the products of the spirit cross and mingle from one end of the world to the other. We must choose between an abominable confusion and the spiritual unity of Christian culture, with all that this unity involves of rigorous formation, discernment and articulate thought. It is towards the establishment of this spiritual unity of a new Christendom that all the ardent desires of the Church of Christ tend today, because the message of Redemption is addressed to all men and because this message must be delivered.

Whatever the partisans of the absolute heterogeneity of languages and culture[4] may say, man is everywhere essentially the same, his mental and affective structure is found to be essentially identical in all climates. The testimony of missionaries is very clear on this point, whether it is a question of so-called primitive peoples or of peoples of the most refined civilizations, such as the Chinese. I am happy to recall in this connection the phrase of Emile Meyerson, one of the most eminent French philosophers of science, affirming the *catholicity of reason*.

And above reason the Church unites again all men in a transcendent and divine unity, which is that of the kingdom of Heaven, of the very life of God participated in here below, and, if I may so put it, of the universe of the Incarnation; and it is when sustained from above by this supernatural unity of the life of grace, that the natural unity of reason succeeds in producing its fruit.

May I be permitted to observe once more: "The Church is universal, because she is born of God, all nations are at home in her, the arms of her crucified Master are extended over all races and all civilizations. She does not bring to peoples *the benefits of civilization,* but the Blood of Christ and supernatural Beatitude . . . This is why she reminds us that her missionaries must renounce every worldly interest, every concern with national propaganda, must know only Christ, and that they are sent to found Churches which will be self-sufficient, complete with their own clergy. She does not affirm that all nations and all races have the same historical vocation and an equal human development, but she does affirm, and in the most significant manner, that they are all called of God, all alike enveloped in His charity, that each has its legitimate place in the spiritual unity of Christendom and is capable of supplying bishops for the flock of Christ." [5]

7. This double unity, this double catholicity of reason and grace, of the human spirit and the Church, needs an intellectual organ to manifest it, strengthen it, and diffuse it.

At a time when East and West are exchanging all their dreams and all their errors, when all the scourges that Europe almost died of—positivist scientism, atheism, either materialism or anti-intellectualism, the religion of automatic Progress and of the deification of man—hurl themselves, exported by Europe, on Africa and Asia as so many gospels of destruction, when in all countries the intelligence is struggling against the most subtle enchantments of the philosophers of this world, are we to believe that Christian culture is not itself obligated to employ a perfectly equipped intelligence, a tried and true doctrine? It is the most highly developed and the most perfect form of Christian thought, it is the lofty wisdom placed under the sign of the Common Doctor of the Church, that provides Christian culture with this indispensable instrument.

"It is from this wisdom that we must draw—under appropriate forms of presentation, and by thoroughly examining it in all its rigor and according to the real exigencies of each problem—the intellectual values which every country in the world needs. A form that preserves all that is universal and lasting, it alone can revive the West, give it back again the free and living use of its spiritual riches, its tradition and its culture; it alone can save also the heritage of the East, and reconcile the two halves of the world." [6]

Let me give an example. In an address delivered in 1928, Louis de la Vallée Poussin, the eminent historian of Buddhism, drew attention to the work accomplished in India by Father Dandoy and his associates: "They publish in Bengal an excellent little paper, called *Christ, the Light of the World*,⁷ in which they show how one can pass, nay, how one must logically pass, from the Vedanta, the traditional philosophy of India, to Christianity. Good Sanskrit scholars, they study in lucid notes the five or six forms of this philosophy which vacillates, in gradations of which Indian scholars have never been able to make head or tail, between a monism which appears absolute and a theism too dualist to be orthodox in our sense.

"Such investigations, from the Indian point of view, are more than praiseworthy. They bring to light especially the religious and mystical character of Indian speculation, even of such of it as offers the most rationalist aspect.

"From the practical point of view, I have a definite feeling that they are hitting the mark. Saint Thomas is right as against Sankara, Ramanuja and the rest: he offers the only solution in which the ends of all the chains are solidly held; he reconciles, in going beyond them, the opposing theses of the Vedantic schools; he is, in a word, the true doctor of the Vedanta. . . .

"Cultured Indians, we are told, found the German scholar Paul Deussen's book, *Das System des Vedânta*, a weak exposition—it is, in fact, a Vedanta concocted of some imperfectly understood Sankara diluted in some Schopenhauer and with a dash of Hegel. . . . On the contrary, the investigations pursued by my friends in Bengal seem to be taken very seriously by the pundits. Father Dandoy and his associates have gone to great trouble to read the texts and the com-

mentaries; you have the feeling that they know in
detail—and this is very important—what they are
talking about; they engage in no polemic, import no
arguments from the West; but they do offer, with an
exactitude of theological learning which I greatly admire and on the most elusive of subjects, a discourse
whose movement is genuinely Indian and a new,
perfectly informed and convincing commentary on the
old Brahmasutras. Without adopting, as did Robert
de Nobili before them, the dress of the Brahmin, these
very modern apologists have fashioned for themselves
a psychology as subtle as you could want, very
Thomistic and yet Bengali." [8]

This example[9] shows us how Saint Thomas Aquinas
has prepared for us the conceptual and notional equipment, the metaphysical equipment of intelligence, that
Christian culture needs, and thanks to which we can
hope that it will achieve its unity in the entire world.

And this is indeed the highest privilege of Western
culture, what makes it precious among all others: the
fact that it itself is basically universal, that, born in
Judea, trained by that strength and piety of natural
reason which characterized ancient Greece and Rome,
and formed then by the Church of Christ, it has been
able to produce first a Plato and an Aristotle, then a
Saint Paul and a Saint Augustine, and then a Saint
Thomas. May the incomparable intellectual instrument thus prepared be put to work not only by
apostles of the white race but also by an elite among
the colored races, who will learn the lesson taught by
Thomas Aquinas as the sons of the Gallic, Celtic or
German "barbarians" have learned the lesson of Aristotle. It is here that that intellectual cooperation
among Christians of all nations referred to above is
more than ever a pressing necessity.

But let it be well understood: nothing solid, nothing lasting, will be achieved without this recourse to the wisdom of Saint Thomas. It would be a tremendous illusion to think that in order to realize more rapidly the work of unity it were necessary to jettison the whole heritage of truths acquired at such a fearful price on the shores of the West. It is precisely this heritage that the world needs; it is the dispersion of it throughout the world that will unite the world. We must not jettison it! We must mobilize it. And to mobilize it is not an easy matter, for the solution to all the new problems which are thus raised is not to be found ready-made in Saint Thomas: to bring out this solution a new and original effort is required, an effort that demands as much boldness in applying one's self to the real as fidelity to the slightest principles of the master.

No philosophy whatever can be baptized as it stands. It must first be corrected and, in most cases, transformed. And often too the task proves to be impossible. If Aristotle could be baptized by Saint Thomas, it is because his metaphysical principles were founded in objective reality. And if the great metaphysical systems of ancient civilizations remain, unlike modern ones, turned toward being and therefore open to universality, by this very fact they have, as it were, a longing for the *emendations* Aristotelianism and Thomism would supply. How much more soothing to our indolence, how much more gratifying to our spirit of adventure, what a relief to play truant and to dispense with the disciplines of the *philosophia perennis!* But culture cannot dispense with these disciplines, it will never be able to dispense with the Greek Aristotle transfigured by the Angelic Doctor.

I do not say that the wisdom of Saint Thomas must

be imposed as a dogma. The Gospel is free of this wisdom. I do not say either that we should keep of the spiritual treasures of the Orient only what would already be formulated in the letter of a system we would regard as complete and closed. Quite the contrary! I say that through love and through respect for these treasures—and in order to have them take on their highest dimensions, as also in order that one may cooperate loyally in upholding them against the forces of destruction—those who want to integrate them in a lasting cultural achievement must fortify themselves with an indefectible doctrinal equipment.

And Thomist philosophy will be the better for it. It will take leave of the eternal controversies of the school, it will go out into the highways and byways, it will spread its wings. What Saint Dominic said with regard to men, must also be said of ideas: "Grain rots in the heap but is fruitful when sown." Thomist philosophy is of its very nature a progressive and assimilative philosophy, a missionary philosophy, a philosophy constantly open to the demands of First Truth. And Saint Thomas is not a relic of the Middle Ages, with whom only history and scholarship would have to concern themselves. He is in all the fullness of the term the apostle of modern times.

III

8. In a more or less narrow and servile way, according as their metaphysical level is more or less elevated, all religions other than the Catholic religion are integral parts of certain determinate cultures, particularized to certain ethnic climates and to certain historical formations. Only the Catholic religion, because it is super-

natural and has come down to us from the pierced Heart of God dying upon the Cross, is absolutely and rigorously transcendent, supra-cultural, supra-racial, supra-national.

This is one of the signs of its divine origin. It is also one of the signs of contradiction which will occasion till the end of time the passion of the Church, raised like her Master between heaven and earth. We can think that the world, from this point of view, is entering a phase of particularly difficult conflicts, comparable perhaps to those of apostolic times, under the Rome of the Caesars. On the one hand, non-Christian peoples do not know how to separate their native cultures, with all their human values, worthy in themselves of respect and filial reverence, from religious creeds stained with error and superstition. And Christian universalism will have to show them how this discernment is to be made, and how the Gospel respects and superelevates—and transfigures little by little—these particular values. This demonstration is not performed, as a rule, without sweat and blood. And the silly dogma of positivist sociologism, taught in all countries in the name of European science, and according to which all religion is but a specific product of the social clan (and Christianity, therefore, a specific product of the European races), will not make it any easier.

On the other hand, it happens that among Christian peoples, when faith and charity diminish in the mass of them, many of them come to think that Christianity, because it has been the vivifying principle of their historical culture, is essentially bound and tied to it. Are not certain apostles of Latin culture (I bear it no grudge, let me assure them) convinced that—this is the way it was put to me one day—*our religion is a*

Graeco-Latin religion? Such an enormity is full of significance. Without knowing of what spirit they are, and forgetting the divine transcendence of that which makes the life of their life, they end up in practice worshipping the true God in the same way as the Ephesians worshipped Diana and as the primitives worship the idols of their tribe. Christian universalism will have to remind them how the Gospel and the Church, without injuring any particular culture or the state or the nation, prevail over them all nevertheless with a pure and unsullied independence, and subordinate them all to the eternal interests of the human being, to the law of God, and to the charity of Christ. And this demonstration too is not made without resistance.

9. One point should, I think, be emphasized here. If the Kingdom of God, for the extension of which we are bound to work unceasingly, belongs to the order of the *spiritual*,[10] that is to say, to the order of eternal and supernatural life already begun here below, what we call *civilization* or *culture*[11] belongs, on the contrary, to the order of the *temporal*, refers immediately to a common good which is not simply material, to be sure, which is also and above all intellectual and moral, but which in itself is of the natural and terrestrial order: though ordered to the Kingdom of God, which superelevates it in its own order, and from which it must receive its highest rule and measure, culture or civilization relates directly to this perishable life and to the development of human nature on earth.

This is why, in this world ravaged by sin, cultures and civilizations are naturally in opposition and at war.

When we speak, therefore, of Christian culture and of its unity we are in reality speaking of the super-elevation produced by Christianity in the various particular ethnic and historical cultures, and which impresses on them, without destroying their diversity, an image of the supra-cultural unity of the Mystical Body of Christ.

In other words, "civilization is the expansion of the truly human life of the body politic. It belongs, of itself, to the *natural* order: art, metaphysics, science, politics are strictly civil virtues. . . . But it can expand fully only under the *supernatural* sky of the Church. . . . Christian civilization is the by-product of the Kingdom of God." [12]

The consequence is clear. A philosophy, a theology even, is part of a culture: if they are to attain to the pure universality required of them by natural reason and by reason enlightened by faith, it is absolutely necessary that they be also superelevated by the influences of grace, assumed by the Mystical Body of Christ. We thus come again to a truth which seems to me essential and on which I have already had occasion to insist.

The privileges inherent in the doctrine of Saint Thomas are to be explained only by the fact that Thomas Aquinas is truly the *Common Doctor of the Church,* because this doctrine (although the Church never imposes it as a dogma of faith, for it is a human synthesis) is the *appropriated instrument* of the intellectual life of the Church. This is what maintains it in a purity of which man by himself alone would not be capable, what assures it that sovereign degree of spirituality and universality which makes it truly *catholic,* and what prevents it from being restricted or particularized by the means it uses.

The metaphysics and the theology of Saint Thomas are expressed in a system of signs, in a language and

an order which are Latin, but in itself this wisdom is
no more bound to Latinism than it is to the astronomy
of Aristotle or Ptolemy. It is bound to no particularity
of climate, of race or of tradition: this is why it alone
is capable of recreating among minds, under the
superior light of the Gospel, a true unity of human
culture, of restoring a spiritual Christendom. For six
centuries now it has been tested in its principles and
in its rational springs, purified, stripped of all that
which weighed it down accidentally. It appears today
in its true youth. Let it be careful to remain "separate,
in order to command," as Anaxagoras said of the
Intellect, to keep itself from being particularized by
any local circumstances of tradition and of culture or
by any one of its partisans. To this end it must remain
jealously attached to the superior virtues on which its
integrity in the souls of men depends, and to its
ministerial role with regard to the Gospel and the holy
contemplation of the Church of Jesus Christ.[13]

If all that has just been said is true, we can understand that if the Thomist synthesis offers us a means
par excellence of achieving the unity of Christian
culture, nevertheless, and by very reason of the fact
that with regard to such a practical goal it is but a
means, an instrument, it does not suffice for this unity.
It would be a great mistake to think that philosophical
or theological science can by itself alone, and taken as
principal agent, so to speak, exercise a truly formative
and rectifying influence on culture.

We must begin with Christ. It is not Saint Thomas,
it is Christ Who makes Christian culture: it is Christ
—through the Church and through Saint Thomas,
through the contemplation of the saints and the love
which joins them to the agony of the Son of Man,
through the labor of the theologians and the philoso-

phers—Who brings into the service of the Son of Man all the virtues of the intellect and all its scattered riches.

It follows from this that the thought of the Common Doctor will shed its light on culture only as it appears together with the Gospel and the Catholic Faith— these two radiances, the one divine, the other human, helping each other and multiplying each other, according to the great law of the reciprocity of causes: *causae ad invicem sunt causae.*

10. Three philosophers were talking together one day in the late nineteen twenties, one Orthodox and two Catholics; a Russian, a German, and a Frenchman— Nicholas Berdyaev, Peter Wust, and the writer. We were wondering how to reconcile two apparently contradictory facts: the fact that modern history seems to be entering, as Berdyaev puts it, a *new middle age*, in which the unity and universality of Christian culture will be recovered, and extended this time to the whole universe; and, on the other hand, the fact that the general movement of civilization seems to be drawing it towards the universalism of Antichrist and his iron rod rather than toward the universalism of Christ and His liberating law, and in any case to prohibit the hope of the unification of the world in a universal Christian "empire."

The answer, in my opinion, is the following. I think that two immanent movements cross each other at each point of the history of the world and affect each of its momentary complexes. One of these movements draws upward everything in the world that participates in the divine life of the Church (which is *in* the world but not *of* the world), and follows the attraction of Christ, Head of the human race. The other movement draws downward everything in the world which belongs to the Prince of this world, head of all evildoers. It is in undergoing these two internal movements that history advances in time.

Thus human affairs are subjected to a distension of ever increasing force, until in the end the fabric gives way. Thus the cockle grows with the wheat; the capital of sin increases throughout the length of history, and the capital of grace increases also and superabounds. In proportion as history approaches Antichrist and undergoes in all its visible structure transformations which prepare his coming, so also does it approach Him Whom Antichrist precedes and Who conceals beneath this same chain of events in the world the holy work He pursues among His own. In this perspective I wrote: "Today the devil has so contrived everything in the regime of terrestrial life that the world will soon be habitable only to saints. The rest will drag their lives out in despair or fall below the level of man. The antinomies of human life are too exasperating, the weight of matter too oppressive; merely to exist, one has to expose himself to too many traps. Christian heroism will one day become the sole answer to the problems of life. Then, as God proportions His graces to needs, and tries no one beyond his strength, we shall doubtless see coincide with the worst state of human history a flowering of sanctity." [14]

Hence it is no doubt true that we are moving toward a new middle age, towards a rediscovered unity and universality of Christian culture. But, whatever may be the more or less lasting terrestrial triumphs we may hope for the Church, we realize that this restoration of Christendom, both in the social order and in the order of the spirit, must be effected in a world more and more tragically contested.

This is to say that instead of being grouped and assembled, as in the Middle Ages, in a homogeneous and integrally Christian body of civilization, limited however to a privileged portion of the inhabited earth, it seems that the unity of Christian culture must now extend over the whole surface of the globe, but, in return, represent only the order and living network of Christian temporal institutions and Christian centers of intellectual and spiritual life spread throughout the world in the great supra-cultural unity of the Church. Instead of a mighty fortress raised up amidst the lands, we should rather think of the army of stars distributed in the sky. Such a unity is not any less real, but it is diffuse instead of being concentrated.

Whatever be the truth of these hypotheses, my object in writing these pages was to show that Saint Thomas Aquinas is our predestined guide in the reconstruction of Christian culture, the steward and minister of that great blessed kingdom which the Church, in the admirable Preface to the Mass of Christ the King, calls the kingdom of truth and of life, of sanctity and of grace, of justice, of love and of peace: *regnum veritatis et vitae, regnum sanctitatis et gratiae, regnum justitiae, amoris et pacis.*

THE APOSTLE OF MODERN TIMES[1]

> *"For knowledge of things so great
> [supernatural truths], the beauty
> of which draws and converts the
> whole man to itself, must not be
> said to be cut off and unproduc-
> tive, but rather very fecund."*
> Pius XI, Encyclical *Studiorum
> Ducem.*

According to the example of his divine Master, Saint
Thomas makes no exception of persons. He invites to
the banquet of wisdom disciple as well as master, both
teacher and the taught, the active and the contemplative, the secular and the regular, poets, artists, scholars
and philosophers, ay, and *the man in the street,* if only
he will lend an ear, as well as priests and theologians.
And his doctrine possesses energies powerful enough
and pure enough to act efficaciously, not only on that
consecrated elite which is being formed in the seminaries (would that it were always sufficiently aware of
the magnitude of its intellectual responsibilities!) but
also on the whole universe of culture; to reestablish
human intelligence in order, and thus, with the grace
of God, to bring back to the ways of Truth a world
that is dying for no longer knowing It.

I

1. The disease afflicting the modern world is above all a disease of the intellect. It began in the mind and has by now penetrated to its very roots. Is it surprising then that the world should seem to us shrouded in darkness? *Si oculus tuus fuerit nequam, totum corpus tuum tenebrosum erit.*[2]

Just as at the moment when the original sin was committed all the harmony of the human being was shattered, because the order which requires that reason be subject to God had first been violated, so at the root of all our disorders we see first and above all a rupture of the supreme ordering of the intellect. The responsibility of philosophers in this respect is of prime importance. In the sixteenth century, but especially by the time of Descartes, the interior hierarchies of the virtues of reason began to crumble. Philosophy separated itself from theology to claim the title of supreme knowledge; then, as a natural result, the mathematical science of the sensible world and its phenomena was to take precedence over metaphysics. The history of modern philosophy shows us how the human intellect progressively affirmed its own independence with respect to God and with respect to being: that is to say, with respect to the supreme Object of every intelligence, and with respect to the connatural object of the intellect as such.

The due order between the intellect and its object was thus shattered. We have difficulty in realizing the frightful significance, charged with blood and tears, of these few abstract words; we have difficulty in realizing the tremendous upheaval, the tremendous invisible catastrophe, to which they point. The intellect! That "divine" activity, as Aristotle termed it, that prodigy of light and life, that glory and supreme perfection of created nature, through which we become spiritually all things, through which we shall one day possess our supernatural beatitude, from which here on earth all our acts (insofar as they are *human* acts) proceed, and on which the rectitude of all we do depends! Can we conceive how ruinous for man is the disturbance of that life—a participation in the divine light—which he bears within him? The revolution begun by Descartes and continued by the philosophers of the eighteenth and nineteenth centuries is a greater historical cataclysm than the most formidable upheavals of the earth's surface or of the economy of nations.

Indocile to the object, to God, to being, the intellect becomes also and to the same extent a rebel against any kind of tradition and spiritual continuity. It retires within itself, locks itself up in the incommunicability of the individual. And if we reflect that *docibilitas,* the capability of being taught, is an essential property of the created intelligence (nay more, of animal faculties themselves insofar as they resemble and foreshadow intelligence, so much so that Aristotle classifies animals according to this criterion, placing on the lowest rung those which are not capable of being taught); if we reflect, further, that this *docibilitas* is for us the true root of social life, man being a political animal primarily because he needs others in order that he may make progress in the work of speculative and practical reason, which is his specific work—then we must conclude, on the one hand, that in losing its heed of human teaching, along with its heed of the object, the intelligence in our time has proceeded in the direction both of a progressive weakening of reason and of a progressive loosening of the most profound and at the same time the most human bonds of social life.

Three main symptoms of the disease afflicting intelligence today down to its very roots may be discerned at the point of evolution which thought has reached since the great changes inaugurated by the Cartesian reform.

Intelligence fancies it affirms its own strength by denying and rejecting as genuine knowledge, first theology, and then metaphysics; by abandoning any attempt to know the First Cause and non-material realities; by cultivating a more or less refined doubt which wounds at once the perception of the senses and the principles of reason, that is to say, the very things all our knowledge depends on. This presumptuous lowering of human knowledge may be described in one word: *agnosticism.*

At the same time intelligence refuses the rights of First Truth, and repudiates the supernatural order, which it regards as impossible—and such a denial is a denial of the whole life of grace. In one word: *naturalism.*

Finally, intelligence lets itself be deceived by the mirage of a mythical conception of human nature, which assigns to that nature conditions peculiar to the pure spirit, supposes it to be in each one of us as perfect and complete as the angelic nature in the angel, and therefore claims for man, as a gift of nature, full self-sufficiency and absolute independence. Such a conception we may term *anthropocentric individualism,* giving to this word its full metaphysical sense, though it would be more exact to call it *angelism:* a term which is justified by historical as well as doctrinal considerations, for it is in the Cartesian confusion between the human soul and the pure spirit, as in the Leibnitzian confusion between substance, whatever it may be, and the angelic monad, that anthropocentric individualism has its ideal origin and its metaphysical type. And naturally this angelist error was to engender its contrary, whether it is a question of the psychological disintegration of the human person in the world of the irrational and of instinct, or of its social and political enslavement to the collective whole.

I say that these three great errors are the symptoms of a radical disease, for it is the very root, the three-fold root—rational, religious, moral—of our life that they attack.

At first they were singularly latent and hidden, in the state of pure spiritual *intentions*. Today everyone sees and feels them, because their cruel point has passed from the intellect right into the flesh of humanity.

Note too, it is the integrity of natural reason, the *simplicity of the eye* of intelligence, to use the Gospel phrase, the fundamental rectitude of common sense which is wounded by these errors. A strange outcome for rationalism! Man, looking for complete emancipation, undertook to reduce everything to the level of reason. And in the end he comes to renounce the real; he no longer dares to use ideas to adhere to being; he forbids himself to know anything beyond the sensible fact and the phenomenon of consciousness; he dissolves every object of thought in a great flowing jelly called Becoming or Evolution; he considers himself a barbarian if he does not suspect every first principle and every rational demonstration, of naïveté; he replaces the effort of thought and logical discernment by a certain refined play of instinct, imagination, intuitive thrills, and visceral emotions; he no longer dares to judge.

2. Now, it is important to realize that nothing below the intellect can remedy this disease which affects the intellect and which sprang from it; it is by intelligence itself that this disease will be cured. If intelligence is not saved, nothing will be saved. However sick it may be, it always conceals in its depths an essential vitality which nothing can injure or corrupt, and it always remains, in the metaphysical order, the highest faculty of the human being. Because of the indefectible energy of its spiritual nature, the disease which affects it, however radical it may be, remains of the accidental order, of the order of operation, and cannot affect it in its essential constitution. And it is precisely when this disease has become most manifest that one is entitled to hope for the salutary reaction: only let the intellect become conscious of the disease and it will immediately rouse itself against it.

Besides, it is no use beating about the bush. We are faced with an ineluctable necessity. The evils afflicting us have penetrated so deeply into the human substance, they have wrought such general havoc, that all the means of defense, all the extrinsic supports, due above all to the social structure, institutions, and the moral order of the family and the body politic—and truth as well as the highest acquisitions of culture have great need of them among men—are, if not actually destroyed, at least gravely shaken. Everything which was humanly solid is in jeopardy, "the mountains slide and leap." Man stands alone before the ocean of being and the transcendentals. It is an abnormal state for human nature and as perilous as can be. But in any case it is indeed the proof that everything depends henceforth on the restoration of the intelligence. Those metaphysical truths which Pascal thought too removed from the common feeling of men are henceforth beyond any doubt the sole refuge and safeguard of the common life and the most immediate interest of humanity. It is no longer a question of wagering heads or tails. It is a question of judging, true or false, and of facing eternal realities.

The attempts at political and social reconstruction to which the pressure of life prompts peoples will not avoid turning into brutal and ephemeral despotisms; they will produce nothing sound and stable—unless the intelligence is restored. The movement of religious renewal appearing in the world will be lasting and truly efficacious, only if the intelligence is restored. Truth first—*veritas liberabit vos.*[3] Woe to us, if we fail to understand that now as in the days of the creation of the world, the Word is at the beginning of the works of God.

II

3. What is the most striking characteristic of all that is most exalted, most divine, most efficacious in Saint Thomas Aquinas, the most striking characteristic of the very *sanctity* of Saint Thomas? "The chief characteristic of the sanctity of Saint Thomas is what Saint Paul calls *sermo sapientiae,* 'the word of wisdom,' and the union of the two wisdoms, the acquired and the infused."[4] Let us say that the sanctity of Saint Thomas is the *sanctity of the intelligence;* and I wish I could vividly convey all the reality contained in those words.

Not only does the philosophy of Saint Thomas uphold better than any other the rights and the nobility of the intellect—affirming its natural primacy over the will; gathering together under its light all the hierarchized diversity of being; identifying it, there where it subsists by itself as Pure Act, with the infinitely holy nature of the living God; and finally, in the practical order, reminding us unceasingly that the life of man, and above all the Christian life, "is grounded on intelligence"—but also, and this goes much further, the very *sanctity* of Thomas Aquinas, his charity, his sacrifice of praise, his consummation in Jesus, all are fulfilled and radiant in him at the summit of the spirit, in that life of the intellect which Aristotle declared to be better than human life, and where the activity of man borders on the activity of pure forms. This is the sense in which we should understand the age-old title of *Doctor Angelicus* so appropriately given to Thomas Aquinas. Saint Thomas is in a supereminent sense *the pure intellectual,* because intelligence itself is his means *par excellence* of serving and loving God, because intelligence itself is his host of adoration.

His principal task, as is well known, was, with the approbation and the encouragement, nay, rather at the instigation of the papacy, to make room in the Christian intelligence for Aristotle—completing him and perfecting him, and purifying him of all dross—and for all the natural wisdom of those philosophers whom Tertullian called "animals of glory." To achieve this he had to fight a very hard battle. For if there is between Aristotle and the Gospel, between the human wisdom which grew up on the soil of Greece and the revelation which came down from the sky of Judea, a kind of preestablished harmony, which is in itself a remarkable apologetic sign; nevertheless, to realize this harmony, to make it actual, by triumphing over the obstacles born of the limitations of the human subject, there was required not only the maturity of the civilization of Saint Louis' age but also all the strength of the great dumb ox of Sicily. As Pascal saw so clearly, it is above all due to the mediocrity of our intellectual wing-span that we fall into error, because we cannot grasp together truths which seem opposed but are in reality complementary. "Exclusion" is thus "the cause of heresy," and more generally of error. The self-styled Augustinians of the thirteenth century, attached materially to the letter of their master, commingled the formal objects of faith and reason, of metaphysical wisdom and the wisdom of the saints: in short, they tended toward what we would today call *anti-intellectualism*. What were they really doing in this, if not refusing the rights of the truth of the natural order? This tendency was to end later in formal heresy, with Luther and his inhuman hatred of reason. The Averroists, in their fanatical devotion to an Aristotle corrupted by the Arabs, disregarded the proper light and the primacy of faith and theology: in short, they tended toward *rationalism*, refusing the rights of supernatural truth. And we know very well to what this tendency was to lead. Saint Thomas crushed them both, and he will crush them again, for it is always the same battle. And at the same time he determined with definitive principles the rational theory of that distinction and that accord between the natural order and the supernatural order which are integral to the Catholic Faith, and more important for the life of the world than the cycle of the stars and the seasons.

But this double battle against the Averroists and the

old benighted Scholasticism, this immense task of integrating Aristotle into Catholic thought, is only the manifestation and the sign of an invisible struggle, greater still and more formidable. The peculiar task of Saint Thomas, the undertaking to which he was appointed by the Lord, was to bring the proudest and most intractable (because the most spiritual) of powers, the intellect—I mean the intellect in all its apparel of riches and majesty, armed with all its speculative energies, with all its logic, all its science, all its art, all the embellishment of its fierce virtues rooted in being itself—to bring the intellect (compelling it to sobriety but never to abdication) whole and entire into the holy light of Christ, into the service of the Child-God lying between the ox and the ass. For the rest of time all the Magi will follow him.

These considerations enable us, I think, to catch a glimpse of the mystery of the very vocation of Saint Thomas. A very astonishing vocation, it has often been observed. For the place that Thomas Aquinas had to leave in order to answer the call of God was not the world, but the cloister, not the society of his day, but Monte Cassino. It was not what the Church calls the ignominy of the habit of the world—*ignominia saecularis habitus*—but the holy Benedictine habit that he abandoned in order to put on the white robe of Saint Dominic. It was not the peril of the world that he left for the state of perfection: it was from one state of perfection to another, and a more difficult one, that he moved. He had to leave the house of blessed Father Benedict from whom, as a little oblate in a black habit, he learned the twelve degrees of humility,[5] and of whom, as an enraptured Doctor finished with his work, he would ask hospitality in order to die. And knowing that such is the will of the

Lord, he obstinately insisted on this departure with the tenacity of an indomitable will.

Brothers, mother, prison, ruse and violence, nothing could stop him. Why this obstinacy? He has to be about his Father's business. What is God? He has to teach us to spell divine things. And this is what Countess Theodora could not understand.

Saint Dominic had asked Saint Benedict for him in Heaven, because the Word of God had asked Saint Dominic for him, to entrust him with a mission to Christian intelligence. He must serve intelligence, but as the priest serves the creature of God. He must instruct it, baptize it, nourish it with the Body of the Lord; he must celebrate the nuptials of the Intellect and the Lamb. On the white pebble given to him, which is also the live coal that purifies his lips, there is written: *Truth.*

Saint Thomas is properly and before everything else *the apostle of the intelligence:* this is the first reason why we must regard him as *the apostle of modern times.*

4. The second reason is what we may call the *absolutism of truth* in his soul and in his work, with this triple consequence: a perfect purity in intellectual quality; a perfect logical rigor and at the same time a harmonious complexity in doctrine; and a perfect docility in obedience to the real. Admittedly every philosopher, every theologian desires and seeks the truth. But do they desire it with such vehemence and so exclusively? Not to mention particularist preoccupations and vices of every kind—self-love, aimless curiosity, the vain desire for originality and novelty pursued for their own sakes—which so often spoil the quest, may not a philosopher, the while he seeks

truth, seek *also* something else? In reality it is very rare that Truth *alone* draws everything to itself in the heaven of the intellect. Giant stars, other transcendentals mingle their attractions with Truth's, and divert thought. And this is a grave disorder, for science as such must be measured only by the true. Is there not at the bottom of Platonism in metaphysics and of Scotism in theology a secret collusion, so to speak, of Beauty or the Good with Truth, of Love with Knowledge? With other philosophers it is more earthly influences that enter into play—convenience, facility, adaptation to the patterns of the age or to the exigencies of teaching, or more generally to the weakness of the human subject, an ill-controlled anxiety as to practical consequences, even an effort to strike a balance between opposed opinions, which one takes for wisdom, though in reality it consists merely in seeking a golden mean between error and truth as between two opposed vices. Thus truths are diminished by the sons of men.

Saint Thomas, on the contrary, leaves truth all its grandeur, a grandeur the measure of which is the Son of God. Philosopher and theologian, he knows nothing but Truth, and is it not so that Philosophy and Theology taken as such must know only Jesus Crucified? His whole rule or measure is in being, he is in a perfectly correct relation to his object. Nothing other than intelligible necessities and the exigencies of supreme principles ever determines his solutions, even if they should be thus rendered more difficult for us, even if they should make men exclaim: *durus est hic sermo.*[6] And if his doctrine rests entirely, in the analytical order, *in via inventionis*, on being, the first datum for the intellect, it depends entirely, in the synthetic order, *in via judicii*, on God, the First Truth, the supreme object of every spirit.[7] Saint Thomas casts his net over the universe and captures all things, to bear them, vivified in the intellect, toward the Beatific Vision. This theology of the peaceful is, under the light of faith, an immense movement of thought between two intuitions: the intuition of being and the first principles of reason, whence it starts and which is given to it here on earth; and the intuition of God clearly seen, towards which it advances and which will be given to it in the hereafter. Ordering the whole discourse to an ineffable supreme end, it remains ever rational, but at the same time it teaches reason not to seek its measure in itself; and before the mysteries from below, such as matter and potency, as before the mysteries from above, such as the influence of divine premotion on created liberty, it asks us to pay tribute both to the rights of being over our spirit and to the divine sublimity. This is why it is so serene and so universal, so open and so free, the most boldly affirmative and the most humbly prudent, the most systematic and the least biased, the most intractable and the most receptive to all the nuances of the real, the richest in certitudes and the most careful to respect the part of the probable and of opinion, the most resolute and uncompromising and the most immune to self-complacency. So transcendent is the object in which it aspires to lose itself!

Now I say that in this respect also Saint Thomas answers in a special way the needs of the present time. The spirit is exposed to such serious dangers today that no palliative can possibly suffice for it. Many restoratives which worked in the past are now powerless to act on minds ploughed to their very depths by modern controversies, and whose critical needs have therefore grown particularly exacting.

The work of disintegrating forces is so much to the fore today that to triumph over them there is required an implacably rigorous doctrine, one that is at the same time so ample that it can do justice to all the diversities in which contemporary thought, for want of an ordering light, exhausts itself. Thus what is really needed is precisely the absolutism of truth; what is expedient and "practical" is doctrinal radicalism, but a radicalism that is free from all narrowness and all brutality, all partiality, all fanaticism, and holding therefore to the only true Absolute, to the transcendence of First Truth, from which all things proceed into being. A thousand doctrines can aggravate the condition of the intelligence, only one can cure it.

5. Thomism—and this is the third reason why Saint Thomas must be called the apostle of modern times— is alone capable of delivering the intelligence from the three radical errors mentioned at the beginning of this chapter.

Scrutinizing the metaphysical secrets of knowledge, the original nature and the mysterious immateriality of which it alone perfectly respects, putting our ideas in continuity with things through the intuition of the senses, and resolving all our knowledge in the evidence of being and the first principles, whose transcendental value enables it to ascend even to God, the doctrine of Saint Thomas is a wisdom high enough to save the intelligence from the deceptions of agnosticism, and to oppose to the idealist demon (already quite decrepit) a realism not naive but soundly critical.

Aware of the infinite elevation and the infinite liberty of the Creator, as of the radically contingent depths of created being, assuring, thanks to a sound notion of the universal, the value of *nature* and its laws, and showing that this nature still remains immensely ductile with respect to God's power, open and penetrable to the divine influx, it reduces to absurdity the naturalist postulate and the metaphysical hypocrisy which, hidden behind the positive sciences, tries to endow the creature with divine aseity.

Understanding all that the very notion of "rational animal" implies of grandeur and servitude, situating the human intelligence on the lowest rung of the ladder of spirits, bluntly dismissing all its claims to play the pure spirit, doing justice both to the autonomy that belongs to us as spirits and to the dependence that belongs to us as creatures, as material creatures, and as wounded creatures, it destroys by the root, by its *angelist* root, an anthropocentric individualism which in reality sacrifices the human person to an illusory and devouring image of man. And at the same time it restores the dignity of the person against all that despairs of reason and liberty and all that deifies the state.

The fact is that Saint Thomas—and this is the most immediate benefit he confers—brings the intellect back to its object, orientates it toward its end, restores it to its nature. He tells it that it is made for being. How could it possibly not give ear? It is as if one told the eye that it is made to see, or wings that they are made to fly. It finds itself again in recovering its object; it orders itself entirely to being; in accordance with the sovereign inclination that things have for their first principle, it tends, above all, towards Subsistent Being Itself.

Simplicity of gaze is at the same time restored to it; artificial obstacles no longer obtrude to make it hesitate before the natural evidence of first principles;

it re-establishes the continuity of philosophy and common sense.

Submissive to the object, but in order to attain to its true liberty, for it is in this submission that it acts with the most spontaneous and the most living activity; heedful of the teaching of masters, but in order to render more intense and more perfect its own grasp of the object (for it is through love of being that it asks to be helped and fortified by the labor of centuries), it re-establishes within itself the essential hierarchies of the intellect and the order of its virtues.

What constitutes the nobility of philosophers, of modern philosophers in particular, is that in spite of their erring ways they love the intellect, even when they ruin it. But for the most part they have loved it more than they have loved God. Saint Thomas loves God more than the intellect, but he loves the intellect more than all the philosophers have loved it. That is why he can restore it, reminding it of its duties. He shames it out of its cowardice, gives it again the courage to face the supreme truths. He shames it out of its vainglory, bends it to measure itself against things and to listen to a tradition. He teaches it again simultaneously the two complementary virtues it had lost together, magnanimity and humility.

6. Apostle of the intelligence, doctor of truth, restorer of the intellectual order, Saint Thomas wrote not for the thirteenth century but for our time. His own time is the time of the spirit, which dominates the ages. I say that he is a contemporary writer, the most "present" of all thinkers. He adheres so purely to the high light of wisdom that as regards the more particular sciences and their moving shadows he enjoys a

liberty such as no philosopher has ever known: all
the considerable coating borrowed from the science
of the thirteenth century can fall away, his philosophical and metaphysical doctrine remains as intact as the
soul when separated from the body. And perhaps the
divestiture effected by the revolutions which have
taken place in the science of phenomena since Nicole
Oresme, Leonardo da Vinci and Galileo, was necessary
to bring Thomism to the state of spirituality, and
therefore of efficacy, which truly corresponds to the
spiritual elevation of the very thought of Saint Thomas.
He stands at the crossroads before us; he holds the
key to the problems which oppress our hearts; he
teaches us how to triumph over both anti-intellectualism and rationalism, over the evil which degrades
reason below, and the evil which exalts it above the
real; he gives us the secret of true humanism, of the
supreme development of the human person and intellectual virtues, but in sanctity, not in concupiscence,
through the spirit and the cross, not through the
grandeurs of the flesh. To an age profoundly tormented
by the desire (too often erratic and turned toward
base things) for a reign of the heart and a life of
love, he teaches the only doctrine which affirms the
absolute practical primacy of charity in our life, and
which invites us to the banquet of true love, I mean
supernatural charity, yet without denying the intellect
and its metaphysical superiority, or adulterating
charity itself by contaminating it with purely human
passions or with clan ambitions. *Charity must ever
increase, in virtue of the first commandment, and this
is why the perfection of charity falls under the commandment, as the end toward which each one must
tend according to his condition.* Such is the law of
gravitation that the Angelic Doctor teaches to a world

all the more haunted by the idea of progress, the more it is ignorant generally of the meaning of progress.

Even William of Tocco in his day never tired of stressing the *modernity* of Friar Thomas. In truth, this modernity is at opposite poles to the modernity pursued nowadays and found so captivating. For Saint Thomas achieves the *new* by accident, seeking to achieve only the *true*, whereas today one achieves the new in willing the new as such: it is the true which is now but an accident. Wherefore one aims much more to destroy the old than to improve it, and to exalt the originality of each thinking subject than to conform thought to the object. It is the reversal of the order: this essentially particularist and negative method is in reality essentially retrograde. All acquired truths must be called into question, one after the other.

Saint Thomas' method, on the contrary, is essentially universalist and positive. It aims indeed at preserving all the acquired knowledge of humanity in order to add to it and to perfect it; and it requires the more and more complete effacement of the personality of the philosopher before the truth of the object. If Thomas attaches himself to Aristotle, it is not because he sees in him a fashionable thinker, recently imported by the Arabs, but because he recognizes him to be the best interpreter of natural reason, the one who established philosophy on foundations in conformity with that which is. And he follows him only in judging him at every step, correcting and purifying him in a higher light, which is not that of Aristotle but of Wisdom incarnate. If he fights the too material disciples of Saint Augustine, it is not to destroy Saint Augustine but rather to follow and understand him in a more living and more profoundly faithful manner, in a more perfect commerce of spirit. And no theologian has had a more devoted love of the common and time-honored wisdom with which the Church is divinely instructed. This is why the Angelic Doctor is also the Common Doctor of the Church. The Common Doctor! An admirable title, and one that points to a truly superhuman grandeur, puts all our sorry vanities in their place, and answers to the most pressing needs of the moment! It is not a special Doctor or a particular Doctor or an original Doctor, or a Doctor peculiar to our person or our community, it is not an illumined Doctor, or a devout or subtle or irrefragable Doctor, or a Doctor *facundus* or *resolutissimus* or *eximius,* or a *venerabilis inceptor,* but a Common Doctor, the Common Doctor of the Church, that we need. He is standing at the threshold of modern times and holding out to us, in the basket wrought of his thousands of arguments, the sacred fruits of wisdom.

Now something much more important than a great many material events that are more easily noticeable, is taking place in our day. At the bidding of the Church, the doctrine of Saint Thomas is not only restored or in process of being restored in Catholic schools and in the education of the clergy, but now it is emerging from the old folios in which it was held in reserve, not itself old but as youthful as truth; it addresses itself to the world and claims its place, that is to say, the first place, in the intellectual life of our age; it cries in the market place, as it is said of wisdom: *sapientia foris praedicat, in plateis dat vocem.*[8] After the long idealist aberration due to Descartes and to the great Kantian heresy, we are now witnessing an attempt at the reintegration of the philosophy of being into Western civilization. The lovers of paradox and novelty should be the first to enjoy this.

There is here an enormous task to be accomplished, and a difficult one, a task not devoid of danger. But it is a beautiful risk, καλὸς κίνδυνος. And should we not imitate Saint Thomas in that also which I called a moment ago his modernity, in his boldness in innovating, in his intellectual courage in risking the new? For it is indeed true, but in a more subtle sense than the devotees of Evolution think, that wherever there is life on earth, there is movement and renewal, and therefore risk to be run and the unknown to be faced. But it is not in revolt that there are the most obstacles to be surmounted, but rather in the restoration of order; it is not for tearing down that the most energy is required, but rather for building up. Saint Thomas Aquinas is the hero of intellectual order; the immense philosophical and theological enterprise which he undertook in his day and which, to be brought to a successful issue, required not only his genius but all the prudence and the energy, the whole perfect organism of the virtues and the gifts of his admirable sanctity, is a much more marvelous adventure than the finest adventures of men—an angelic adventure. He told his companion that he would never be anything in his Order or in the Church. On his shoulders weighed the whole future of Christian civilization and of the intellect, and the greatest mission the Church ever assigned to one of her children.

Each of us, insignificant as we may be in comparison with this giant, must yet have some part in his spirit, since we are his disciples. We are certainly not childish enough to aim, as some would have us, to do again with modern philosophers, in taking them for our masters and adopting their principles, to do again with Descartes, even with Kant or Hegel or Bergson, what Thomas did with Aristotle. As if one could do with error the same as one can do with truth, and as if to build a house one should keep changing its foundations endlessly! No, what is required of us is that, while rejecting decidedly the ferment of error which has been at work in modern philosophy from its very beginning and which tends to equate the human creature with God, and while attaching ourselves to the principles of Saint Thomas with a fidelity which will never be pure enough, without admitting the least diminution or any admixture (for assimilation is possible only if the organism is whole and intact)—what is required is that we transmit the light of Saint Thomas into the intellectual life of our time, that we think our time in this light, and that we apply ourselves to informing, animating, and ordering by this light all the materials, palpitating with life and sometimes rich with such a precious human quality, which the world and its art, its philosophy, its science, its culture have prepared, and spoiled, alas! in the past four centuries. What is required is that we save all that is still viable in the modern world, and that we recover possession in order to bring into the perfect order of wisdom, of these constellations in movement, these spiritual milky ways, those things which, through the weight of sin, are sinking towards dissolution and death. Of course I do not think that such an undertaking can succeed fully; to indulge such a hope would suppose great illusions about the nature of man and the course of his history. But what is necessary—and it is sufficient—is that the deposit be saved and that those who love the truth may be able to recognize it.

7. Nothing below the intellect, we said above, can cure the intellect. But what is better here on earth than intelligence, infused charity, must also be in-

voked. If the return to intellectual order must be the work of the intelligence itself, nevertheless the intelligence, in this work which is its own, needs to be aided by Him Who is the principle of its light and Who reigns in spirits only through charity. If the philosophy and the theology of Saint Thomas are exclusively founded on and stabilized by the pure objective necessities which impose themselves either on natural reason or on reason illuminated by faith, nevertheless the human intellect is so weak by nature, and so weakened further by the first sin, and the thought of Saint Thomas is of such a high intellectuality, that in actual fact, so far as the knowing subject is concerned, there was required, for this thought to be given us, all the supernatural graces of whose aid the eminent sanctity and the unique mission of the Angelic Doctor assured him. And it follows, too, let us note, that if this thought is to live without alteration, there is required, and there will always be required, the superior strengthening of those gifts of the Holy Ghost which are present in every Christian and which develop in us with sanctifying grace and charity.

To ignore these truths would be to labor under a serious delusion. They are, more particularly, made only the more urgent by the very diffusion of Thomism. Once a doctrine of wisdom passes amongst men, it must be more apprehensive of becoming one day fashionable than of the sophisms of its adversaries. Are not even our French centers of higher learning, forgetting the famous darkness of the Middle Ages, beginning to take some interest in Saint Thomas? I am told that an impressive number of the doctoral theses presented to the Sorbonne are devoted to Thomist philosophy. We feel most gratified, naturally.

But we do not conceal from ourselves that in proportion as minds insufficiently prepared and armed, and more or less influenced by modern prejudices, take to examining this philosophy, it will run the risk of being studied without the proper light and thus of suffering inadequate, fragmentary and distorting interpretations. This is already apparent, and not only in the works of academic historians.

Saint Thomas himself tells us how to guard against this danger, both by his doctrine and, perhaps more efficaciously still, by his example. Did he not confess to his companion Reginald that his learning had been acquired above all through the means of prayer? Each time he wanted to study, to debate, to write or to dictate, did he not first have recourse to the secrecy of prayer, shedding tears before God in order that he might be instructed in truth? Were not metaphysical wisdom and theological wisdom for him the footstool and the throne of the wisdom of the Holy Ghost? Was not this greatest of all Doctors raised to such a high mystical life that in the end what he had tasted of God in ecstasy made distasteful to him all knowledge of the human mode? For having glimpsed too much of the eternal light, he died before having finished his work.

Recent books have excellently described, and the encyclical *Studiorum Ducem* has admirably shown, the union in him of the life of study and the life of prayer. It is the secret both of his sanctity and of his wisdom.

It is the secret, too, of the unique splendor of his teaching. Teaching, he tells us, belongs to the sphere of the active life, and it must be confessed that one finds too often in teaching the burdens and encumbrances peculiar to action; there is even a certain danger for the life of the spirit in the ponderous handling of concepts which constitutes the labor of teaching and which always runs the risk, if you are not constantly on your guard, of becoming material and mechanical.

Saint Thomas was an accomplished teacher because he was a great deal more than a teacher, because in him the pedagogic *discourse* came down entirely from the very simple heights of contemplation.

Observe him in that great disputation he held at Paris just before Easter in 1270, on the most controverted point of his teaching, the thesis on the oneness of the substantial form—a disputation in which he opposed John Peckham, Regent of the Friars Minor and later Archbishop of Canterbury. The Bishop of Paris, the masters in theology, all the doctors were determined to ruin him. Inflamed with jealousy or exasperated by the calm manner in which he broke with hallowed routine, they menaced him with looks and words.

And in truth they had reason enough to be disconcerted, for he was not one of them, he had the origin of his wisdom in a source higher than theirs, in the very pure silence which is the father of preaching. *Nisi efficiamini sicut parvuli.*[9] With all his learning, this great theologian, whose confession, according to the testimony of Friar Reginald, was like that of a child of five, stood in the midst of them, in his simplicity—which was not disarmed, certainly, but candid, natural (*ex Deo nata*) and unstudied, humble and severe as innocence—the likeness and configuration of the Child Jesus among the doctors.

Such is the way there is accomplished in him the sacred saying which must be accomplished in one way or another in all Christians, and which insists that wisdom is to be given to the little ones—to those who are "in their own eyes little children," as it is said in the Book of Kings—and that God chooses "what is not" to confound "what is." For no more than art or any superior human achievement, knowledge does not prevent the saintly soul, as a certain false spirit of interior poverty would sometimes have us believe, from being in its own estimation a mere nothing, without any self-assurance, since, all its achievements being purely in the service of love, absolutely none of them is the foundation of its hope. Its hope rather passes over the whole of created being to rest in God alone; absolutely nothing of all its achievements is for it a personal possession securing it in its own well-being.

Because he kept his whole soul attached only to the wounds of the humanity of Christ, the portal to the mysteries of deity, Thomas Aquinas was perfectly poor in spirit amid the riches of the intelligence; because he knew the rights, all the rights, of First Truth, he pursued learning only in order to attain to wisdom, he delivered himself over without reserve to the Spirit of Truth. By his life and by his teaching he showed that the contemplative life is better than the active, and that it constitutes, when it superabounds in apostolic activity, the state of life purely and simply the most perfect; that the contemplation of the saints is better than the speculation of the philosophers; that the highest intellectuality is not diminished but corroborated and brought to the summit of the spirit by the humility of the science of the Cross. Thus Saint Thomas teaches the intelligence the highest condition of its salvation. And for this too he deserves to be called the apostle of modern times, times which have thought they were giving so much to intellectuality but have so cruelly ignored its very conditions, times whose great misery is to have forgotten the union of the intellectual life and the spiritual life, and whose deepest need, more or less obscurely felt, is to recover this union.

III

8. There is a final reason why it is fitting to give this title of apostle of modern times to Saint Thomas Aquinas. The apostle is not only the one sent into the world to preach the Word of God to the ignorant and the infidel, to convert souls to truth, and thus to dilate the Mystical Body of the Savior. He is also the one who preserves and increases the faith in souls, the one who is given to the Church to be a pillar, a rampart and a light therein, and to serve, as a doctor of truth, the growth of her mysterious life of grace and sanctity. We know well the absolutely unique role played from this point of view in modern times by him of whom the Church proclaims, in the Oration for the Mass of his feast-day, that his admirable learning enlightens her and that his holy activity makes her fruitful, and whose doctrine she implores God to enable us to penetrate: *et quae docuit intellectu conspicere.* Now one feature appears here as the consummate touch, so to speak, of the divine art, ever attentive to fashion perfectly the countenance of its saints: the prince of metaphysics and of sacred science is also the Doctor of the Blessed Sacrament. He thus achieves and consummates his office of servant of the eternal Word, the Word which illumines intelligences, the Word archetype of every splendor, the Word become flesh and hidden among us under the white-

ness of bread. There is the divine immensity, there the benignity and humanity of the Truth he serves, and which we serve too, and which wills that we be called not only its servants, but also its friends: *vos dixi amicos*. It is the same Truth which desires to give itself to all of us in light and in substance in the Beatific Vision, and which meanwhile gives itself in light through doctrine and contemplation, in substance through the Eucharist. Distributed to all, partaken of by all, through teaching or in the Sacrament, it remains whole and unbroken. Here it gathers spirits together into the light which descends from the Uncreated Word; there it unites the Mystical Body of Christ in the communion of the Body and Blood of the Incarnate Word. And is it not with a same love that Thomas watched over its integrity in doctrine, a created participation in First Truth, and adored its presence in the Sacrament, where First Truth is in person? He held it in his hands, this Truth that he loved, and his heart fainted with ecstasy as he contemplated it. And then it happened that the Pope asked him to compose for the whole Church a hymn to this great mystery of faith; another Pope, six centuries and a half later, was to bestow on him the title of Eucharistic Doctor.

Now, is not an immense development in devotion to the Blessed Sacrament, preceding and enveloping devotion to the Sacred Heart, the main feature of Catholic piety in modern times? Is not the feast of Corpus Christi the great modern feast in the Church? While the world stumbles and falls, is not the Church, which prepares ascents in her heart, gathering souls together—with a more and more pressing maternal solicitude—around the Body of the Lord? Eucharistic Doctor, Saint Thomas is in a supereminent degree the apostle and teacher of modern times. Listen to the Christian multitude singing the divine chants that come from the soul and lips of the Theologian. I said above that all the Magi are following him. He has the whole body of the faithful following him. Carrying the monstrance, he walks at the head of the ages.

9. If Saint Thomas is for us all that I have just said he is, with what confident fervor ought we not to ask him for the secret of wisdom and of the apostolic conquest of the modern world? We will cling to his cloak, we will not let him go until he has divulged this secret. The Church, through the voice of Peter, exhorts us to do so with extraordinary insistence. Shall we not listen to her entreaties?

If you are looking for the truth, she cries aloud, go to this doctrine. I show you the way; go, open your eyes, see for yourselves.

Let us be sorry for those who, slow to see or seeing only with the eyes of prejudice, are loath to think that their own sight has perhaps need of being nursed by study and prayer and prefer to think that it is the Church of God which has a beam in her eye.

But for those who wish to follow the will of the Church and to go to school to Saint Thomas, let us note that there are two ways of studying Saint Thomas. And if it is true that man attains to science only if he is first taught, if it is true that Thomas Aquinas, the Common Doctor of the Church, is, after Christ Jesus, the Master *par excellence,* the ever living Master who from the heart of the Beatific Vision watches over his doctrine here below and fecundates souls with it, then it must be said that of the two ways of studying

Saint Thomas, one is sound, the other spoiled from the beginning. I am so strongly convinced of this that I should wish at all costs to persuade young students of its truth. There is a way of studying Saint Thomas which consists in reading Kant, Hegel, and our most up-to-date philosophers, to begin with, then the Fathers, then Avicenna and Averroes, then, as occasion arises, Peter Lombard or Alexander of Hales, and then finally the writings of Saint Thomas in chronological order (bits of all these, of course, for life is short), in order *to clarify Saint Thomas* in the light of modern philosophy and to discern everything he received from his predecessors, everything he added to them, everything he received from himself and added to himself in the course of his individual development. This method, taken as a rule of intellectual discipline, is sterile and useless. What it comes to after all is treating Saint Thomas as an object to be judged—and behaving as if one already had science, whereas it is a question of acquiring science.

On condition that they are pursued with the necessary light, and that one does not expect too much of them, such investigations and comparisons are good and even necessary—particularly the intensive study of modern philosophers—but for those who have arrived at the adult age of knowing. For beginners, they beget bombast, not science.

The other way consists in really placing oneself before Saint Thomas as a living being who receives before a living being who gives, as one who is formed and enlightened before the one who does the forming and enlightening: so that Saint Thomas may teach us to think and to see, so that we may make progress, under his guidance, in the conquest of intelligible being. This method is good and fruitful, for it puts the soul in the truth of its own condition, in order to lead it to the truth of things.

If we follow this method faithfully, it will develop in us a profound love for the vivifying thought of Saint Thomas, and for the text itself, superior to any commentary, which delivers this thought to us, with a wondrous limpidity and a special grace, as it were, of light and simplicity. It will teach us to study this text as a whole and according to the order of the articles. It will teach us also, by the progressive development itself of the Thomist *habitus,* to use in the right way the great commentators, and to discern in its formal line the authentic tradition that we need if we are to attain to a genuine understanding of so exalted a doctrine. For the thought of Saint Thomas is singularly vast and profound. To penetrate it in its essential vitality, as also to meet the new difficulties raised by the course of time, is the text alone, precious and enlightening though it be, sufficient to instruct us? Do we not need to have explained to us more, through the movement and progress characteristic of every living organism, the hidden articulations and the inflexible hierarchy of the theses that rule this immense spiritual universe? And if it is true, as Plato says, that the written word, not being able to defend and explain itself unaided, always needs the help of its father, shall we believe that God, in raising up Saint Thomas, did not give him, in a living tradition, the means of coming to the aid of his doctrine and of communicating its spirit to us? It is in this sense that Leo XIII, in recommending in his encyclical *Aeterni Patris* that we above all study the doctrine of Saint Thomas in the living spring itself, *ex ipsis ejus fontibus,* advised us also to drink from the pure and limpid streams which have flowed from that spring, *rivi integri et illimes*, as opposed to other streams that have become swollen with alien and noxious waters, *rivi qui exinde fluxisse dicuntur, re autem alienis et non salubribus aquis creverunt.*

But all our personal talents and all the human aids of tradition, all the commentators and glossarists, will avail us nothing if that itself which is the object and the end of the intelligence, the goal of its *natural* inclination, is not also the object and the goal of our *voluntary* inclination, of the desire which draws us totally towards our good—if we do not love the truth with our whole heart, if we do not love it as he himself loved it, this great Doctor whose tranquil eyes often flowed with tears, so heavy was his heart with waiting for the vision.

If we love the truth in souls, if we understand the thirst with which the world agonizes, if we are ready to give everything in order that this thirst may be assuaged; if we love the truth in the Church, if we understand the significance of Benedict XV's words, taken up by Pius XI: "The Church has declared the doctrine of Saint Thomas to be her own doctrine"— then we shall not be greatly deterred by scholastic quibbling and controversies, we shall be able to hope to share in the light of Saint Thomas, to understand truly—*intellectu conspicere*—the things he taught, and to be of use according to the best of our abilities, poor though they be, in that universal task of restoration in truth entrusted to him by the Master of History.

THE COMMON DOCTOR

> *Because Thomas illuminated the Church more than all the other Doctors.* John XXII (1318).
>
> *The Church declared Thomas' doctrine to be her own.*
> Benedict XV (1921).

I would wish that no one misunderstand the intention of this chapter, in which, considering the philosophy of Saint Thomas in abstraction from the theology, which latter maintains an intrinsic and essential relationship with faith, I try to characterize the attitude of the Catholic Church in regard to this philosophy. In publishing it I am fully aware that it would be absurd to try to replace by the argument from authority or by a kind of constraint the reasons of intrinsic evidence which alone can motivate scientific adherence to a system of philosophy. It is not in religious faith nor in the authority of the Church that Thomist philosophy has its principles and its *raison d'être*, and one would be greatly deceived if he were to see in it a doctrine reserved for clerics and for sacred offices. It is a philosophy, it is founded on evidence alone, it lives by reason alone. Of itself it belongs to the same secular cycle as the *liberal arts*. I even think that the time has come for it to spread into every order of secular speculative activity, to leave the walls of the school, the seminary or the college in order to assume in the whole world of culture the role that befits a wisdom of the natural order: its place is among its sister sciences, it must converse with politics and anthropology, history and poetry; formed in the open air, in the free conversations of peripateticism, it desires, though all the while remaining apart from the traffic of men, to take an interest in everything that concerns the life of men, it is essential for it to keep contact with sensible experience; to maintain its own vitality it needs a vast breathing space and incessant exchanges.

But the body politic, with all its secular culture, is enveloped by the Church as the earth is enveloped by the heavens; the Christian *lay* is part of the Church. The more lay it becomes, and the more it advances boldly toward the most exposed frontiers, the more will the perennial philosophy, to preserve its integrity, have to remain in continuity with the superhuman sources without which the human weakens, with the sacred wisdom which transcends it and whose native land is the contemplative activity of the Church. This is why it was normal and consonant with the eternal order that, venturing into the universe, it should first be *commissioned* by the Papacy.

This predilection of the Church, these recommendations, these exhortations of the Popes, do not constitute and do not claim to constitute an intrinsic demonstration of the truth of Thomism. They are extrinsic arguments and guarantees, signs which induce in the intelligence of the believer a well-founded confidence. Unbelievers, no doubt, are unmoved by them; nay more, such recommendations rather render suspect to them a philosophy thus patronized. For all that, the

Church does not lower her voice; she does not mind *compromising* philosophers with her company and that of Jesus Christ; she doubtless considers that if these unbelievers do not listen to First Truth, they would listen still less to metaphysical reasonings, because their hearts are prejudiced; let them take scandal at seeing a science honored by faith, she regards their scandal as pharisaical. In any event, it would be ridiculous to present before them evidence based on the feeling of the Church in favor of one philosophy.

As for believers, they are well aware that a philosophy can in no way be imposed on them as a dogma. But if the philosophy of Saint Thomas does not thus receive in their eyes, by reason of its recommendation by the Church, either the supra-rational value of an article of faith or, in the proper order of rational disciplines, that evidence compelling assent which a philosophy has by itself or will never have—if this is so, the fact remains that among the extrinsic signs likely to lead to right judgment and capable of disposing a mind in good faith to place trust in a doctrine, then to examine it, to study it with respect and confidence, indeed with that joy which the reasonable hope of encountering the true gives, they can find no recommendation more persuasive and more notable than this one.

In the proper sphere of science, the argument from authority is the weakest of all.[1] But in the sphere of apprenticeship, in the order of preparation for science, of the *via ad scientiam*, in which, precisely, the mind, supported by extrinsic signs and arguments, accustoms itself little by little to advance by itself *with steps of evidence*, the authority of a master has in fact a preponderant role. For we are not angel-mathematicians, constituted by the natural light of our reason in a virtual scientific state that we would only have to expand through discourse, we are, alas! children of men, who learn in order to know, and who, knowing, keep on learning. Many misunderstandings concerning the attitude of the Church in regard to the philosophy of Saint Thomas would vanish of themselves, if it were understood that it is above all a question here of pedagogy and of *education:* of "educing," of bringing to existence, of engendering philosophical knowledge from the potency of an intellect which is at first but a *tabula rasa.*

It is in this perspective, and in order to grasp more exactly how a philosophy which of itself relates only to evidence and to reason may nevertheless be recommended by the Church with a unique and extraordinarily significant insistence, that I offer the following observations. They will show, I hope, that it is equally false either to accuse the Catholic Church of imposing on its faithful an "ideological conformism" in matters of philosophy, or to regard the philosophy of Saint Thomas as something "indifferent" for a Catholic, and which would propose itself for his consideration in the same manner and under the same conditions as any other philosophical doctrine.

In this discussion—in which, as I indicated at the beginning of the chapter, I am considering simply what concerns Saint Thomas the philosopher, leaving aside what concerns Saint Thomas the theologian— my whole desire is to put the reader face to face with texts of the Supreme Pontiffs, texts of which the public does not always appear to be fully enough informed. We shall therefore above all consider, from the point of view of the facts, historically and documentarily, what has actually been the attitude of the Popes in regard to Saint Thomas.

However, to light us on our way, we must first try, by way of introduction, to attain a summary but exact idea of the general truths which command the whole discussion, that is to say, the role and the authority of the Church in philosophical matters.

I

On this point certain elementary truths impose themselves logically on every man who admits a revelation from God, propounded by the Church of Christ, elementary truths which the Church herself has been careful to embody in dogmatic definitions.[2] I recall them here for the sake of clarity.

1) Truth cannot contend against truth, for this would be to tear to pieces the very first principle of reason; and the theory of the double truth, invented in the Middle Ages by the Averroists and taken up again in our day by some "modernists"—the theory according to which the same thing can be true according to faith and false according to reason, or inversely—is a pure absurdity. "Although faith is above reason," the Vatican Council declares, "yet there can be no genuine disagreement between faith and reason; for it is the same God Who, on the one hand, reveals the mysteries and infuses faith into souls and, on the other, has endowed the human mind with the light of reason, and God cannot possibly deny Himself or the true ever contradict the true. When the vain appearance of such a contradiction occasionally arises, it is above all because the dogmas of faith are not understood and expounded according to the mind of the Church, or because erroneous opinions are taken for affirmations of reason." Whence it follows that:

2) Philosophy, like every science, is independent of revelation and faith in its own work and in its principles, and develops in an autonomous manner starting from these principles, having for its proper light the natural light of reason, and for sole criterion, evidence;

3) Philosophy is nevertheless subject to the magisterium of faith, every enunciation of a philosopher that is destructive of a revealed truth being clearly an error, and *reason enlightened by faith* alone having authority to judge whether such an enunciation of a philosopher (that is to say, of a man who uses more or less well *natural reason* alone) is or is not contrary to faith.

Thus revelation plays the role of *norm* or *negative rule* in regard to philosophy, which is to say that without encroaching on its principles or intervening in its procedures and in its own proper work, it has a right of inspection over its *conclusions*.

4) It is evident, from the moment one admits the fact of revelation, that philosophy cannot suffer any harm from this indirect subordination to faith. Like art and every human discipline, it is free and autonomous in its own sphere, but this sphere is limited and subordinate; it does not therefore enjoy an *absolute* freedom, but who then is *absolutely free* but God Himself? To be limited in one's freedom *to be wrong*, to have an external reference-mark and a hand-rail, as it were, against error, is in reality a great benefit for philosophy. For if it is true, as Cicero says, that there is no folly in the world but has found some philosopher to maintain it—which comes to saying with Scripture that there is no end to the number of fools (even among philosophers)—then it must be admitted that philosophy, in order to perform suc-

cessfully the work of reason, must have need—I do not say in itself, I say in man—of the help afforded it by the inspection exercised by revelation, protecting it against many unfortunate accidents.

The better to appreciate the importance and even, in a sense, the necessity of this benefit, let us recall that, according to the common teaching of theologians, confirmed by the Vatican Council, the natural weakness of man is so great that without a special help from God human reason is incapable of attaining to the possession, all at once (*collective*) and without admixture of error, of the great truths of the natural order, though each one, considered separately, is within its reach. We realize then that over and above the essential function of negative norm or external reference-mark I just spoke of, faith has also a positive office in regard to philosophical reason, that of indicating the goal and of orienting the mind, *veluti stella rectrix,* like a guiding star.

5) Lastly, philosophy can be considered no longer in itself and in its own proper sphere, but insofar as it enters into the contexture of a more exalted science: theology, the science of revealed truths, which is in us, Saint Thomas says, like a participation in the science proper to God and the blessed. Theology cannot develop in the human mind without making use of philosophical truths, which are established by reason, and which it puts in contact with the data of faith in order to have emerge from these data the consequences they virtually contain. It thus superelevates philosophy and then *uses* it as an instrument. One sees immediately that these living bonds confirm on still another ground the subordination of philosophy to the magisterium of revelation and faith: theology, independent in itself of every philosophical system,

having to judge the enunciations of philosophers in its own light and to take up, from among the different philosophical systems, the one which will be in its hands the best *instrument of truth*.

Such are the elementary notions that impose themselves logically on the mind, once the fact of Catholic Revelation is posited.

What follows? It follows that those who have received the grace of faith cannot philosophize in utter disregard of this faith, *stella rectrix*, and of theology, by practicing a system of water-tight compartments. Philosophy remains in them rigorously *distinct* from faith and admits only the rational into its own proper structure, but it cannot be *separated* from faith. And it is clear that the natural inclination of every believer is to reject as false the philosophical opinions he sees to be contrary to revealed truth. Each one is bound to defend his goods and God's goods against error.

But will the Church abandon each one here to his own individual resources? If she did, she would fail the mandate imposed on her to preserve the deposit of faith, fail her duty to protect souls. She will therefore intervene, and when confronted with a philosophical error she considers sufficiently grave (whether this error destroys directly a revealed truth, or destroys a truth *connected* with the deposit of revelation) she will condemn it; she will also recommend positively the philosophical doctrine she judges to be most capable of confirming and strengthening the mind in relation to faith; she will exercise her sacred magisterium over the sphere of philosophy.

When we speak of the Church—allow me this parenthesis—let us think of what she truly is. Let us not have an attenuated conception of her; let us not picture to ourselves a mere spiritual administration.

Let us remember that she is herself a mystery, that she is the Mystical Body of Christ, a living person, at once divine and human, whose head is Christ and all of whose members the Holy Ghost joins together, the great Contemplative who aspires to beget all men unto eternal life, and all of whose movements—so far as the Church herself is concerned (whatever the human frailty of individuals may be)—proceed from divine wisdom and the most pure gifts of grace. We shall not then bargain over the terms of our allegiance, we shall not follow her like peevish children who have to be dragged along; we shall understand that her doctrinal authority is not limited to defining solemnly what one cannot deny without being a heretic, but extends, on the contrary, according to all the degrees and all the nuances that what one calls the ordinary magisterium of the Church admits of in the tone of its voice and the authority of its affirmations, to all that concerns the integrity of faith in souls.

From the principles just laid down, a final conclusion emerges. When the Church exercises her authority over the philosophical sphere, she does this essentially *with reference to faith, with reference to revealed truth,* the deposit of which it is her mission to guard. But since faith presupposes reason, as grace presupposes nature, it happens that in order to accomplish perfectly her office of guardian of the faith the Church is also, and secondarily, constituted by God guardian of the health of reason, guardian of the natural order (as also of the natural law). Let us say then that she has a double mission: to safeguard the deposit of revelation and, secondarily, to safeguard the natural rectitude of reason itself. And it is in the name of this double mission that in exercising her authority over the philosophical sphere, she works in fact for the greater good of reason. The Church is not for the world, said Saint Augustine; and yet she acts as though she were there for the good of the world.

II

It is well known that the great doctrinal synthesis accomplished by Saint Thomas in the thirteenth century appeared to his contemporaries as a bold innovation. Why? Because Saint Thomas, following his master Albert the Great, had adopted the philosophy of Aristotle in order to bring it into the service of the faith, and Aristotle, who had but recently arrived in the Christian world through the compromising intermediary of Arab translators and commentators, had the worst reputation. Certain routine minds were so astounded that, a few years after the death of Saint Thomas, and in spite of the enormous influence already achieved by his doctrine, some of the theses he taught were censured by the Bishop of Paris, Etienne Tempier, and by two English bishops. But Etienne Tempier was not the Church. As for the *novelty* of Saint Thomas, it did not derive from the fact that he changed or altered the theological thought inherited from the Fathers and elaborated in the schools of the Middle Ages; it derived on the contrary from the fact that he brought theology to its point of scientific perfection, using for this as instrument, but not without superelevating and purifying it, the most vigorously rational, the most highly developed, the most analytical philosophy that the Greek genius was able to conceive.

Now it is highly significant that from the very beginning the Popes have not only encouraged Saint

Thomas in his work[3] but have also discerned in the Thomist synthesis an incomparable value and *quality*, and have considered that in this synthesis the whole of the Christian tradition bore its fruit. John XXII, who canonized Friar Thomas Aquinas in 1323, fifty years after his death, declared that his doctrine could have proceeded only from a miraculous intervention by God, *"doctrina ejus non potuit esse sine miraculo,"* and that by himself alone he enlightened the Church more than all the other Doctors. Twenty years later, on the 6th of February, 1344, Clement VI testified to the spread of Saint Thomas' thought in the universal Church, and in 1346 he enjoined the Dominican Order not to deviate from his doctrine. The Dominicans, who had already in their general Chapters of 1279 and 1286 chosen Thomas Aquinas for their Doctor, were thus commissioned by the Pope to defend and maintain intact the teaching of Saint Thomas, the teaching rightfully appointed, under the sign of the Angelic Doctor, to the protection of the Catholic mind.

Urban V in 1368 ordered the University of Toulouse "to follow the doctrine of the blessed Thomas as being true and Catholic and to exert itself to the utmost to develop it." There would be no end to reporting in detail the testimonies of the Supreme Pontiffs: Nicholas V, Pius IV, Saint Pius V (who proclaimed Thomas Aquinas a Doctor of the Church), Sixtus V, Clement VIII, Paul V, Alexander VII, Innocent XI, Innocent XII, Benedict XIII, Clement XII, Benedict XIV. . . . Let it suffice to recall Innocent VI's declaration that "those who have a firm grasp of the doctrine of Saint Thomas are never found far astray from the path of truth, and whoever has opposed it has always been suspect of error," and to observe that in the stout volume[4] devoted by Father Berthier to *St. Thomas Aquinas, the Common Doctor of the Church,* these testimonies of the Popes fill no less than 280 octavo pages. Ever since the Council of Lyons, held in 1274, the very year of the death of Saint Thomas (he died at Fossanova on his way to the Council, but his thought was present there and it is from it that the Council borrowed the formulas with which it condemned the "errors of the Greeks"), and the Council of Vienna (1311-1312), at which the Church defined the substantial unity of the human being in the very words of Saint Thomas, the Fathers of all the Councils, it may be asserted, have had recourse to the intellectual tools prepared by Thomas and have always shown themselves to be strictly faithful to his principles. This is nowhere more evident than in the definitions of the Council of Trent. "For ever since the glorious death of the saintly Doctor," wrote Pius X, "the Church has not held a single Council in which Thomas has not participated through the treasures of his doctrine." [5] If, however, the mark of human limitations with regard to the divine mysteries was not lacking even in such a Doctor, in this respect that the privilege of the Immaculate Conception, much controverted in his time, was not taught by him (it was even bitterly opposed for some centuries by *a part* of his school), we must yet note that the reserve he maintained on this point derived from the fact that he kept (out of theological prudence and in order not to anticipate the judgment of the Roman Church) to the implicit, not pushing on to definitive assertions; this reserve discloses no defect in his principles, which, in reality, like a "rudder" [6] ensuring the right course, prepared the way no less than the fervor and "steam" of Scotus and the Franciscan school for the dogmatic definition promulgated by Pius IX in 1854.

But let us come to the last quarter of the nineteenth century. Here things take on a new aspect. Saint Thomas no longer appears as simply the master of sacred science, whose doctrine presides over the solemn acts of the ecclesiastical magisterium and constitutes the *theological* store of the Church. The Pope addresses himself to human reason, he entreats it to return to the Angelic Doctor, to ask him the way of light; he entreats it—this human reason which has known so many negations, intoxications and revulsions—to restore the great affirmations of Thomist *philosophy*. On August 4, 1879, Leo XIII published the encyclical *Aeterni Patris,*[7] and from this dates the renaissance of Scholastic studies. Everyone will find it profitable to read (or re-read) this whole encyclical, for it contains a defense of Philosophy, of its value as knowledge, of its dignity and its utility among men and in Christian society, which, coming from the Vicar of Christ speaking to the universe, has a singular gravity and nobility.

After a brief summary of the history of philosophy in the Christian centuries, in the ages of the Fathers and of the Scholastics, the Pope says:

Above all the Scholastic Doctors towers Thomas Aquinas, prince and master of them all, who, as Cajetan observes, "because he profoundly revered the holy Doctors who preceded him inherited in a way the intellect of all, *intellectum omnium quodammodo sortitus est.*" Thomas gathered their doctrines together, as if they were the scattered members of the same body, and knitted them into one whole. He assembled them in an admirable order, and so increased them with valuable additions that he is rightly and deservedly esteemed the special guardian and glory of the Catholic Church.

Leo XIII then stressed very remarkably the outstanding importance of a Thomist renaissance, not only in regard to religious truth and the sacred goods to be protected in souls, but also in regard to secular culture and the whole movement of art and science. The arts indeed

borrow from philosophy, as from the wisdom that moderates, their supreme regulation, and draw from it, as from a common source of life, the spirit which animates them.

As for the natural sciences,

supreme injustice is done to [Scholastic philosophy] to accuse it of putting obstacles in the path of the progress and development of these sciences. [On the contrary] as the Scholastics, following in this the teachings of the holy Fathers, teach at each step in anthropology that the intellect can rise to knowledge of immaterial things only through the intermediary of sensible things, they themselves have understood that nothing is more useful to the philosopher than to scrutinize diligently the secrets of nature, and to give much time and care to the study of physical things . . . Far from suffering the least harm, the sciences of nature themselves, which are held in such high esteem today, and which through so many splendid discoveries attract everywhere an admiration without parallel, would singularly gain from a restoration of the ancient philosophy . . . For to ascertain the facts does not suffice, one must rise to a higher plane . . . Scholastic philosophy, widely made use of, would bring to these investigations a marvelous increase of strength and light.

And the Pope concludes:

We most urgently exhort you, for the defense and the glory of the Catholic faith, for the good of society, for the advancement of all the sciences, to restore the precious wisdom of St. Thomas and to propagate it as far as possible.

We are witnessing today a great intellectual movement launched by the will and the words of the watchman at the summit of the Church's towers; this is one of the best examples of what we might call the healing action of the papacy on wounded humanity.

Innumerable are the acts in which Leo XIII confirmed and further defined the exhortations contained in the encyclical *Aeterni Patris*. The defense of the faith, "the progress of science, the welfare of society are at stake." [8] Whether he was addressing the whole Church, or the Redemptorists, the Franciscans, the Dominicans, the Benedictines, the Jesuits, Bishops, universities, or seminaries, throughout twenty-five years he unceasingly urged—in encyclicals, briefs, letters and audiences—the return to Saint Thomas, and couched his recommendations, each time the occasion presented itself, in words as imperative as they are precise:

Those who are desirous of truly being philosophers— and religious especially ought to desire this—are obliged [he tells the Friars Minor[9]] to establish the principles and bases of their doctrine on St. Thomas Aquinas.

If doctors are found who disagree with St. Thomas [he writes to the Jesuits[10]], however great their merits be in other respects, hesitation is not permitted, the former must be sacrificed for the latter.

On January 18, 1880, he ordered the Dominicans to publish, at the expense of the Holy See, a monumental edition of Saint Thomas; on August 4 of the same year he placed "all Catholic universities, academies, faculties, and schools" under the patronage of Thomas Aquinas; and in the Brief he published on this occasion he affirmed his conviction that "Thomist doctrine possesses, with an eminent superiority, a singular force and virtue for curing the evils with which our age is afflicted."

He continued:

The doctrine of St. Thomas is so vast that it contains, like a sea, all the wisdom that flows from the ancients. All the true that had been said, all that had been wisely sifted by the pagan philosophers, by the Fathers and the Doctors of the Church, by the eminent men who flourished before him, not only was Thomas fully acquainted with it all, but he added to it, perfected it, ordered it with such a penetrating grasp of the essential principles, with such a perfection of method and such a propriety of terms, that he seems to have left his successors only the possibility of imitating him, having deprived them of the possibility of rivaling him.

And there is this also to be considered: his doctrine, being formed and as it were armed with principles of great breadth of application, answers the needs, not of an age only, but of all time, and is sovereignly fitted to conquer the ever recurring errors.

Leo XIII himself, "to prove the timeliness of this doctrine and its suitableness for the problems of the day, made use of it continually in the teaching of the Church." [11] He encouraged and supported in every way institutions and enterprises designed to spread it, particularly the work pursued at Louvain, not without strenuous opposition, by the courageous and dedicated man who would become Cardinal Mercier.

Finally, in his encyclical letter of September 8, 1899, to the French clergy, he insisted on the matter again and once more opposed Saint Thomas to subjectivism and Kantian rejection of metaphysics as knowledge, which he denounced as the danger *par excellence:*

We said in Our Encyclical *Aeterni Patris,* which We once more recommend your seminarians and their teachers carefully to peruse, and We based Ourselves on the authority of St. Paul to say it: it is through the vain subtleties of bad philosophy, *per philosophiam et inanem fallaciam*,[12] that the minds of the faithful let themselves most often be deceived, and that the purity of the faith is corrupted among men. We added (and the events of the last twenty years have sadly confirmed the reflections and apprehensions We then expressed): "If one considers the critical conditions of the times in which we live, if he reflects on the state of public and private affairs, he will easily perceive that the cause of the evils which oppress us, as of those which threaten us, consists in this, that erroneous theories on all things, divine and human, propounded in the schools of the philosophers, have little by little penetrated all ranks of society and have come to be accepted by a great number of minds."

We again condemn these doctrines, which have of true philosophy only the name, and which, shaking the very foundations of human knowledge, lead logically to universal scepticism and to irreligion. We are profoundly grieved to learn that for some years now some Catholics have been thinking that they can follow a philosophy which, under the specious pretext of freeing the human reason of every preconceived idea and of every illusion, denies it the right to affirm anything beyond its own operations, thus sacrificing to a radical subjectivism all the certitudes that the traditional metaphysics, consecrated by the authority of the most vigorous minds, laid down as necessary and unshakeable foundations for the demonstration of the existence of God, of the spirituality and the immortality of the soul, and of the objective reality of the external world.

Let us note that about the same time Rudolf Eucken, on the Protestant side, was also contrasting Saint Thomas with Kant as two worlds in irreducible conflict.[13]

We have not finished. Pius X, Benedict XV, Pius XI, and Pius XII have continued and confirmed in every way the intellectual work of Leo XIII. It is more than ever important here to have the texts themselves before our eyes.[14] Let us call to mind again these lines from the encyclical *Pascendi* (September 8, 1907):

In the first place, with regard to studies, We will and expressly order that the Scholastic philosophy constitute the foundation of sacred studies. It goes without saying that "if anything is taken up with too great subtlety by the Scholastic doctors, or too carelessly stated—if there be anything that ill agrees with the discoveries of a later age, or, in a word, improbable in whatever way—it does not enter Our mind to propose that for imitation to Our age." [15] But what is of capital importance is that when We prescribe that the Scholastic philosophy is to be followed, We mean especially that philosophy which has been bequeathed to us by St. Thomas Aquinas. We therefore declare that all that has been laid down by Our Predecessor remains in full force, and, if need be, We renew it again and confirm it, and order that it be rigorously observed by all. Let Bishops impose and require its observance in any seminary in which it may have been neglected. The same injunction applies also to Superiors of religious orders. And let teachers bear in mind that to deviate from St. Thomas, especially in metaphysical questions, is always attended by grave detriment.

In his Motu Proprio *Sacrorum Antistitum* (September 1, 1910), addressed to all Bishops and to the Superiors-General of religious Orders charged with the duty of supervising the development of young clerics, Pius X reiterated these instructions:

With regard to studies, We will and expressly order that the Scholastic philosophy constitute the foundation of sacred studies . . . And what is of capital importance is that when We prescribe that the Scholastic philosophy is to be followed, We mean especially that philosophy which has been bequeathed to us by St. Thomas Aquinas."

Especially, the Pope said.

In the Motu Proprio *Doctoris Angelici,*[16] which gathers together and sums up all the pontifical teachings on Saint Thomas, and which powerfully testifies to the indivisibility of his doctrine, the Pope was to insist:

Now because We said [in the Encyclical *Pascendi* and in the Motu Proprio *Sacrorum Antistitum*] that the philosophy of Thomas Aquinas *especially* was to be followed, without saying that it *exclusively* was to be followed, many have persuaded themselves that they were complying with Our will, or at least were not acting contrary to it, if they indiscriminately adopted and adhered to what any other of the Scholastic doctors taught in philosophy, even though this might be in opposition with the principles of St. Thomas. But in this way they have been gravely mistaken. When We gave St. Thomas to Our own as supreme guide in Scholastic philosophy, it goes without saying that We wanted this to be understood as referring above all to the principles taught by him, which principles are the foundations on which this philosophy rests. For just as, in fact, the opinion of certain ancients is to be rejected, according to which it makes no difference to the truth of the Faith that one have such or such a view on the subject of created things, provided only that one thinks correctly on the subject of God, for error concerning nature entails a false knowledge about God: so must the principles of philosophy laid down by Thomas Aquinas be religiously and inviolably safeguarded—thanks to which principles there is conjointly procured of created things a science which accords fully with the Faith (*Contra Gent.* II, 3, 4); all the errors of all times are refuted; one is enabled to discern with certitude what must be attributed to God alone and to no other (*Ibid.,* 3; *Sum. Theol.,* I, 12, 4; 54, 1); and, lastly, both the diversity and the analogy between God and His works are admirably brought to light . . .

. . . Sound reason will not sanction anyone's neglecting, and religion will not permit anyone's attenuating such a magnificent patrimony of wisdom, which Thomas, after receiving it from the ancients, perfected and increased by the power of his genius—a genius worthy of the angels, and which he applied to preparing, illustrating and protecting Sacred Doctrine in human intelligences (*In librum Boethii de Trinitate*, q. 2, a. 3). This is especially true since, if Catholic truth is once deprived of this powerful support, it would be in vain that in order to defend it one would ask help from a philosophy whose principles are either in common with *materialist, monist, pantheist, socialist* errors, and with the different forms of *modernism*, or, in any case, are not opposed to them. The fact is that the capital points of St. Thomas' philosophy must not be placed in the category of opinions that can be debated one way or the other, but they must rather be regarded as the foundations on which the whole science of natural and divine things is established; and if they are removed or altered in any way whatsoever, it necessarily follows that the students of the sacred sciences no longer even perceive the meaning of the words through which the dogmas God has revealed are proposed by the Church's magisterium.

It is for this reason that We desired that all who are teaching philosophy and sacred theology be warned that if they deviated so much as a step, especially in metaphysics, from Thomas Aquinas, they would not do so without grave detriment.—We now go further and declare that those who pervert in their interpretations or hold in complete scorn what in this philosophy constitutes the principles and the great theses (*principia et pronuntiata majora*), not only do not follow St. Thomas, but they stray very far from the holy Doctor. And We declare that if the doctrine of any writer or any saint has ever been recommended by Us or by Our predecessors with such singular commendation and in such a way that to the commendation were added the invitation and the order to spread it and defend it, it is easy to understand that it was recommended in the measure in which it was in accord with the principles of St. Thomas Aquinas or was in no way opposed to them.

One step only remained to be taken: to make, for professors appointed to Church institutions, the teach-

ing of the philosophy of Saint Thomas an obligation
of their office, by a law inscribed in the very Code
of the decrees of the Church. This was done; and such
an enactment goes further still than all that the Popes
had done up till then. In the new Code of Canon
Law promulgated by Benedict XV, teachers in Catholic
schools are ordered:

to treat in every particular the studies of rational philosophy and theology, and the formation of students in these
sciences, according to the method, the doctrine, and the
principles of the Angelic Doctor, and to adhere religiously
to them.[17]

Thus Thomas Aquinas is no longer proposed only as
a doctor eminent among others. He is the Doctor *par
excellence*, he occupies an absolutely unique place. He
now realizes in its fullness the title of *Doctor Communis Ecclesiae* which had already been given to him.
Insofar as a philosopher carries to an exceptionally
eminent degree the characteristics of a certain spiritual
community, we can say that Descartes, Malebranche or
Auguste Comte are philosophers specifically French,
Fichte or Hegel philosophers specifically German.
Saint Thomas, for his part, is the Doctor specifically
Catholic; he is the philosopher and the theologian
of Peter and of Catholicity.

Later Benedict XV was to write—and this is one of
the highest commendations that have been bestowed
on Saint Thomas—that "the Church has proclaimed
that the doctrine of Thomas Aquinas is her own,"
*cum Thomae doctrinam Ecclesia suam propriam edixit
esse.*[18] Then Pius XI, in his Apostolic Letter on the
education of the clergy:[19]

Once the program of literary studies has been completed, the young clerics must, as a preparation for the-

ology, apply themselves with the greatest care, for two years at least, to the study of philosophy. We mean the Scholastic philosophy, which has been diligently worked out by the labors of the holy Fathers and the Doctors of the School, and which the labor and the genius of Thomas Aquinas carried to its highest perfection, that philosophy which Our illustrious Predecessor Leo XIII did not hesitate to call "the rampart of the Faith and the solid fortress of religion." [20] It is, in fact, the glory of Leo XIII to have restored to honor the Christian philosophy, by rekindling love and devotion for the Angelic Doctor; and We are so convinced that this was the greatest of all the so precious services which in the course of his long pontificate he rendered to the Church and to civil society, that, even if he lacked other merits, this alone would suffice to immortalize the name of this great Pope.

The teachers of philosophy, therefore, in teaching this science to seminarians, will take special pains to follow not only the method of St. Thomas, but also his doctrine and his principles; they will put all the more fervor into being faithful to him, the more they realize that the modernists and the other enemies of the Catholic Faith fear and dread no Doctor of the Church as much as St. Thomas.[21]

Finally, the encyclical *Studiorum Ducem,* by clearly revealing the union of sanctity and doctrine in the Angelic Doctor, and pointing out in him, with the grace of the *eloquence of wisdom,* "the union of the two wisdoms, the acquired and the infused," renders sensibly present to us, as it were, all that there is of love, of holy apostolic vigor, and of ever-present vitality in the thought of Saint Thomas. It insists also on the *catholicity* of this thought, and, taking up the very important phrase of Benedict XV, it gives an official consecration to the oldest, and doubtless the most beautiful, of the titles of Saint Thomas:

We Ourselves find so justified the magnificent tributes of praise bestowed on this truly divine genius, that We think it proper to call, not only the Angelic Doctor, but also the Common or Universal Doctor of the Church, him whose doctrine the Church has made her own, as so many documents of every kind show." [22]

At the same time this Encyclical, by emphasizing and sanctioning with its authority certain points taught by Saint Thomas, gives us some notable statements of the reasons for the adoption of his doctrine by the Church:

Accustomed [writes Pius XI] to contemplating all things in God, the first cause and last end of all that has been made, Thomas was naturally inclined to guide himself in his life, as in the *Summa Theologiae,* according to the two wisdoms We have spoken of and which he describes in these words: "The wisdom that man acquires through study . . . enables him to bring to bear on divine things a right judgment according to the perfect use of reason . . . But the other wisdom is a gift which comes down from heaven . . . and it judges of divine things in virtue of a certain community of nature (connaturality) with them. It is a gift of the Holy Ghost . . . through which man is rendered perfect in the order of divine things, not learning only, but experiencing these things within himself" (II-II, 45, 1, ad 2; 2, c.).

This wisdom emanating from God, this infused wisdom, accompanied by the other gifts of the Holy Ghost, continually grew and increased in St. Thomas, in the same measure as charity, mistress and queen of all the virtues. Indeed it was for him a most certain doctrine that the love of God must never cease to increase, "as the very words of the precept imply: *Thou shalt love the Lord thy God with thy whole heart; with thy whole heart* or *perfectly* come to the same thing . . . Charity, says the Apostle, is the end of the precept: now it is not the end which admits of a measure, but only the means which lead to it" (*Ibid.,*

184, 3). It is for this reason that the perfection of charity is included in the precept, as the end towards which all must tend, each according to his condition.

Thus are affirmed two important theses of the Common Doctor—one distinguishing the wisdom acquired through study (philosophical and theological wisdom) from the infused wisdom, which is a gift of the Holy Ghost and is linked with charity; the other declaring that the perfection of charity falls under the precept as the end towards which each must tend according to his condition.

As far as philosophy in particular is concerned, the Encyclical unreservedly commends Saint Thomas' conception (quite Aristotelian) of the structure and essential divisions of the highest knowledge of the natural order, and it cites these fundamental sentences of the *Commentary on the Ethics:*

"It belongs to the wise man to make order. The reason is that wisdom is the most mighty perfection of reason, whose property it is to know order. For though the sensitive powers know some things taken absolutely, it belongs to intellect alone or to reason *to know the order of one thing to another* . . . Now there are as many different sciences as there are different orders which reason considers. The order that speculative reason establishes in its own act belongs to the philosophy of reason, or *logic,* which considers the order of the parts of the discourse among themselves, and the order that the principles have among themselves and with respect to the conclusions. To the philosophy of nature, or *physics,* it belongs to consider the order which human reason observes in things but does not itself make; and in this respect we may here link *metaphysics* with the philosophy of nature. Finally, the order of voluntary acts pertains to the sphere of moral philosophy, or *ethics*, which is divided into three parts: the first considers the operations of the individual in their relation to the end, and is called *monastics* (or individual ethics); the second, the operations of the family collectivity, and is called *economics;* the third, the operations of the civil collectivity, and is called *politics*" (*In I Ethic.*, lect. 1).

All these parts of philosophy [the Pope continues], St. Thomas studied deeply, each according to its proper method—starting with that which is nearest to human reason in order to rise gradually to that which is farthest from it, and to stop finally "at the pinnacle of all things," *in supremo rerum omnium vertice* (*Contra Gent.*, II, 56; IV, 1).

His teaching on the power or the value of the human mind must be held as irrefragable (*sanctum*). "By nature, our intelligence knows being and that which, in virtue of its very notion, holds of being as such, and it is on this knowledge that the certitude of first principles is based" (*Contra Gent.*, II, 83). This insight reduces to naught the theories and the errors of modern philosophers who maintain that in the act of intellection it is not being itself which is perceived, but the modification in the one perceiving—errors that end in agnosticism, which was so vigorously condemned in the Encyclical *Pascendi*.

As to the arguments through which St. Thomas shows that God exists and that He alone is Subsisting Being Itself, they remain today as in the Middle Ages the most solid proof of these truths; they clearly confirm the Catholic dogma solemnly promulgated at the Vatican Council and which Pius X formulates so succinctly: "God, as principle and end of all things, can be known with certitude and even demonstrated by the natural light of reason, by means of what has been made, that is to say, the visible works of creation, as the cause is known and demonstrated through its effects" (Motu Proprio *Sacrorum Antistitum,* September 1, 1910). His metaphysical doctrine, though it has often been and is still today exposed to the bitter attacks of unjust critics, still retains, like gold which no acid can mar, all its force and its full radiancy. Our Predecessor was therefore right in affirming (Encyclical *Pascendi,* September 8, 1907): "To deviate from Thomas Aquinas, especially in metaphysics, is always attended with grave detriment." [23]

Finally,

if we are to guard against the errors which are the source and fountainhead of all the miseries of our time, we must remain more than ever faithful to the doctrine of St. Thomas. In all spheres, Thomas decisively refutes the theories contrived by the modernists: in philosophy, by safeguarding, as We have said, the value and the power of the human intelligence and by establishing through irrefutable arguments the existence of God; in dogma, by distinguishing the supernatural order from the natural order and by elucidating the reasons for believing and the dogmas themselves; in theology, by showing that all that is the object of faith rests not on opinion, but on truth, and cannot change; in Biblical matters, by establishing the true notion of divine inspiration; in matters of morals, of social life, and of law, by formulating with precision the principles of legal and social, of commutative and distributive justice and by explaining the relations between justice and charity; in ascetics, by giving the rules of the perfect life, as also by refuting those of his contemporaries who attacked religious orders. Lastly, against that independence of human reason in regard to God that is so ostentatiously displayed today, he affirms the rights of First Truth and the authority over us of the sovereign Master. We see then that the modernists have sufficient reasons for fearing no Doctor of the Church as much as Thomas Aquinas.

Accordingly, just as it was said of old to the Egyptians in time of famine: *Go to Joseph,* that they might receive from him a supply of wheat to nourish their bodies, so

We now say to all without exception who today are seeking the truth: *Go to Thomas,* go and ask him for the food of sound doctrine, which nourishes souls for eternal life, and which he possesses in rich abundance.

III

Two things seem to me particularly striking here. First, the Church commits herself completely, so to speak, to Saint Thomas and his philosophy, and she thus proposes to us, not this or that particular truth, but a whole body of doctrine. Secondly, note the dramatic accent of the admonitions which, ever since Leo XIII, she has been addressing on this point to her faithful and still more to her clergy. One gathers that in her eyes the issue is of immense importance, that it is a question vital for the interests of faith and of civilization.

Why is this so?

It is because we do not have to do today with particular and determinate heresies, but with a global, universal heresy, with a rupture at the foundations: reason is giving way, one no longer believes in truth, neither in the natural order nor in the supernatural order, one separates human life from truth; this is the core of that *modernism* condemned by Pius X in 1907 in the encyclical *Pascendi,* and characterized by him as the cesspool of all errors. Such a peril must be countered not with a particular truth, but with the whole of faith, as far as heaven comforts us, and the whole light of the infused gifts, but also, as far as we labor on earth, with the whole of a philosophy, with the whole of *Philosophy,* taken globally in its universality and in its doctrinal unity.

The various aspects of the essential harmony between dogma and reason cannot be studied in a few
pages. I should like only to recall here the extreme
solicitude with which the Church, who has, however,
far superior, far more beautiful objects to contemplate,
busies herself in defending and guaranteeing the value
and dignity of natural reason, in which she admires
a created participation of the God Whom she loves,
of the Light which enlightens every man coming
into this world. In 1567 against Baius, in 1713 against
Quesnel, she affirmed the validity of the knowledge of
the moral law and of the existence of God which
natural reason attained among the pagans. In 1840 she
required from Abbé Bautain, and in 1855 from Abbé
Bonnetty, the acknowledgment that "reasoning can
prove with certitude the existence of God, the spirituality of the soul, the freedom of man," that "the use
of reason precedes faith and leads man to it with the
help of revelation and grace." In 1870, at the Vatican
Council, she solemnly defined that "God, principle and
end of all things, can be known with certitude (*certo
cognosci*) by the natural light of human reason, starting from created things"; and, more precisely, that
He can be so "demonstrated (*adeoque demonstrari
posse*) by means of the *visible* works of creation, as
the cause by its effects." [24] She whom false reason has
so calumniated thus protects reason against itself,
when in a surge of philosophical frenzy this erstwhile
goddess has recourse to suicide to end its torments.

All this is easily explained, if it is true that grace
perfects nature and that man is by nature an animal
endowed with reason. Destroy the force of reason and
you destroy the natural strata themselves by which
grace *takes* in the human being; you erect a divine

monument, and an exceedingly weighty one, on ground already undermined. The Christian life is not easy, Saint Christopher needs good shoulders to carry the infant Jesus. It takes a good mind to carry supernatural truth.

I do not say that it necessarily takes the reason of the philosophers, a reason technically developed and cultivated! If Philosophy, with its choicest intellectual splendors, is part of the treasure of the Church, if it is necessary for the integrity and the full development of her doctrinal life on earth, it is not necessary to every believer, at least not to the simple and the ignorant. On the other hand, the truths of faith, taken in themselves, are *independent* of any philosophical system (I say independent of any system, I do not say indifferent to any system) because, descending directly from God, they are *superior* to any philosophical conception. Thus it is that nowhere in the Gospel does Christ philosophize: He was wisdom itself, and therefore He had no need to seek for it.

But what is necessarily required is reason in its *natural* vigor, that spontaneous and naturally right use of the intelligence that we call *common sense.*

Now it is the fundamental rectitude of common sense, the very health of natural reason, which is wounded and destroyed by the great errors to which modern philosophy is prone. The natural vigor of reason and common sense, destroyed by philosophers, can henceforth be restored only if the mind rights itself in philosophy, in the knowledge of the superior truths naturally accessible to man. Faith and grace—*gratia sanans*—will aid in this work of recovery; they do not make reason useless or superfluous; on the contrary, they require it.

What then, from our present point of view, are the most striking characteristics of the philosophy of Saint Thomas?

This philosophy has already appeared to us as incorporated into the intellectual life of the Church, as the best proportioned to faith, as Pius X observed in his Motu Proprio *Doctoris Angelici,* and as the instrument *par excellence* of theology (no other philosophical doctrine having been able actually to enter into the contexture of theology without causing it some damage). Heretics themselves pay it this testimony. "Take away Thomas and I will destroy the Church," exclaimed Martin Bucer; and Jansenius: "Thomas nauseates me, but I relish Augustine" (as though it were a question of relishing that which one must first understand!) Let us note in passing that this typical relation with theology is for Thomist philosophy a remarkable *sign* of truth: I said at the beginning of this chapter that theology, the superior knowledge, independent in itself of any philosophy, must take into its service, from all the philosophical systems, the one which will be in its hands the best instrument of truth. Could it possibly be the best instrument of truth, if it were not itself *true?*

But we come now to a second characteristic of the philosophy of Saint Thomas. It is *par excellence* the philosophy of reason, the *philosophy of common sense.*[25]

Certainly I do not mean this in the same sense as in the philosophy of the Scottish school! For it is not based on the authority of the common consent of mankind; it is based only on the evidence of the object.

I mean this in an altogether different sense: that

common sense itself is an embryonic and rudimentary philosophy, a philosophy which has not yet reached the scientific state. Does not common sense firmly believe that what is is, that one cannot at the same time affirm and deny the same thing, that in affirming and denying, if we speak truly, we attain to that which is, that all that happens has a cause, that the sensible world exists, that man has a substantial self, that our wills are free, that the fundamental laws of morality are universal, and, lastly, that the world did not make itself and that its author is intelligent? Now this spontaneously right reason, this common sense which precedes faith and without which the words that faith puts on our lips no longer have any meaning for us, is at work, too, in the philosophy of Saint Thomas, but transfigured here by the light of science; not only does the Thomist doctrine establish demonstratively the conclusions instinctively laid down by common sense, but there is perfect continuity between its principles, even the loftiest and the most subtle, and the primary evidences of the intelligence enveloped in the certitudes of common sense.[26] Based on objective evidence, subject to the most rigorous method, scrupulously concerned with critical and analytical reflection, leading metaphysical thought to the highest and craggiest peaks, Thomist philosophy is the discipline of wisdom which corresponds in the scientific order to the natural certitudes of reason. They perceive this clearly who, making their way through it after a long sojourn in the artificial paradises of modern philosophy, feel all the fibers of their intelligence coming to life again. Here again we can note in passing a remarkable *sign* of truth. For if intelligence is worth anything—and if it is not it would be better to be a vegetable than a philosopher—is not the doctrine which develops best in the natural line of intelligence also the truest?

At the same time, the philosophy of Saint Thomas is the only philosophy capable of maintaining and defending against every assault, the only philosophy which, in fact, undertakes to maintain and defend, the integrity of reason, and of justifying—and this is the proper office of metaphysical wisdom—the principles of human knowledge. Consequently, intellectual positions, a great deal more clearly drawn today than they were a hundred or two hundred years ago, thanks to the evolution of modern philosophy, compel us in the last analysis to choose between the two terms of this alternative: integral realism in the sense of Saint Thomas, or pure irrationality.

Philosophy *par excellence* in regard to faith and revealed truth, philosophy *par excellence* in regard to natural reason and common sense: one can note many other characteristics in Thomism, but these two are the ones which make it easiest for us to understand the unique confidence placed in it by the Church.

Must it then be said that the Church has *canonized* the philosophy of Saint Thomas? Yes, certainly, in the sense that she has included the teaching of this philosophy among the prescriptions of Canon Law. We must say in this sense that the philosophy of Saint Thomas is the philosophy of the Church, the philosophy the Church makes use of in her own proper life, the philosophy she commands her masters to teach, the philosophy she desires (and what an unceasingly manifested desire!) to see adopted by her faithful.

But has she canonized it in the sense that she would impose it on minds in the name of her doctrinal magisterium? No! From this point of view, no philosophy, that is to say, no purely human doctrine of wisdom, can be called, strictly speaking, "the Catholic philosophy." There cannot be any "philosophical system which a man would have to adopt in order to be a Christian." [27] The philosophy of Saint Thomas is not a dogma; the Church can define as a truth of faith only what is contained, at least implicitly, in the divine deposit of revelation. One or another truth professed by the Thomist philosophy may very well be so defined one day (if the Church judges that it was contained in the deposit of faith, and in fact this has already happened)—but never the whole philosophy, the body of Thomist doctrine; and the truth in question will never be defined *as philosophical,* since it can be defined only *as contained in the deposit of revelation.* By the very fact of the elevation of dogma and its independence in regard to every philosophical system, any such truth will be raised above philosophical language and formulations. This is what happened, for example, when the Council of Vienna defined that *the rational soul is in itself and essentially the form of the human body.* This definition, as Pius IX explained in 1877, affirms only the substantial unity of human nature, composed of two partial substances, the body and the rational soul; it does not impose the philosophical sense, the strictly Aristotelian sense of the word *form*—although in fact (but this is another matter, which concerns our reason) we cannot find any philosophical doctrine except Aristotle's which fully answers the truth defined.

However, as we said at the beginning of this chapter, the doctrinal magisterium of the Church is not strictly limited to the definitions of faith. And it is proper for every Catholic to receive the philosophy of Saint Thomas for what it actually is—the philosophy the Church has adopted for her own and which she declares to be "according to Christ" [28]—and therefore with the respect due to such an approbation.

The Church, acting as a perfect society having its own proper executive organs, *commands* her masters to teach the philosophy of Saint Thomas, and by this very fact she *recommends* to her faithful that they adhere to it; she throws every possible light on this philosophy, she uses every kind of signal, she cries out: there is where you will find the living waters. But she does not force, she does not constrain anyone to go there.

She even shows great leniency and forbearance towards her own professors, professors being everywhere, we know, a cross-grained and pernickety tribe.

Leo XIII in the encyclical *Aeterni Patris,* and Pius X later in the encyclical *Pascendi,* took pains, as we saw above,[29] to observe:

if anything is taken up with too great subtlety by the Scholastic doctors, or too carelessly stated—if there be anything that ill agrees with the discoveries of a later age, or, in a word, improbable in whatever way—it does not enter Our mind to propose that for imitation to Our age.

Certain professors availed themselves of this to treat as so much refuse the very principles of Saint Thomas, doubtless regarded as sinning through excess of subtlety.

Pius X, it will be remembered, in the Motu Proprio *Doctoris Angelici*, protested vigorously against this abuse,[30] and ordered professors to be piously faithful to the *principia et pronuntiata majora*, to the principles and the main points of doctrine, of the Thomist philosophy (a prescription later inscribed in the new Code of Canon Law). Yet a question could be asked: What are precisely these main points of doctrine?

On July 27, 1914, the Congregation of Studies published by order of Pius X twenty-four theses which, it declared, "plainly contain the principles and main points of doctrine of the Holy Doctor." [31] This was the last public act of Saint Pius X.

Certain professors thereupon asked if all of these twenty-four theses were *imposed* on them in their teaching. On March 7, 1916, the Congregation of Studies, which in the meantime had become the Congregation of Seminaries and Universities, while confirming that the twenty-four theses did in fact express the authentic teaching of Saint Thomas (*Omnes illae viginti quatuor theses philosophiae germanam S. Thomae doctrinam exprimunt*), replied by ordering only that they be *proposed* by the professors to their students as safe rules of guidance: "*proponantur veluti tutae normae directivae.*"

Let us admire the prudence (not exempt from some irony) the Church uses in the government of minds, because she knows human weakness. She first imposes the teaching of the philosophy of Saint Thomas on those to whom she entrusts the task of teaching; then she declares that twenty-four theses, which she publishes, express the main points of doctrine in the philosophy of Saint Thomas; and she is then asked if she imposes the teaching of these twenty-four theses, and her answer is "No, I do not impose them on you."

It is so, I assume, because she thinks: "They will finally come to see for themselves that, if they must teach Saint Thomas, they must also teach the twenty-four theses which faithfully express the mind of Saint Thomas. But so long as they do not see this, I will let them be. I will give them time to draw this consequence for themselves, and to convince themselves of the truth of what I ask them to teach on my behalf."

Does the Church impose on her faithful a sort of "ideological conformism" in philosophy? No.

Is then the philosophy of Saint Thomas something "indifferent" for the Catholic, something which would present itself for his examination in the same way and under the same conditions as any other philosophical doctrine? No.

Like every philosophy, the philosophy of Saint Thomas presents itself for examination by our reason, but it alone among all philosophies presents itself with this recommendation and, if I may so put it, this formidable coefficient of being the philosophy that the Mystical Body of Christ, the Church of whom we are the members, uses in her own intellectual life. If the authority of masters plays in the genesis of human knowledge the role we were recalling to mind in the first pages of this chapter, if in knowledge itself, and however secondary it may then be, it still has a part to play, with how much greater reason will the authority of the Church—and perhaps even more than her injunctions, her example, this very fact that in her own intellectual life she makes constant use of the philosophy of the Common Doctor—incline an attentive mind to turn to him, and induce it to seek patiently, under the bitter rind of Scholasticism, the promised fruit of knowledge. Doubtless there is only one way to judge a philosophy properly, and that is to study it in itself and to appraise its intrinsic evidence. But meanwhile, what a *sign* it is for a Christian, to see the Church officially putting her confidence in one man, in one Doctor! The fact is that in Saint Thomas, according to the profound saying of John of St. Thomas, something greater than Saint Thomas is received and defended, *magis aliquid in Sancto Thoma quam Sanctus Thomas suscipitur et defenditur.* It is proper to remember that God in His highest works proceeds by way of privileges and exceptions and unique cases. He once sent His Son on earth, He gave Him a precursor, He once gave the Law through Moses —is there anything surprising in that He should once have given to His Church a Doctor *par excellence* in philosophical and theological wisdom?

For anyone who would have an adequate idea of the wisdom of the Church, the sign I refer to, though all the while remaining, as regards the philosophy itself of Saint Thomas, an extrinsic sign, something of the order of well-founded confidence rather than of the order of science—this sign, I say, would take on, as regards the value of this philosophy considered as a whole, the character of certitude, and would beget an absolutely solid intellectual determination. Once again, it is not a question of substituting in this way for the labor of philosophizing, but rather of preparing for it and stimulating it; it is not a question of imposing by force adherence to a philosophy, but rather of inviting men, out of love and compassion, to go and see the truth there where it is. This is the meaning

of those great signs in the heavens that we have seen
succeeding one another ever since the time of Leo
XIII. *Come and see:* this is always the way good tidings
are announced. "We now say to all such as are desirous
of the truth: Go to Thomas." [32]

Thus it is that the Catholic Church asks those who
believe in her not to make capital out of a few texts
cut out here and there from the *Summa Theologiae*
for the benefit of one's particular doctrine but rather
to go to Saint Thomas in his living unity. She desires
that he be *the master of their philosophical education,*
the master in whom one puts his trust in order to learn
to think for himself and in order to acquire science. As
she commissioned Saint Thomas to go and speak to
the intellect, so she urges the intellect to go and
listen to Saint Thomas. It is to be hoped that his
modern disciples understand the task that is therefore
theirs. The time has long since passed for them to be
quarreling with the Scotists and the Occamists, the
Molinists, the Augustinians, the Suarezians and the
Vasquezians over scholastic questions which must be
regarded as having been decided for centuries. (Let no
one despise these great questions, for to do so would
be great weakness of mind; one is not a philosopher
if he has not examined them thoroughly, but other
problems must be posed and grappled with.) The
philosophy of Saint Thomas is entering, it seems, into
a period of its development at once more *apostolic* and
more *lay;* it is needed in all the problems of culture.
The intellect, which needs it everywhere, would never
forgive it if it went to sleep at its post.

It demands a *living Thomism,* a Thomism that will
enter into the life of the age and work for the good of
the world. In virtue of a profound law, which can
appear paradoxical only to a mind nourished on

appearances, the more *lay* such a Thomism becomes and the more it works in the secular order, the more will it be, at the same time, *of the Church.* For in order that it may go, without alienating its essence and with genuine efficacy, to the extreme limits to which it is summoned, a virtue must pass through it which comes to it from something higher than itself, from the energies of the Church of Christ. This supposes that a living, actual, active bond unites this whole intellectual effort to the prayer of the contemplatives, in their solitudes and their charterhouses, and that this work among men is really borne up by this prayer in God.

They who will follow Saint Thomas in such a disposition will share in that sort of *poverty* of spirit which gave this greatest of Doctors the demeanor and the simplicity of a child. Their confidence will not be in their own science, they will trust only in the God of compassion, to Whom they themselves and their own science are delivered up as instruments. Not that they therein warp science, as happens each time one makes it the instrument of a human interest. They will on the contrary carefully preserve all its rigor and all its disinterestedness, for they will be employing it only in the service of Him Who conserves all things in their integrity and their loyalty.

But because of this very poverty and this instrumental role, they may hope to serve efficaciously the good of souls and the good of the human community; because they will be ordering their effort to something higher than the human community, that is, to the extension of the Kingdom of God, to the evangelization of the world—an end more exalted than culture, and on which culture depends.

As Saint Thomas combated both the Averroists and

the pseudo-Augustinians, so we must now avoid a double error: one error which we may place under the sign of Cartesian optimism and which hopes for, and demands, a final completion of culture and history in a totally self-sufficient natural perfection achieved by human reason, as if human nature were not wounded and in need of grace, and as if the ultimate end did not transcend culture and history; and another error which we may place under the sign of Lutheran pessimism, and which despairs completely of the world and of culture, abandoning it to the powers of the devil, as if Christ had not really redeemed us.

The Gospel tells us that we are *in* the world and not *of* the world. This is to tell us that the effort we make in the world will remain incomplete in the world, but that we must nevertheless make it with all the more hope, in the assurance that it is completed elsewhere, and that the little good we are able to manage here below, and ever so much more still our sufferings and our very infirmities, are turned to good account by Him Whom we love.

APPENDICES

A LIST OF ST. THOMAS' WORKS[1]

A. *Theological Syntheses*

Scripta super libros Sententiarum—c. 1256
Summa contra Gentiles—1261-1263
Summa theologiae—1265-1273

B. *Academic Disputations*

Quaestiones disputatae:
De veritate—1256-1259
De potentia Dei—1259-1268
De spiritualibus creaturis—1269
De anima—1269-1270
De unione Verbi incarnati—1268-1272
De malo—1263-1271

[1] For the most recent, most exhaustive, detailed, and painstakingly accurate descriptive catalogue of the works, embodying the results of decades of research by himself and others concerning the authenticity and chronology of those works, see I. T. Eschmann, O.P., "A Catalogue of St. Thomas' Works: Bibliographical Notes" in the Appendix to Etienne Gilson's *The Christian Philosophy of Saint Thomas Aquinas*, Random House, New York, 1956, pp. 381-439. This list is following Father Eschmann's classification and order. One has but to consult his work to appreciate how provisional many of the dates in this list are.

161

De virtutibus—1269-1272

?De immortalitate animae?

?Utrum anima conjuncta cognoscat seipsam per essentiam?

Quaestiones de quolibet I-XII:

I-VI—1269-1272

VII-XI—1256-1259

XII—c. 1270

C. *Expositions of Holy Scripture*

Expositio in Job ad litteram—c. 1260

In Psalmos Davidis expositio—1272-1273

Expositio in Canticum Canticorum—a lost work

Expositio in Isaiam prophetam—1256-1259

Expositio in Jeremiam prophetam—1267-1268

Expositio in Threnos Jeremiae prophetae—1267-1268

Glossa continua in Matthaeum, Marcum, Lucam, Joannem—1263-1264 (The Glossa is commonly called the Catena aurea)

Expositio in evangelium s. Matthaei—1269-1272

Expositio in evangelium s. Joannis—1269-1272

Expositio in s. Pauli Epistolas—1259-1272

D. *Expositions of Aristotelian Works*

In libros Peri Hermeneias expositio—1269-1271

In libros posteriorum Analyticorum expositio—1268

In octo libros Physicorum expositio—1268-1271

In libros De caelo et mundo expositio—1272-1273

In libros De generatio et corruptione expositio—1272-1273

In libros Meteorologicorum expositio—1269-1273

In libros De anima expositio—1268-1271

In librum De sensu et sensato expositio—1267-1271

In librum De memoria et reminiscentia expositio—
1267-1271

In duodecim libros Metaphysicorum expositio—1270-
1272

In decem libros Ethicorum expositio—1271-1272

In libros Politicorum expositio—1265-1272

E. *Other Expositions*

Expositio super librum Boethii De Trinitate—1257-
1259

Expositio in librum Boethii De hebdomadibus—1257-
1259

Expositio in Dionysium De divinis nominibus—c. 1261

Super librum De causis expositio—1271

F. *Polemical Writings*

Contra impugnantes Dei cultum et religionem—1256

De perfectione vitae spiritualis—1270

Contra pestiferam doctrinam retrahentium pueros a
religionis ingressu—1270

De unitate intellectus, contra Averroistas—1270

De aeternitate mundi, contra murmurantes—1271

G. *Treatises on Special Subjects*

De fallaciis ad quosdam nobiles artistas—1244-1245

De propositionibus modalibus—1244-1245

De ente et essentia—before 1256

De principiis naturae ad fratrem Sylvestrum—before
1256

Compendium theologie ad fratrem Reginaldum socium
suum carissimum—1260-1273

De substantiis separatis, seu de angelorum natura, ad

fratrem Reginaldum, socium suum carissimum—
   after 1270

De Regno (De regimine principum), ad regem Cypri
   —1267

H. *Expert Opinions*

Contra errores Graecorum, ad Urbanum IV Pontificem
   Maximum—1263

Responsio ad fr. Joannem Vercellensem, Generalem
   Magistrum Ordinis Praedicatorum, de articulis
   CVIII ex opere Petri de Tarentasia—1264-1266

Responsio ad fr. Joannem Vercellensem, Generalem
   Magistrum Ordinis Praedicatorum, de articulis
   XLII—1271

De forma absolutionis, ad Generalem Magistrum
   Ordinis—1269-1272

De secreto—1269

I. *Letters*

To the Archbishop of Palermo: De articulis fidei et
   Ecclesiae sacramentis, ad archiepiscopum Panor-
   mitanum—1261-1262

To Bernard Ayglier, Abbot of Monte Cassino: Ad
   Bernardum, abbatem Cassinensem—1274

To the Archdeacon of . . . ? Expositio super primam
   decretalem "De fide catholica et sancta Trinitate"
   et super secundam "Damnamus autem"—1259-
   1268

To the Cantor of Antioch: De rationibus fidei contra
   Saracenos, Graecos et Armenos, ad Cantorem
   Antiochiae—1261-1264

To Master Philippus: De motu cordis, ad Magistrum
   Philippum—1270-1271

To Master Philippus: De mixtione elementorum—
1270-1271

To Brother Baxianus da Lodi: Responsio ad lectorem
Venetum de articulis XXXVI—1271

To Brother Gerald of Besançon: Responsio ad lectorem
Bisuntinum de articulis VI—date unknown

To Brother Johannes of Viterbo: De emptione et
venditione ad tempus—1262

To Brother Johannes: De modo studendi

To the Duchess of Brabant: De regimine Judaeorum,
ad Ducissam Branantiae—1270-1272

To Sir James of . . . ? De sortibus ad Dominum Jaco-
bum de . . . ?—1269-1272

To a Gentleman from beyond the Alps: De occultis
operationibus naturae, ad quendam militem ultramontanum—date unknown

To a Gentleman from beyond the Alps: De judiciis
astrorum, ad quendam militem ultramontanum—
date unknown

J. *Liturgical Pieces and Sermons*

Officium de festo Corporis Christi, ad mandatum
Urbani Papae IV—1264

Adoro te and other prayers

Sermons:

De duobus praeceptis caritatis et decem legis praeceptis—1273

Devotissima expositio super symbolum apostolorum
—1273

Expositio devotissima orationis dominicae—1273

Devotissima expositio super salutatione angelica—
1269-1273

and many other sermons

K. *Works of Uncertain Authenticity*

De instantibus
De natura verbi intellectus
De principio individuationis
De natura generis
De natura accidentium
De natura materiae
De quatuor oppositis
De demonstratione

TESTIMONIES OF THE POPES

Alexander IV (1254-1261)	9-23[1]	7-24[1]
Urban IV (1261-1264)	24-30	24-28
Clement IV (1265-1268)	31-36	29-31
Gregory X (1271-1276)	37-41	32-33
Innocent V (1276)	42-44	34-35
Nicholas III (1277-1280)	47-50	36-38
Martin IV (1281-1285)	51 P	38-39
Honorius IV (1285-1287)	52-53	39-40
Nicholas IV (1288-1292)	54 P	40-41
Celestine V (1294)	55 P	41
Boniface VIII (1294-1303)	56-57	42-43
Benedict XI (1303-1304)	58-59 P	43
Clement V (1305-1314)	60	44
John XXII (1316-1344)	61-69	44-53

March 1, 1318. Declares
his doctrine miraculous.
"He alone enlightened
the Church more than all
the other doctors."

July 18, 1323. Bull of

[1] These references are to: J. J. Berthier, O.P., *Sanctus
Thomas Aquinas "Doctor Communis" Ecclesiae,* vol. I:
Testimonia Ecclesiae, Roma, 1914. The column on the
left refers to the paragraphs, the one on the right to the
pages. The letter P indicates an explicit testimony in
regard to the Preachers, which implicitly designates Saint
Thomas.

Canonization: "Redemptionem misit Dominus."	62	45
Benedict XII(1335-1342)	70 P	53-54
Clement VI (1342-1352)	71-78	54-61
1346. Orders the Preachers not to deviate from the doctrine of St. Thomas.		
Innocent VI (1352-1362)	79	62
Urban V (1362-1370)	80-86	62-66
Gregory XI (1370-1378)	87-88	66-67
Urban VI (1378-1389)	89 P	68
Boniface IX (1389-1404)	90	68-69
Innocent VII (1404-1406)	91	70
July 6, 1406. Confirms the doctrine of the Preachers, which is the Doctrine of St. Thomas; Const. "Decens reputamus."	91	70
Gregory XII (1406-1415)	92	71
Alexander V (1409-1410)	93	71-72
John XXIII (1410-1415)	94	72
Martin V (1417-1431)	95 P	73-74
Eugene IV (1431-1447)	96-97	74-76
Nicholas V (1447-1455)	98-99	76-78
Calixtus III (1455-1458)	100-101	78-80
Pius II (1458-1464)	102	80-81
Paul II (1464-1471)	103 P	81-82
Sixtus IV (1471-1484)	104	82-83
Innocent VIII (1484-1492)	105	83-84
Alexander VI (1492-1503)	106	84
Julius II (1503-1513)	108 P	85-86
Leo X (1513-1521)	109-111 P	86-87
Clement VII (1523-1534)	113-115 P	88-90

Paul III (1534-1549)	116-118 P	90-92
Julius III (1550-1555)	119 P	93
Paul IV (1555-1559)	121	94-95
Pius IV (1559-1565)	122	95-96
Pius V (1566-1572)	123-125	97-101
April 11, 1567. Proclaims St. Thomas Doctor in the Const. "Mirabilis Deus."	124	97
1570. Orders an edition of the complete works of Saint Thomas.	125	100
Gregory XIII (1572-1585)	126-127 P	101-103
Sixtus V (1585-1590)	128-130	103-106
Clement VIII (1592-1605)	134-140	108-115
1594. Recommends adhering to Saint Thomas to the Fathers of the Society of Jesus.	140	114-115
Leo XI (1605)	141	116
Paul V (1605-1621)	142-144	116-119
Urban VIII (1624-1644)	146-147 P	120-121
Alexander VII (1655-1667)	149-151	122-125
Clement X (1670-1676)	153	127-128
Innocent XI (1676-1689)	154-155	128-132
Alexander VIII (1689-1691)	156	133-134
Innocent XII (1691-1700)	157-158	134-136
Clement XI (1700-1721)	159-165	136-141
April 23, 1718. Gives his solemn approbation to the statutes of the Academy of St. Thomas in Rome. Const. "Inscrutabili."	159	136-138
Innocent XIII (1721-1724)	166 P	142-143

December 30, 1892. Invites the members of the Society of Jesus to follow the teaching of Saint Thomas. Brief: "Gravissime Nos."	318-325	244-252
November 25, 1898. The same invitation addressed to the Friars Minor.	352	264
May 9, 1895. Approves the new constitutions of the Roman Academy of St. Thomas. Apostolic letter "Constitutiones."	341	258-260
September 8, 1899. Encyclical letter to the French clergy "Depuis le jour."	355	265-267
Pius X (1903-1914)	366-388 680-682	271-280 695-702
September 8, 1907. Encyclical "Pascendi."	376	276
September 1, 1910. Motu proprio "Sacrorum Antistitum."	AAS,[2] 2 (1910) 655-680	
June 29, 1914. Motu proprio "Doctoris Angelici."	680-681 AAS, 6 (1914)	695-699 336-341
July 27, 1914. Publication of the XXIV Thomist theses.	682 AAS, 6 (1914)	699-702 383-386

[2] *Acta Apostolicae Sedis;* commentarium officiale. Città del Vaticano, Libreria editrice Vaticana, 1909 seq.

Benedict XV (1914-1922)

December 31, 1914. Motu proprio "Non multo" on the Roman Academy of St. Thomas. ... AAS, 7 (1915) 5-7

March 7, 1916. Answer given by the Congregation of Seminaries and Universities on the XXIV theses. ... AAS, 8 (1916) 156-157

May 27, 1917. Promulgation of the new Code of Canon Law. (Canon 1366, par. 2: "Teachers shall adhere religiously to the method, doctrine and principles" of Saint Thomas.) ... AAS, 9 (1917), Part 2

June 29, 1921. Encyclical "Fausto appetente die." ... AAS, 13 (1921) 329-335

Pius XI (1922-1939)

August 1, 1922. Apostolic letter on the education of the clergy. ... AAS, 14 (1922) 449-458

June 29, 1923. Encyclical "Studiorum Ducem" for the sixth centenary of Saint Thomas. ... AAS, 15 (1923) 309-326

May 24, 1931. Apostolic Constitution "Deus scientiarum Dominus," especially Art. 29. ... AAS, 23 (1931) 241-262

December 20, 1935. "Ad Catholici Sacerdotii" on the priesthood.	AAS, 28 (1936)	5-53

Pius XII (1939-   ):

June 24, 1939. "Sollemnis conventus," a sermon to ecclesiastical students in Rome.	AAS, 31 (1939)	245-251
	Discorsi,[3] I,	211-218
March 7, 1942. "Quandoquidem qui sacris," a letter to the Master General of the Order of Friar Preachers: St. Thomas Aquinas, patron of all schools.	AAS, 34 (1942)	96-99
	Discorsi, IV,	429-432
September 17, 1946. "Quamvis inquieti," allocution to the newly elected General of the Society of Jesus and his electors.	AAS, 38 (1946)	381-385
	Discorsi, VIII,	229-234
September 22, 1946. "Par est laeto," allocution to the Master General of the Dominican Order and the Capitular Fathers.	AAS, 38 (1946)	385-389
	Discorsi, VIII,	243-247

September 25, 1949. "De grand coeur," address to

[3] *Discorsi e radiomessaggi di Sua Santità Pio XII.* Milano, Società editrice "Vita e Pensiero," 1941, seq.

the members of the International Congress of Humanistic Studies.	AAS, 41 (1949) 555-556 Discorsi, XI, 217-218
August 12, 1950. "Humani generis," encyclical concerning some false opinions which threaten to undermine the foundations of Catholic doctrine.	AAS, 42 (1950) 561-578
September 17, 1950. "Singulari animi erga," allocution to the third International Thomistic Congress organized by the Pontifical Roman Academy of St. Thomas.	AAS, 42 (1950) 734-735 Discorsi, XII, 205-206
September 23, 1950. "Menti Nostrae," Apostolic exhortation to the priests of the world: spiritual perfection.	AAS, 42 (1950) 657-702
August 12, 1953. "Opportuno sane consilio," letter to the Rector of the Pontifical Gregorian University on the fourth centenary of its founding.	AAS, 45 (1953) 658-664 Discorsi, XV, 661-667
October 17, 1953. "Animus Noster gaudio," address to the faculty, stu-	

dents and alumni of the Pontifical Gregorian University: fourth centenary.

AAS, 45 (1953) 682-690
Discorsi, XV,   405-414

September 14, 1955. "Nous vous souhaitons," address to members of the Fourth International Thomistic Congress, on Thomistic philosophy and modern thought.

AAS, 47 (1955) 683-691

March 9, 1956. "C'est bien volontiers," address to the International Union of Archaeological Institutes.

AAS, 48 (1956) 210-216

FOUR PAPAL DOCUMENTS

AETERNI PATRIS

DOCTORIS ANGELICI

STUDIORUM DUCEM

HUMANI GENERIS

AETERNI PATRIS

ON THE RESTORATION OF CHRISTIAN PHILOSOPHY IN SCHOOLS

Introductory Remarks on the Encyclical by Etienne Gilson

Published on August 4, 1879, the encyclical letter *Aeterni Patris* prescribes that Christian philosophy, as contained in the works of Thomas Aquinas, should be taught in schools in conformity with the teaching of the Church. The abbreviated title commonly given to it, "On Christian Philosophy," is therefore correct. Its other title, "On Scholastic Philosophy," is correct only to the extent that the scholastic philosophy at stake is that of Thomas Aquinas himself, not a more or less corrupt version of it.

The conclusions of this encyclical were implemented, one year later, by an apostolic letter establishing Thomas Aquinas the common patron of *all* the Catholic schools (A.S.S., 13, 56-59). This latter document explicitly refers to *Aeterni Patris* as to "Our Letter on the Restoring in Catholic Schools of the Christian Philosophy in the Spirit of St. Thomas Aquinas." This doctrine is said to be applicable in all times because of the amplitude of its principles. The remarkable revival of Thomism in modern times has found a powerful incentive in these documents. The critical edition of the complete works of Thomas Aquinas (Leonine edition), the development of historical research work in the history of mediaeval philosophies and theologies, the creation of research centers, collections and journals devoted to the study of Thomism as well as of its sources and its influence all bear witness to the fecundity of the directives issued in 1879.

In his first encyclical, on the evils that threaten society,

179

Pope Leo XIII had already recalled the warning of St. Paul: "Beware lest any man cheat you by philosophy and vain deceit, according to the tradition of man, according to the principles of the world, and not according to Christ" (Col. 2:8). The safest way to keep false philosophies out of the schools is to have them teach the true one. In defining the method of Christian philosophy or, rather, the Christian way of philosophizing, Pope Leo XIII was therefore laying down the doctrinal foundation of the social and philosophical order.

Summary

1) Doctrinal mission of the Church and teaching office of the Popes. 2) False philosophy has crept into all the orders of the State. 3) Usefulness of philosophy to call back the people to the paths of faith and salvation. 4) Philosophy, if rightly used, is a stepping stone to faith, but, inversely, faith completes and strengthens the light of reason. 5) Services rendered to faith by reason. 6) Philosophy helps theology to assume the nature, form, and character of a science. 7) Philosophy helps in defending divinely revealed truth. 8) Philosophy waits as a handmaid and attendant upon the revealed doctrines which are beyond the reach of human reason; it makes use of its own principles and methods of demonstration in the case of truths accessible to human reason. 9) The best way to philosophize is to unite the study of philosophy to obedience to the Christian faith. 10) This is confirmed by the history of philosophy, especially by the sight of the errors committed by the ancient philosophers who were not guided by the light of the divine revelation. 11) Not so in the case of the apologists, especially Justin Martyr. 12) Contribution of early patristics to the work of Christian philosophy. 13) Outstanding contribution of Augustine and his successors up to Anselm of Canterbury. 14-15) In praise of the Scholastics, especially St. Thomas and St. Bonaventure. 16) This praise of Scholastic theology applies to Scholastic philosophy. 17) Thomas Aquinas, the chief and master of all the Scholastic doctors; characteristics of his method. 18) Because it chiefly dealt with the prin-

ciples of things, his doctrine contains, so to say, the seeds of almost infinite truths. 19) Nearly all the founders of religious orders have prescribed to their members to adhere to the teachings of St. Thomas. 20) Many European universities have recognized his authority. 21) Many Popes have praised his teaching as the true and catholic doctrine. 22) The ecumenical councils have held Thomas in singular honor. 23) Heretics have considered him their main adversary. 24-26) Dangers arising from the new systems of philosophy and necessity of a return to Thomas Aquinas as to the fountainhead of philosophic truth. 27) Outside of divine grace, nothing is better calculated than the doctrine of the Fathers and the Scholastics to satisfy the minds which claim reason as their sole mistress and guide. 28) It provides the domestic and civil society with the safest guarantee of peace. 29) Not only the social order, but all studies would find promise of advancement and assistance in the restoration of this philosophic training. 30) The examples of Albert the Great and Thomas Aquinas show that there is no opposition between the study of such a philosophy and that of natural sciences; rather, the reverse is true. 31) Universities should, therefore, restore the wisdom of St. Thomas, without feeling bound to maintain what Scholastic doctors could have said with too much subtlety or that which, in their doctrines, might contradict modern scientific discoveries. 32) This undertaking cannot succeed without the help of the God of all knowledge, who is also the Father of lights. 33) Following the example of St. Thomas, we should beseech God to grant us the gifts of knowledge and of understanding. 34) Apostolic benediction.

AETERNI PATRIS

ENCYCLICAL LETTER OF OUR
MOST HOLY LORD
POPE LEO XIII

On Christian Philosophy
To All Our Venerable Brethren
the Patriarchs, Primates, Archbishops and Bishops
of the Catholic World in grace and
communion with the Apostolic See,
Leo XIII, Pope

Venerable Brethren,
Greeting and the Apostolic Benediction.

1) The only-begotten Son of the Eternal Father, who came on earth to bring salvation and the light of divine wisdom to men, conferred a great and wonderful blessing on the world when, about to ascend again into heaven, He commanded the Apostles to go and teach all nations,[1] and left the Church which He had founded to be the common and supreme teacher of the peoples. For men whom the truth had set free were to be preserved by the truth; nor would the fruits of heavenly doctrines by which salvation comes to men have long remained had not the Lord Christ appointed an unfailing teaching authority to train the minds to faith.[a] And the Church built upon the promises of its own divine Author, whose charity it imitated, so faith-

fully followed out His commands that its constant aim and chief wish was this: to teach religion and contend forever against errors. To this end assuredly have tended the incessant labors of individual bishops; to this end also the published [b] laws and decrees of councils, and especially the constant watchfulness of the Roman Pontiffs, to whom, as successors of the blessed Peter in the primacy of the Apostles, belongs the right and office of teaching and confirming their brethren in the faith. Since, then, according to the warning of the Apostle, the minds of Christ's faithful are apt to be deceived and the integrity of the faith to be corrupted among men by philosophy and vain deceit,[2] the supreme pastors of the Church have always thought it their duty to advance, by every means in their power, science truly so called, and at the same time to provide with special care that all studies should accord with the Catholic faith, especially philosophy, on which a right interpretation [c] of the other sciences in great part depends. Indeed, venerable brethren, on this very subject among others, We briefly admonished you in Our first encyclical letter; but now, both by reason of the gravity of the subject and the condition of the time, we are again compelled to speak to you on the mode of taking up the study of philosophy which shall respond most fitly to the excellence [d] of faith, and at the same time be consonant with the dignity of human science.[e]

2) Whoso turns his attention to the bitter strifes of these days and seeks a reason for the troubles that vex public and private life must come to the conclusion that a fruitful cause of the evils which now afflict, as well as those which threaten, us lies in this: that false conclusions concerning divine and human things,

which originated in the schools of philosophy, have
now crept into all the orders of the State, and have
been accepted by the common consent of the masses.
For, since it is in the very nature of man to follow
the guide of reason in his actions, if his intellect sins
at all his will soon follows; and thus it happens that
false opinions,[f] whose seat is in the understanding,
influence human actions and pervert them. Whereas,
on the other hand, if men be of sound mind and take
their stand on true and solid principles, there will result a vast amount of benefits for the public and
private good. We do not, indeed, attribute such force
and authority to philosophy as to esteem it equal to
the task of combating and rooting out all errors; for,
when the Christian religion was first constituted, it
came upon earth to restore it to its primeval dignity
by the admirable light of faith, diffused "not by persuasive words of human wisdom, but in the manifestation
of spirit and of power"; so also at the present time we
look above all things to the powerful help of Almighty
God to bring back to a right understanding the minds
of men and dispel the darkness of error. But the
natural helps with which the grace of the divine
wisdom, strongly and sweetly disposing all things,
has supplied the human race are neither to be despised
nor neglected, chief among which is evidently the
right use of philosophy. For, not in vain did God set
the light of reason in the human mind; and so far is
the superadded light of faith from extinguishing or
lessening the power of the intelligence that it completes it rather, and by adding to its strength renders
it capable of greater things.

3) Therefore, Divine Providence itself requires that,
in calling back the people to the paths of faith and

salvation, advantage should be taken of human science also—an approved and wise practice which history testifies was observed by the most illustrious Fathers of the Church. They, indeed, were wont neither to belittle nor undervalue the part that reason had to play, as is summed up by the great Augustine when he attributes to this science "that by which the most wholesome faith is begotten . . . is nourished, defended, and made strong." [3]

4) In the first place, philosophy, if rightly made use of by the wise, in a certain way tends to smooth and fortify the road to true faith, and to prepare the souls of its disciples for the fit reception of revelation; for which reason it is well called by ancient writers sometimes a stepping-stone to the Christian faith,[4] sometimes the prelude and help of Christianity,[5] sometimes the Gospel teacher.[6] And, assuredly, the God of all goodness, in all that pertains to divine things, has not only manifested by the light of faith those truths which human intelligence could not attain of itself, but others, also, not altogether unattainable by reason, that by the help of divine authority they may be made known to all at once and without any admixture of error. Hence it is that certain truths which were either divinely proposed for belief, or were bound by the closest chains to the doctrine of faith,[g] were discovered by pagan sages with nothing but their natural reason to guide them, were demonstrated and proved by becoming arguments. For, as the Apostle says, the invisible things of Him, from the creation of the world, are clearly seen, being understood by the things that are made: His eternal power also and divinity;[7] and the Gentiles who have not the Law show, nevertheless, the work of the Law written in their hearts.[8] But it is

most fitting to turn these truths, which have been discovered by the pagan sages even, to the use and purposes of revealed doctrine, in order to show that both human wisdom and the very testimony of our adversaries serve to support the Christian faith—a method which is not of recent introduction, but of established use, and has often been adopted by the holy Fathers of the Church. What is more, those venerable men, the witnesses and guardians of religious traditions, recognize a certain form and figure of this in the action of the Hebrews, who, when about to depart out of Egypt, were commanded to take with them the gold and silver vessels and precious robes of the Egyptians, that by a change of use the things might be dedicated to the service of the true God which had formerly been the instruments of ignoble and superstitious rites. Gregory of Neo-Caesarea[9] praises Origen expressly because, with singular dexterity, as one snatches weapons from the enemy, he turned to the defense of Christian wisdom and to the destruction of superstition many arguments drawn from the writings of the pagans. And both Gregory of Nazianzen[10] and Gregory of Nyssa[11] praise and commend a like mode of disputation in Basil the Great; while Jerome[12] especially commends it in Quadratus, a disciple of the Apostles, in Aristides, Justin, Irenaeus, and very many others. Augustine says: "Do we not see Cyprian, that mildest of doctors and most blessed of martyrs, going out of Egypt laden with gold and silver and vestments? And Lactantius, also, and Victorinus, Optatus and Hilary? And, not to speak of the living, how many Greeks have done likewise?" [13] But if natural reason first sowed this rich field of doctrine before it was rendered fruitful by the power of Christ, it must assuredly become more prolific after the grace of the Saviour has renewed and added to the native faculties of the human mind. And who does not see that a plain and easy road is opened up to faith by such a method of philosophic study?

5) But the advantage to be derived from such a school of philosophy[h] is not to be confined within these limits. The foolishness of those men who "by these good things that are seen could not understand Him, that is, neither by attending to the works could have acknowledged who was the workman," [14] is gravely reproved in the words of Divine Wisdom. In the first place, then, this great and noble fruit is gathered from human reason, that it demonstrates that God *is;* for by the greatness of the beauty and of the creature the Creator of them may be seen so as to be known thereby.[15] Again, it shows God to excel in the height of all perfections, especially in infinite wisdom before which nothing lies hidden, and in absolute justice which no depraved affection could possibly shake; and that God, therefore, is not only true but truth itself, which can neither deceive nor be deceived. Whence it clearly follows that human reason finds the fullest faith and authority united in the word of God. In like manner, reason declares that the doctrine of the Gospel has even from its very beginning been made manifest by certain wonderful signs, the established proofs, as it were, of unshaken truth; and that all, therefore, who set faith in the Gospel do not believe rashly as though following cunningly devised fables,[16] but, by a most reasonable consent, subject their intelligence and judgment to an authority which is divine. And of no less importance is it that reason most clearly sets forth that the Church instituted by Christ (as laid down in the

Vatican Council), on account of its wonderful spread, its marvelous sanctity, and its inexhaustible fecundity in all places, as well as of its Catholic unity and unshaken stability, is in itself a great and perpetual motive of belief and an irrefragable testimony of its own divine mission.[17]

6) Its solid foundations having been thus laid, a perpetual and varied service is further required of philosophy, in order that sacred theology may receive and assume the nature, form, and genius of a true science. For in this, the most noble of studies, it is of the greatest necessity to bind together, as it were, in one body the many and various parts of the heavenly doctrines, that, each being allotted to its own proper place and derived from its own proper principles, the whole may join together in a complete union; in order, in fine, that all and each part may be strengthened by its own and the others' invincible arguments. Nor is that more accurate or fuller knowledge of the things that are believed, and somewhat more lucid understanding, as far as it can go, of the very mysteries of faith which Augustine and the other Fathers commended and strove to reach, and which the Vatican Council itself[18] declared to be most fruitful, to be passed over in silence or belittled. Those will certainly more fully and more easily attain that knowledge and understanding who to integrity of life and love of faith join a mind rounded and finished by philosophic studies, as the same Vatican Council teaches that the knowledge of such sacred dogmas ought to be sought as well from analogy of the things that are naturally known as from the connection of those mysteries one with another and with the final end of man.[19]

7) Lastly, the duty of religiously defending the truths divinely delivered, and of resisting those who dare oppose them, pertains to philosophic pursuits. Wherefore, it is the glory of philosophy to be esteemed as the bulwark of faith and the strong defense of religion. As Clement of Alexandria testifies, the doctrine of the Saviour is indeed perfect in itself and wanteth naught, since it is the power and wisdom of God. And the assistance of the Greek philosophy maketh not the truth more powerful; but, inasmuch as it weakens the contrary arguments of the sophists and repels the veiled attacks against the truth, it has been fitly called the hedge and fence of the vine.[20] For, as the enemies of the Catholic name, when about to attack religion, are in the habit of borrowing their weapons from the arguments of philosophers, so the defenders of sacred science draw many arguments from the store of philosophy which may serve to uphold revealed dogmas. Nor is the triumph of the Christian faith a small one in using human reason to repel powerfully and speedily the attacks of its adversaries by the hostile arms which human reason itself supplied. This species of religious strife St. Jerome, writing to Magnus, notices as having been adopted by the Apostle of the Gentiles himself; Paul the leader of the Christian army and the invincible orator, battling for the cause of Christ, skillfully turns even a chance inscription into an argument for the faith; for he had learned from the true David to wrest the sword from the hands of the enemy and to cut off the head of the boastful Goliath with his own weapons.[21] Moreover, the Church herself not only urges, but even commands, Christian teachers to seek help from philosophy. For, the Fifth Lateran Council, after it had decided that "every assertion contrary to

the truth of revealed faith is altogether false, for the reason that it contradicts, however slighly, the truth," [22] advises teachers of philosophy to pay close attention to the exposition of fallacious arguments; since, as Augustine testifies, "If reason is turned against the authority of sacred Scripture, no matter how specious it may seem, it errs in the likeness of truth; for true it cannot be." [23]

8) But in order that philosophy may be found equal to the gathering of those precious fruits which we have indicated, it behooves it above all things never to turn aside from that path which the Fathers have entered upon from a venerable antiquity, and which the Vatican Council solemnly and authoritatively approved. As it is evident that very many truths of the supernatural order which are far beyond the reach of the keenest intellect must be accepted, human reason, conscious of its own infirmity, dare not affect to itself too great powers, nor deny those truths, nor measure them by its own standard, nor interpret them at will; but receive them, rather, with a full and humble faith, and esteem it the highest honor to be allowed to wait upon heavenly doctrines like a handmaid and attendant, and by God's goodness attain to them in any way whatsoever. But in the case of such doctrines as the human intelligence may perceive, it is equally just that philosophy should make use of its own method, principles, and arguments—not, indeed, in such fashion as to seem rashly to withdraw from the divine authority. But, since it is established that those things which become known by revelation have the force of certain truth, and that those things which war against faith war equally against right reason, the Catholic philosopher will know that he violates at once faith and

the laws of reason if he accepts any conclusion which he understands to be opposed to revealed doctrine.

9) We know that there are some who, in their overestimate of the human faculties, maintain that as soon as man's intellect becomes subject to divine authority it falls from its native dignity, and, hampered by the yoke of this species of slavery, is much retarded and hindered in its progress toward the supreme truth and excellence. Such an idea is most false and deceptive, and its sole tendency is to induce foolish and ungrateful men wilfully to repudiate the most sublime truths, and reject the divine gift of faith, from which the fountains of all good things flow out upon civil society. For the human mind, being confined within certain limits, and those narrow enough, is exposed to many errors and is ignorant of many things; whereas the Christian faith, reposing on the authority of God, is the unfailing mistress of truth, whom whoso followeth he will be neither enmeshed in the snares of error nor tossed hither and thither on the waves of fluctuating opinion. Those, therefore, who to the study of philosophy unite obedience to the Christian faith, are philosophizing in the best possible way;[1] for the splendor of the divine truths, received into the mind, helps the understanding, and not only detracts in nowise from its dignity, but adds greatly to its nobility, keenness, and stability. For surely that is a worthy and most useful exercise of reason when men give their minds to disproving those things which are repugnant to faith and proving the things which conform to faith. In the first case they cut the ground from under the feet of error and expose the viciousness of the arguments on which error rests; while in the second case they make themselves masters

of weighty reasons for the sound demonstration of truth and the satisfactory instruction of any reasonable person. Whoever denies that such study and practice tend to add to the resources and expand the faculties of the mind must necessarily and absurdly hold that the mind gains nothing from discriminating between the true and the false. Justly, therefore, does the Vatican Council commemorate in these words the great benefits which faith had conferred upon reason: *Faith frees and saves reason from error, and endows it with manifold knowledge.*[24] A wise man, therefore, would not accuse faith and look upon it as opposed to reason and natural truths, but would rather offer heartfelt thanks to God, and sincerely rejoice that, in the density of ignorance and in the flood-tide of error, holy faith, like a friendly star, shines down upon his path and points out to him the fair gate of truth beyond all danger of wandering.

10) If, venerable brethren, you open the history of philosophy, you will find all We have just said proved by experience. The philosophers of old who lacked the gift of faith, yet were esteemed so wise, fell into many appalling errors. You know how often among some truths they taught false and incongruous things; what vague and doubtful opinions they held concerning the nature of the Divinity, the first origin of things, the government of the world, the divine knowledge of the future, the cause and principle of evil, the ultimate end of man, the eternal beatitude, concerning virtue and vice, and other matters, a true and certain knowledge which is most necessary to the human race; while, on the other hand, the early Fathers and Doctors of the Church, who well understood that, according to the divine plan, the restorer

of human science is Christ, who is the power and
the wisdom of God,[25] and in whom are hid all the
treasures of wisdom and knowledge,[26] took up and
investigated the books of the ancient philosophers,
and compared their teachings with the doctrines of
revelation, and, carefully sifting them, they cherished
what was true and wise in them and amended or
rejected all else. For, as the all-seeing God against the
cruelty of tyrants raised up mighty martyrs to the
defense of the Church, men prodigal of their great
lives, in like manner to false philosophers and heretics
He opposed men of great wisdom, to defend, even by
the aid of human reason, the treasure of revealed
truths. Thus, from the very first ages of the Church,
the Catholic doctrine has encountered a multitude of
most bitter adversaries, who, deriding the Christian
dogmas and institutions, maintained that there were
many gods, that the material world never had a beginning or cause, and that the course of events was
one of blind and fatal necessity, not regulated by the
will of Divine Providence.

11) But the learned men whom We call apologists
speedily encountered these teachers of foolish doctrine
and, under the guidance of faith, found arguments in
human wisdom also to prove that one God, who stands
pre-eminent in every kind of perfection, is to be
worshiped; that all things were created from nothing
by His omnipotent power; that by His wisdom they
flourish and serve each their own special purposes.
Among these St. Justin Martyr claims the chief place.
After having tried the most celebrated academies of
the Greeks, he saw clearly, as he himself confesses, that
he could only draw truths in their fullness from the
doctrine of revelation. These he embraced with all the

ardor of his soul, purged of calumny, courageously and fully defended before the Roman emperors, and reconciled with them not a few of the sayings of the Greek philosophers.

12) Quadratus, also, and Aristides, Hermias, and Athenagoras stood nobly forth in that time. Nor did Irenaeus, the invincible martyr and Bishop of Lyons, win less glory in the same cause when, forcibly refuting the perverse opinions of the Orientals, the work of the Gnostics, scattered broadcast over the territories of the Roman Empire, he explained (according to Jerome) the origin of each heresy and in what philosophic source it took its rise.[27] But who knows not the disputations of Clement of Alexandria, which the same Jerome thus honorably commemorates: "What is there in them that is not learned, and what that is not of the very heart of philosophy?" [28] He himself, indeed, with marvelous versatility treated of many things of the greatest utility for preparing a history of philosophy, for the exercise of the dialectic art, and for showing the agreement between reason and faith. After him came Origen, who graced the chair of the school of Alexandria, and was most learned in the teachings of the Greeks and Orientals. He published many volumes, involving great labor, which were wonderfully adapted to explain the divine writings and illustrate the sacred dogmas; which, though, as they now stand, not altogether free from error, contain nevertheless a wealth of knowledge tending to the growth and advance of natural truths. Tertullian opposes heretics with the authority of the sacred writings; with the philosophers he changes his fence and disputes philosophically; but so learnedly and accurately did he confute them that he made bold to

say: "Neither in science nor in schooling are we equals, as you imagine." [29] Arnobius, also, in his works against the pagans, and Lactantius in the divine *Institutions* especially, with equal eloquence and strength strenuously strive to move men to accept the dogmas and precepts of Catholic wisdom, not by philosophic juggling, after the fashion of the Academicians, but vanquishing them partly by their own arms, and partly by arguments drawn from the mutual contentions of the philosophers.[30] But the writings on the human soul, the divine attributes, and other questions of mighty moment which the great Athanasius and Chrysostom, the prince of orators, have left behind them are, by common consent, so supremely excellent that it seems scarcely anything could be added to their subtlety and fulness. And, not to cover too wide a range, we add to the number of the great men of whom mention has been made the names of Basil the Great and of the two Gregories, who, on going forth from Athens, that home of all learning, thoroughly equipped with all the harness of philosophy, turned the wealth of knowledge which each had gathered up in a course of zealous study to the work of refuting heretics and preparing Christians.

13) But Augustine would seem to have wrested the palm from all. Of a most powerful genius and thoroughly saturated with sacred and profane learning, with the loftiest faith and with equal knowledge, he combated most vigorously all the errors of his age. What topic[j] of philosophy did he not investigate?[k] What region of it did he not diligently explore, either in expoundng the loftiest mysteries of the faith to the faithful, or defending them against the full onslaught of adversaries, or again when, in demolishing the

fables of the Academicians or the Manichaeans, he laid the safe foundations and sure structure of human science, or followed up the reason, origin, and causes of the evils that afflict man? How subtly he reasoned on the angels, the soul, the human mind, the will and free choice, on religion and the life of the blessed, on time and eternity, and even on the very nature of changeable bodies. Afterwards, in the East, John Damascene, treading in the footsteps of Basil and of Gregory of Nazianzen, and in the West, Boethius and Anselm following the doctrines of Augustine, added largely to the patrimony of philosophy.

14) Later on, the doctors of the middle ages, who are called Scholastics, addressed themselves to a great work—that of diligently collecting, and sifting, and storing up, as it were, in one place, for the use and convenience of posterity the rich and fertile harvests of Christian learning scattered abroad in the voluminous works of the holy Fathers. And with regard, venerable brethren, to the origin, drift, and excellence of this scholastic learning, it may be well here to speak more fully in the words of one of the wisest of Our predecessors, Sixtus V: "By the divine favor of Him who alone gives the spirit of science, and wisdom, and understanding, and who through all ages, as there may be need, enriches His Church with new blessings and strengthens it with new safeguards, there was founded by Our fathers, men of eminent wisdom, the scholastic theology, which two glorious doctors in particular, the angelic St. Thomas and the seraphic St. Bonaventure, illustrious teachers of this faculty, . . . with surpassing genius, by unwearied diligence, and at the cost of long labors and vigils, set in order and beautified, and when skilfully arranged and

clearly explained in a variety of ways, handed down to posterity.

15) "And, indeed, the knowledge and use of so salutary a science, which flows from the fertilizing founts of the sacred writings, the sovereign Pontiffs, the holy Fathers and the councils, must always be of the greatest assistance to the Church, whether with the view of really and soundly understanding and interpreting the Scriptures, or more safely and to better purpose reading and explaining the Fathers, or for exposing and refuting the various errors and heresies; and in these late days, when those dangerous times described by the Apostle are already upon us, when the blasphemers, the proud, and the seducers go from bad to worse, erring themselves and causing others to err, there is surely a very great need of confirming the dogmas of Catholic faith and confuting heresies."

16) Although these words seem to bear reference solely to Scholastic theology, nevertheless they may plainly be accepted as equally true of philosophy and its praises. For, the noble endowments which make the Scholastic theology so formidable to the enemies of truth—to wit, as the same Pontiff adds, "that ready and close coherence of cause and effect, that order and array as of a disciplined army in battle, those clear definitions and distinctions, that strength of argument and those keen discussions, by which light is distinguished from darkness, the true from the false, expose and strip naked, as it were, the falsehoods of heretics wrapped around by a cloud of subterfuges and fallacies" [31]—those noble and admirable endowments, We say, are only to be found in a right use of that

philosophy which the Scholastic teachers have been accustomed carefully and prudently to make use of even in theological disputations.[1] Moreover, since it is the proper and special office of the Scholastic theologians to bind together by the fastest chain human and divine science, surely the theology in which they excelled would not have gained such honor and commendation among men if they had made use of a lame and imperfect or vain philosophy.

17) Among the Scholastic Doctors, the chief and master of all, towers Thomas Aquinas, who, as Cajetan observes, because "he most venerated the ancient doctors of the Church, in a certain way seems to have inherited the intellect of all." [32] The doctrines of those illustrious men, like the scattered members of a body, Thomas collected together and cemented, distributed in wonderful order, and so increased with important additions that he is rightly and deservedly esteemed the special bulwark and glory of the Catholic faith. With his spirit at once humble and swift, his memory ready and tenacious, his life spotless throughout, a lover of truth for its own sake, richly endowed with human and divine science, like the sun he heated the world with the warmth of his virtues and filled it with the splendor of his teaching. Philosophy has no part which he did not touch finely at once and thoroughly; on the laws of reasoning, on God and incorporeal substances, on man and other sensible things, on human actions and their principles, he reasoned in such a manner that in him there is wanting neither a full array of questions, nor an apt disposal of the various parts, nor the best method of proceeding, nor soundness of principles or strength of argument, nor

clearness and elegance of style, nor a facility for explaining what is abstruse.

18) Moreover, the Angelic Doctor pushed his philosophic inquiry[m] into the reasons and principles of things, which because they are most comprehensive and contain in their bosom, so to say, the seeds of almost infinite truths, were to be unfolded in good time by later masters and with a goodly yield. And as he also used this philosophic method in the refutation of error, he won this title to distinction for himself: that, single-handed, he victoriously combated the errors of former times, and supplied invincible arms to put those to rout which might in after-times spring up. Again, clearly distinguishing, as is fitting, reason from faith, while happily associating the one with the other, he both preserved the rights and had regard for the dignity of each; so much so, indeed, that reason, borne on the wings of Thomas to its human height, can scarcely rise higher, while faith could scarcely expect more or stronger aids from reason than those which she has already obtained through Thomas.

19) For these reasons most learned men, in former ages especially, of the highest repute in theology and philosophy, after mastering with infinite pains the immortal works of Thomas, gave themselves up not so much to be instructed in his angelic wisdom as to be nourished upon it. It is known that nearly all [n] the founders and lawgivers[o] of the religious orders commanded their members to study and religiously adhere to the teachings of St. Thomas, fearful lest any of them should swerve even in the slightest degree from the footsteps of so great a man. To say nothing of the family of St. Dominic, which rightly claims this great

teacher for its own glory, the statutes of the Benedictines, the Carmelites, the Augustinians, the Society
of Jesus, and many others all testify that they are
bound by this law.

20) And, here, how pleasantly one's thoughts fly
back to those celebrated schools and universities which
flourished of old in Europe—to Paris, Salamanca,
Alcala, to Douay, Toulouse, and Louvain, to Padua
and Bologna, to Naples and Coimbra, and to many
another! All know how the fame of these seats of
learning grew with their years, and that their judgment,
often asked in matters of grave moment, held great
weight everywhere. And we know how in those great
homes of human wisdom, as in his own kingdom,
Thomas reigned supreme; and that the minds of
all, of teachers as well as of taught, rested in wonderful harmony under the shield and authority of the
Angelic Doctor.

21) But, furthermore, Our predecessors in the
Roman pontificate have celebrated the wisdom of
Thomas Aquinas by exceptional tributes of praise and
the most ample testimonials. Clement VI in the bull
In Ordine; Nicholas V in his brief to the friars of the
Order of Preachers, 1451; Benedict XIII in the bull
Pretiosus, and others bear witness that the universal
Church borrows lustre from his admirable teaching;
while St. Pius V declares in the bull *Mirabilis* that
heresies, confounded and convicted by the same teach-
ing, were dissipated, and the whole world daily freed
from fatal errors; others, such as Clement XII in the bull
Verbo Dei, affirm that most fruitful blessings have
spread abroad from his writings over the whole
Church, and that he is worthy of the honor which

is bestowed on the greatest Doctors of the Church, on Gregory and Ambrose, Augustine and Jerome; while others have not hesitated to propose St. Thomas for the exemplar and master of the universities and great centers of learning whom they may follow with unfaltering feet. On which point the words of Blessed Urban V to the University of Toulouse are worthy of recall: "It is Our will, which We hereby enjoin upon you, that ye follow the teaching of Blessed Thomas as the true and Catholic doctrine, and that ye labor with all your force to profit by the same." [33] Innocent XII followed the example of Urban in the case of the University of Louvain, in the letter in the form of a brief addressed to that university on February 6, 1694, and Benedict XIV in the letter in the form of a brief addressed on August 26, 1752, to the Dionysian College in Granada; while to these judgments of great Pontiffs on Thomas Aquinas comes the crowning testimony of Innocent VI: "His teaching above that of others, the canonical writings alone excepted, enjoys such a precision of language, an order of matters, a truth of conclusions, that those who hold to it are never found swerving from the path of truth, and he who dare assail it will always be suspected of error." [34] [p]

22) The ecumenical councils, also, where blossoms the flower of all earthly wisdom, have always been careful to hold Thomas Aquinas in singular honor. In the Councils of Lyons, Vienna, Florence, and the Vatican one might almost say that Thomas took part and presided over the deliberations and decrees of the Fathers, contending against the errors of the Greeks, of heretics and rationalists, with invincible force and with the happiest results. But the chief and special

glory of Thomas, one which he has shared with none of the Catholic Doctors, is that the Fathers of Trent made it part of the order of the conclave to lay upon the altar, together with sacred Scripture^q and the decrees of the supreme Pontiffs, the *Summa* of Thomas Aquinas, whence to seek counsel, reason, and inspiration.

23) A last triumph was reserved for this incomparable man—namely, to compel the homage, praise, and admiration of even the very enemies of the Catholic name. For it has come to light that there were not lacking among the leaders of heretical sects some who openly declared that, if the teaching of Thomas Aquinas were only taken away, they could easily battle with all Catholic teachers, gain the victory, and abolish the Church.[35] A vain hope, indeed, but no vain testimony.

24) Therefore, venerable brethren, as often as We contemplate the good, the force, and the singular advantages to be derived from his philosophic discipline^r which Our Fathers so dearly loved, We think it hazardous that its special honor should not always and everywhere remain, especially when it is established that daily experience, and the judgment of the greatest men, and, to crown all, the voice of the Church, have favored the Scholastic philosophy. Moreover, to the old teaching a novel system of philosophy has succeeded here and there, in which We fail to perceive those desirable and wholesome fruits which the Church and civil society itself would prefer. For it pleased the struggling innovators of the sixteenth century to philosophize without any respect for faith, the power of inventing in accordance with his own pleasure and

bent being asked and given in turn by each one. Hence, it was natural that systems of philosophy multiplied beyond measure, and conclusions differing and clashing one with another arose about those matters even which are the most important in human knowledge. From a mass of conclusions men often come to wavering and doubt; and who knows not how easily the mind slips from doubt to error? But, as men are apt to follow the lead given them, this new pursuit seems to have caught the souls of certain Catholic philosophers, who, throwing aside the patrimony of ancient wisdom, chose rather to build up a new edifice than to strengthen and complete the old by aid of the new—ill-advisedly, in sooth, and not without detriment to the sciences. For, a multiform system of this kind, which depends on the authority and choice of any professor, has a foundation open to change, and consequently gives us a philosophy not firm, and stable, and robust like that of old, but tottering and feeble. And if, perchance, it sometimes finds itself scarcely equal to sustain the shock of its foes, it should recognize that the cause and the blame lie in itself. In saying this We have no intention of discountenancing the learned and able men who bring their industry and erudition, and, what is more, the wealth of new discoveries, to the service of philosophy; for, of course, We understand that this tends to the development of learning. But one should be very careful lest all of his chief labor be exhausted in these pursuits and in mere erudition. And the same thing is true of sacred theology, which, indeed, may be assisted and illustrated by all kinds of erudition, though it is absolutely necessary to approach it in the grave manner of the Scholastics, in order that, the forces of revelation and reason being united in it, it may continue to be "the invincible bulwark of the faith." [36]

25) With wise forethought, therefore, not a few of the advocates of philosophic studies,[s] when turning their minds recently to the practical reform of philosophy, aimed and aim at restoring the renowned teaching of Thomas Aquinas and winning it back to its ancient beauty.

26) We have learned with great joy that many members of your order, venerable brethren, have taken this plan to heart; and while We earnestly commend their efforts, We exhort them to hold fast to their purpose, and remind each and all of you that Our first and most cherished idea is that you should all furnish to studious youth a generous and copious supply of those purest streams of wisdom flowing inexhaustibly from the precious fountainhead of the Angelic Doctor.[t]

27) Many are the reasons why We are so desirous of this. In the first place, then, since in the tempest that is on us the Christian faith is being constantly assailed by the machinations and craft of a certain false wisdom, all youths, but especially those who are the growing hope of the Church, should be nourished on the strong and robust food of doctrine, so that, mighty in strength and armed at all points, they may become habituated to advance the cause of religion with force and judgment, "being ready always, according to the apostolic counsel, to satisfy every one that asketh you a reason of that hope which is in you," [37] and that they may be able to exhort in sound doctrine and to convince the gainsayers.[38] Many of those who, with

minds alienated from the faith, hate Catholic institutions, claim reason as their sole mistress and guide. Now, We think that, apart from the supernatural help of God, nothing is better calculated to heal those minds and to bring them into favor with the Catholic faith than the solid doctrine of the Fathers and the Scholastics, who so clearly and forcibly demonstrate the firm foundations of the faith, its divine origin, its certain truth, the arguments that sustain it, the benefits it has conferred on the human race, and its perfect accord with reason, in a manner to satisfy completely minds open to persuasion, however unwilling and repugnant.

28) Domestic and civil society even, which, as all see, is exposed to great danger from this plague of perverse opinions, would certainly enjoy a far more peaceful and secure existence if a more wholesome doctrine were taught in the universities and high schools[u]—one more in conformity with the teaching of the Church, such as is contained in the works of Thomas Aquinas.

29) For, the teachings of Thomas on the true meaning of liberty, which at this time is running into license, on the divine origin of all authority, on laws and their force, on the paternal and just rule of princes, on obedience to the higher powers, on mutual charity one toward another—on all of these and kindred subjects—have very great and invincible force to overturn those principles of the new order which are well known to be dangerous to the peaceful order of things and to public safety. In short, all studies ought to find hope of advancement and promise of assistance in this restoration of philosophic discipline which We

have proposed. The arts were wont to draw from philosophy, as from a wise mistress, sound judgment and right method, and from it, also, their spirit, as from the common fount of life. When philosophy stood stainless in honor and wise in judgment, then, as facts and constant experience showed, the liberal arts flourished as never before or since; but, neglected and almost blotted out, they lay prone, since philosophy began to lean to error and join hands with folly. Nor will the physical sciences themselves, which are now in such great repute, and by the renown of so many inventions draw such universal admiration to themselves, suffer detriment, but find very great assistance in the restoration of the ancient philosophy. For, the investigation of facts and the contemplation of nature is not alone sufficient for their profitable exercise and advance; but, when facts have been established, it is necessary to rise and apply ourselves to the study of the nature of corporeal things, to inquire into the laws which govern them and the principles whence their order and varied unity and mutual attraction in diversity arise. To such investigations it is wonderful what force and light and aid the Scholastic philosophy, if judiciously taught, would bring.

30) And here it is well to note that our philosophy can only by the grossest injustice be accused of being opposed to the advance and development of natural science. For, when the Scholastics, following the opinion of the holy Fathers, always held in anthropology that the human intelligence is only led to the knowledge of things without body and matter by things sensible, they well understood that nothing was of greater use to the philosopher than diligently to search into the mysteries of nature and to be earnest

and constant in the study of physical things. And this they confirmed by their own example; for St. Thomas, Blessed Albertus Magnus, and other leaders of the Scholastics were never so wholly rapt in the study of philosophy as not to give large attention to the knowledge of natural things; and, indeed, the number of their sayings and writings on these subjects, which recent professors approve of and admit to harmonize with truth, is by no means small. Moreover, in this very age many illustrious professors of the physical sciences openly testify that between certain and accepted conclusions of modern physics and the philosophic principles of the schools there is no conflict worthy of the name.

31) While, therefore, We hold that every word of wisdom, every useful thing by whomsoever discovered or planned, ought to be received with a willing and grateful mind, We exhort you, venerable brethren, in all earnestness to restore the golden wisdom of St. Thomas, and to spread it far and wide for the defense and beauty of the Catholic faith, for the good of society, and for the advantage of all the sciences. The wisdom of St. Thomas, We say; for if anything is taken up with too great subtlety by the Scholastic doctors, or too carelessly stated—if there be anything that ill agrees with the discoveries of a later age, or, in a word, improbable in whatever way—it does not enter Our mind to propose that for imitation to Our age. Let carefully selected teachers endeavor to implant the doctrine of Thomas Aquinas in the minds of students, and set forth clearly his solidity and excellence over others. Let the universities already founded or to be founded by you illustrate and defend this doctrine, and use it for the refutation of prevailing

errors. But, lest the false for the true or the corrupt for the pure be drunk in,ᵛ be ye watchful that the doctrine of Thomas be drawn from his own fountains, or at least from those rivulets which, derived from the very fount, have thus far flowed, according to the established agreement of learned men, pure and clear; be careful to guard the minds of youth from those which are said to flow thence, but in reality are gathered from strange and unwholesome streams.

32) But well do We know that vain will be Our efforts unless, venerable brethren, He helps Our common cause who, in the words of divine Scripture, is called the God of all knowledge;[39] by which we are also admonished that "every best gift and every perfect gift is from above, coming down from the Father of Lights";[40] and again: "If any of you want wisdom, let him ask of God, who giveth to all men abundantly, and upbraideth not: and it shall be given him." [41]

33) Therefore in this also let us follow the example of the Angelic Doctor, who never gave himself to reading or writing without first begging the blessing of God, who modestly confessed that whatever he knew he had acquired not so much by his own study and labor as by the divine gift; and therefore let us all, in humble and united prayer, beseech God to send forth the spirit of knowledge and of understanding to the children of the Church and open their senses for the understanding of wisdom. And that we may receive fuller fruits of the divine goodness, offer up to God the most efficacious patronage of the Blessed Virgin Mary, who is called the seat of wisdom; having at the same time as advocates St. Joseph, the most chaste spouse of the Virgin, and Peter and Paul, the

chiefs of the Apostles, whose truth renewed the earth which had fallen under the impure blight of error, filling it with the light of heavenly wisdom.

34) In fine, relying on the divine assistance and confiding in your pastoral zeal, most lovingly We bestow on all of you, venerable brethren, on all the clergy and the flocks committed to your charge, the apostolic benediction as a pledge of heavenly gifts and a token of Our special esteem.

Given at St. Peter's, in Rome, the fourth day of August, 1879, the second year of our pontificate.

LEO XIII, *Pope.*

VARIANTS

The abbreviations used here are as follows: P., Paulist Press; H., J. Husslein, S. J., *Social Wellsprings;* L., official Latin text of the encyclicals; F., text of the French translation published at Paris, with the official Latin text, in *Actes de Léon* XIII.

[a] L. *erudiendis ad fidem mentibus.*—P. for the instruction of the faith.—H. to train the minds of men to faith.—Note that the verb *erudire* points out the kind of teaching given to beginners.

[b] L. *perlatae leges et decreta.*—H. the sanctioned laws and decrees.

[c] L. *ceterarum scientiarum recta ratio.*—P. a right apprehension of the other sciences.—H. the proper ordering of the other sciences.—F. la sage direction des sciences.—The word *ratio* is difficult to translate because its meaning covers a wide field. In its wider interpretation, it means that the knowledge of true philosophy is necessary to the proper understanding and interpretation of the other sciences.

ᵈ L. *bono fidei.*—P. which shall respond most fitly to true faith.—H. which shall be suitable and advantageous to faith.—F. qui respecte . . . les règles de la foi.

ᵉ L. *humanarum scientiarum dignitati;* that is, to the dignity of scientific knowledge possessed by man.—P. with the dignity of human knowledge.—H. to the dignity of human science.—F. la dignite des sciences humaines.

ᶠ L. *pravitas opinionum.*—P. looseness of intellectual opinions.—H. bad opinions, whose seat is the intelligence.

ᵍ L. *cum doctrina fidei;* note that the word *doctrina* always connotes a certain notion of teaching: that which is taught by faith.

ʰ L. *ex illo philosophandi instituto;* that is, from this way of philosophizing.—H. rightly: from this method of philosophizing.—P. from such a school of philosophy; can be maintained with the sense: the school of philosophy which unites the light of faith with the light of reason.

ⁱ L. *Quapropter qui philosophiae studium cum obsequio fidei christianae conjungunt, ii optime philosophantur.*—P. Those, therefore, who to the study of philosophy unite obedience to Christian faith are philosophers indeed.—H. Therefore, they who add the study of philosophy to obedience to Christian faith philosophize well.

ʲ L. *locum.*—P. what height of philosophy.—H. (rightly) topic.

ᵏ L. *investigavit.*—P. reach.—H. (rightly) has he left untouched?

ˡ L. *ejus philosophiae, quam magistri scholastici, data opera et sapienti concilio, in disputationibus etiam theologicis passim usurpare consueverunt.*—H. of that philosophy which the Scholastic masters, exercising the utmost industry and consummate wisdom, were accustomed always to employ in theological disputations.

ᵐ P. conclusions.—H. philosophic conclusions with regard to the reasons and principles of things which, being most comprehensive, and containing in themselves the germs of truths almost countless in number, were to be developed by later teachers at a proper time and with abundant fruit.

ⁿ L. *prope.*

ᵒ L. *legiferos.*—H. all the founders and lawgivers of

religious orders.—P. all the founders and framers of laws of the religious orders.

[p] The references inserted in the original text have been restored to their respective places. In this paragraph, the Latin text uses the words *Academiis et magnis Lycaeis* in a sense approximately the same as that of "universities and high schools." It is possible to adhere more closely to the Latin terminology. For instance, P: the academies and great colleges; or H: the great academies and lyceums; but impossible to translate (with P): "the academy of Toulouse," for the document at stake was addressed by Urban V to the university, not to any academy.

[q] P. with the code of sacred Scripture.

[r] L. *ejus disciplinae philosophicae.*—P. and H. philosophic system.—We are keeping "discipline" in the archaic sense of "branch of instruction," but without excluding the modern connotation of mental training and intellectual formation acquired through the study of the "discipline" at stake, namely Scholasticism.

[s] L. *cultores disciplinarum philosophicarum;* that is, those who dedicate themselves to the study of philosophy in its various branches.

[t] P. that you should all furnish a generous and copious supply to studious youth of those crystal rills of wisdom flowing in a never-ending and fertilizing stream from the fountainhead of the Angelic Doctor.—H. that you all supply for the benefit of young students, plentifully and abundantly, those pure streams of wisdom that flow from the Angelic Doctor as from an inexhaustible and precious fountain.

[u] L. *in Academiis et scholis.*

[v] L. *Ne autem supposita pro vera, neu corrupta pro sinceri bibatur;* that is, But lest a false wisdom be drunk in for the true, or a corrupt wisdom for the pure.

NOTES TO *Aeterni Patris*

[1] Matt. 28:19.

[2] Col. 2:8.

[3] *De Trinitate,* 14, 1, 3 (PL 42, 1037); quoted by Thomas Aquinas, *Summa theologiae,* 1, 1, 2.

[4] Clement of Alexandria, *Stromata*, 1, 16 (PG 8, 795); 7, 3 (PG 9, 426).

[5] Origen, *Epistola ad Gregorium* (PG 11, 87-91).

[6] Clement of Alexandria, *Stromata*, 1, 5 (PG 8, 718-719).

[7] Rom. 1:20.

[8] Rom. 2:14-15.

[9] Gregory of Neo-Caesarea (also called Gregory Thaumaturgus, that is, "the miracle worker"), *In Origenem oratio panegyrica*, 6 (PG 10, 1093A).

[10] Carm., 1. Iamb. 3 (PG 37, 1045A-1047A).

[11] *Vita Moysis* (PG 44, 359).

[12] *Epistola ad Magnum*, 4 (PL 22, 667). Quadratus, Justin, Irenaeus, are counted among the early Christian apologists, who devoted their works to the defence of Christian truth against the pagans.

[13] *De doctrina christiana*, 1, 2, 40 (PL 34, 63).

[14] Wisd. 13:1.

[15] Wisd. 13:5.

[16] 2 Peter 1:16.

[17] *Const. Dogm. de Fid. Cath.*, c.3.

[18] *Const. cit.*, c.4.

[19] *Loc. cit.*

[20] *Stromata*, 1, 20 (PG 8, 818).

[21] *Epistola ad Magnum*, 2 (PL 22, 666).

[22] Bulla *Apostolici regiminis*.

[23] *Epistola 147, ad Marcellinum*, 7 (PL 33, 589).

[24] *Const. Dogm. de Fid. Cath.*, c.4.

[25] 1 Cor. 1:24.

[26] Col. 2:3.

[27] *Epistola ad Magnum*, 4 (PL 22, 667).

[28] *Loc. cit.*

[29] Tertullian, *Apologet.*, 46 (PL 1, 573).

[30] Lactantius, *Div. Inst.*, 7, 7 (PL 6, 759).

[31] Bulla *Triumphantis*, an. 1588.

[32] Cajetan's commentary on *Sum. theol.*, IIa-IIae 148, 9. Art. 4; Leonine edit., Vol. 10, p. 174, n.6.

[33] *Constitutio 5a, data die 3 Aug. 1368*, ad Cancell. Univ. Tolos.

[34] *Sermo de S. Thoma*.

[35] Bucer.

[36] Sixtus V, Bulla *Triumphantis*.

[37] 1 Peter 3:15.

[38] Titus 1:9.
[39] 1 Kings 2:3.
[40] James 1:17.
[41] James 1:5.

DOCTORIS ANGELICI

Motu Proprio for Italy and the adjacent islands, to encourage the study of the philosophy of St. Thomas Aquinas in Catholic Schools.

No true Catholic has ever ventured to call in question the opinion of the Angelic Doctor that: The regulation of studies is the special concern of the authority of the Holy See by which the universal Church is governed and the need is met by the establishment of Universities (Opusc. *Contra impugnantes Dei cultum et religionem, iii*). We have already discharged this great duty of Our office elsewhere, and more particularly on the 1st September, 1910, when in the Letter *Sacrorum Antistitum,* addressed to all Bishops and Superiors of Religious Orders duly charged with the duty of educating young men for the priesthood, We counselled them in the first place as follows: "So far as studies are concerned, it is Our will and We hereby explicitly ordain that the Scholastic philosophy be considered as the basis of sacred studies. . . . And what is of capital importance in prescribing that Scholastic philosophy is to be followed, We have in mind particularly the philosophy which has been transmitted to us by St. Thomas Aquinas. It is Our desire that all the enactments of Our Predecessor in respect thereto be maintained in full force; and, where need be, We renew and confirm them and order them to be strictly observed by all concerned. Let Bishops urge and compel their observance in future in any Seminary in which they may have been neglected. The same injunction applies also to Superiors of Religious Orders."

Now because the word We used in the text of that letter recommending the philosophy of Aquinas was 'particularly,' and not 'exclusively,' certain persons persuaded themselves that they were acting in conformity to Our Will or at any rate not actively opposing it, in adopting indiscriminately and adhering to the philosophical opinions of any other Doctor of the School, even though such opinions were contrary to the principles of St. Thomas. They were greatly deceived. In recommending St. Thomas to Our subjects as supreme guide in the Scholastic philosophy, it goes without saying that Our intention was to be understood as referring above all to those principles upon which that philosophy is based as its foundation. For just as the opinion of certain ancients is to be rejected which maintains that it makes no difference to the truth of the Faith what any man thinks about the nature of creation, provided his opinions on the nature of God be sound, because error with regard to the nature of creation begets a false knowledge of God; so the principles of philosophy laid down by St. Thomas Aquinas are to be religiously and inviolably observed, because they are the means of acquiring such a knowledge of creation as is most congruent with the Faith (*Contra Gentiles,* II, 2, 3); of refuting all the errors of all the ages, and of enabling man to distinguish clearly what things are to be attributed to God and to God alone (*ibid.,* iii; and *Sum. Theol.,* I, xii, 4: and liv, 1). They also marvellously illustrate the diversity and analogy between God and His works, a diversity and analogy admirably expressed by the

Fourth Lateran Council as follows: "The resemblance between the Creator and the creature is such that their still greater dissimilarity cannot fail to be observed" (*Decretalis* iii, *Damnamus ergo*, etc. Cf. St. Thomas, *Quaest, disp. De Scientia Dei*, a. 11).—For the rest, the principles of St. Thomas, considered generally and as a whole, contain nothing but what the most eminent philosophers and doctors of the Church have discovered after prolonged reflection and discussion in regard to the particular reasons determining human knowledge, the nature of God and creation, the moral order and the ultimate end to be pursued in life.

St. Thomas perfected and augmented still further by the almost angelic quality of his intellect all this superb patrimony of wisdom which he inherited from his predecessors and applied it to prepare, illustrate and protect sacred doctrine in the minds of men (*In Librum Boethii de Trinitate,* quaest, ii, 3). Sound reason suggests that it would be foolish to neglect it and religion will not suffer it to be in any way attenuated. And rightly, because, if Catholic doctrine is once deprived of this strong bulwark, it is useless to seek the slightest assistance for its defence in a philosophy whose principles are either common to the errors of materialism, monism, pantheism, socialism and modernism, or certainly not opposed to such systems. The reason is that the capital theses in the philosophy of St. Thomas are not to be placed in the category of opinions capable of being debated one way or another, but are to be considered as the foundations upon which the whole science of natural and divine things is based; if such principles are once removed or in any way impaired, it must necessarily follow that students of the sacred sciences will ultimately fail to perceive so much as the meaning of the words in which the dogmas of divine revelation are proposed by the magistracy of the Church.

We therefore desired that all teachers of philosophy and sacred theology should be warned that if they deviated so much as a step, in metaphysics especially, from Aquinas, they exposed themselves to grave risk.— We now go further and solemnly declare that those who in their interpretations misrepresent or affect to despise the principles and major theses of his philosophy are not only not following St. Thomas but are even far astray from the saintly Doctor. If the doctrine of any writer or Saint has ever been approved by Us or Our Predecessors with such singular commendation and in such a way that to the commendation were added an invitation and order to propagate and defend it, it may easily be understood that it was commended to the extent that it agreed with the principles of Aquinas or was in no way opposed to them.

We have deemed it Our apostolic duty to make this declaration and order so that the clergy, both regular and secular, may clearly know Our will and mind in a matter of the gravest importance, and fulfil Our desire with the appropriate alacrity and diligence. Teachers of Christian philosophy and sacred theology will be particularly zealous in this respect, for they must bear in mind that they have not been entrusted with the duty of teaching in order to impart to their pupils whatever opinions they please, but to instruct them in the most approved doctrines of the Church.

As for sacred theology itself, it is Our desire that the study of it be always illuminated by the light of the philosophy before referred to, but in ordinary clerical seminaries, provided suitable teachers are available, there is no objection to the use of text books containing summaries of doctrines derived from the source of Aquinas. There is an ample supply of excellent works of the kind.

But for the more profound study of this science, as it ought to be studied in Universities and Colleges and in all Seminaries and institutions which are empowered to grant academic degrees, it is of the first importance that the old system of lecturing on the actual text of the *Summa Theologica*—which should never have been allowed to fall into disuse—be revived; for the reason also that prelections on this book make it easier to understand and to illustrate the solemn decrees of the teaching Church and the acts passed in consequence. For ever since the happy death of the saintly Doctor, the Church has not held a single Council, but he has been present at it with the wealth of his doctrine. The experience of so many centuries has shown and every passing day more clearly proves the truth of the statement made by Our Predecessor John XXII: "He (Thomas Aquinas) enlightened the Church more than all the other Doctors together; a man can derive more profit from his books in one year than from a lifetime spent in pondering the philosophy of others" (Consistorial address of 1318). St. Pius V confirmed this opinion when he ordered the feast of St. Thomas as Doctor to be kept by the universal Church: "But inasmuch as, by the providence of Almighty God, the power and truth of the philosophy of the Angelic Doctor, ever since his enrolment amongst the citizens of Heaven, have confounded, refuted and routed many subsequent heresies, as was so often clearly seen in the past and was lately apparent in the sacred decrees of the Council of Trent, We order that the memory of the Doctor by whose valour the world is daily delivered from pestilential errors be cultivated more than ever before with feelings of pious and grateful devotion" (Bull *Mirabilis Deus* of the 11th April, 1567). To avoid recapitulating the many other resounding praises of Our Predecessors, We may adopt the following words of Benedict XIV as a summary of all the commendations bestowed upon the writings of Thomas Aquinas, more particularly the *Summa Theologica:* "Numerous Roman Pontiffs, Our Predecessors, have borne glorious testimony to his philosophy. We also, in the books which We have written on various topics, after by diligent examination perceiving and considering the mind of the Angelic Doctor, have always adhered and subscribed with joy and admiration to his philosophy, and candidly confess that whatever good is to be found in Our own Writings is in no way to be attributed to Us, but entirely to so eminent a teacher" (*Acta Cap. Gen. O.P., vol IX*, p. 196).

Therefore that "the philosophy of St. Thomas may flourish incorrupt and entire in schools, which is very dear to Our heart," and that "the system of teaching which is based upon the authority and judgement of the individual teacher" and therefore "has a changeable foundation whence many diverse and mutually conflicting opinions arise . . . not without great injury to Christian learning" (Leo XIII, *Epist, Qui te* of the 19th June, 1886) be abolished forever, it is Our will and We hereby order and command that teachers of sacred theology in Universities, Academies, Colleges, Seminaries and Institutions enjoying by apostolic indult the privilege of granting academic degrees and doctorates in philosophy, use the *Summa Theologica* of St. Thomas as the text of their prelections and comment upon it in the Latin tongue, and let them take particular care to inspire their pupils with a devotion for it.

Such is already the laudable custom of many

Institutions. Such was the rule which the sagacious founders of Religious Orders, with the hearty approval of Our Predecessors, desired should be observed in their own houses of study; and the saintly men who came after the time of St. Thomas Aquinas took him and no other for their supreme teacher of philosophy. So also and not otherwise will theology recover its pristine glory and all sacred studies be restored to their order and value and the province of the intellect and reason flower again in a second spring.

In future, therefore, no power to grant academic degrees in sacred theology will be given to any institution unless Our present prescription is religiously observed therein. Institutions or Faculties of Orders and Regular Congregations, also, already in lawful possession of the power of conferring such academic degrees or similar diplomas, even within the limits of their own four walls, shall be deprived of such a privilege and be considered to have been so deprived if, after the lapse of three years, they shall not have religiously obeyed for any reason whatsoever, even beyond their control, this Our injunction.

This is Our Order, and nothing shall be suffered to gainsay it.

Given at Rome, at St. Peter's, on the 29th day of June, 1914, the eleventh year of Our Pontificate."

PIUS PP. X.

STUDIORUM DUCEM
ENCYCLICAL LETTER OF OUR
MOST HOLY LORD
POPE PIUS XI

ON THE OCCASION OF
THE SIXTH CENTENARY OF
THE CANONIZATION OF THOMAS AQUINAS

To Our Venerable Brethren,
the Patriarchs, Primates, Archbishops,
Bishops and other Ordinaries
in grace and communion with the Apostolic See
Pius XI, Pope
Venerable Brethren,
Greeting and the Apostolic Benediction

In a recent apostolic letter confirming the statutes of Canon Law, We declared that the guide to be followed in the higher studies by young men training for the priesthood was Thomas Aquinas. The approaching anniversary of the day when he was duly enrolled, six hundred years ago, in the calendar of the Saints, offers Us an admirable opportunity of inculcating this more and more firmly in the minds of Our students and explaining to them what advantage they may most usefully derive from the teaching of so illustrious a Doctor. For science truly deserving of the name and piety, the companion of all the virtues, are related in a marvellous bond of affinity, and, as God is very Truth and very Goodness, it would assuredly not be sufficient to procure the glory of God by the salvation of souls—the chief task and peculiar mission of the Church—if ministers of religion were not well disciplined in knowledge and not also abundantly provided at the same time with the appropriate virtues.

Such a combination of doctrine and piety, of erudition and virtue, of truth and charity, is to be found in an eminent degree in the Angelic Doctor and it is not without reason that he has been given the sun for a device; for he both brings the light of learning into the minds of men and fires their hearts and wills with the virtues. God, the Source of all sanctity and wisdom, would, therefore, seem to have desired to show in the case of Thomas how each of these qualities assists the other, how the practice of the virtues disposes to the contemplation of truth, and the profound consideration of truth in turn gives lustre and perfection to the virtues. For the man of pure and upright life, whose passions are controlled by virtue, is delivered as it were of a heavy burden and can much more easily raise his mind to heavenly things and penetrate more profoundly into the secrets of God, according to the maxim of Thomas himself: "Life comes before learning: for life leads to the knowledge of truth" (*Comment. in Matth.*, v); and if such a man devotes himself to the investigation of the supernatural, he will find a powerful incentive in such a pursuit to lead a perfect life; for the learning of such sublime things, the beauty of which is a ravishing ecstasy, so far from being a solitary or sterile occupation, must be said to be on the contrary most practical.

These are among the first lessons, Venerable Brethren, which may be learned from the commemoration of this centenary; but that they may be the more clearly apparent, We propose to comment briefly in this Letter on the sanctity and doctrine of Thomas Aquinas and to show what profitable instruction may be derived therefrom by priests, by seminarians especially, and, not least, by all Christian people.

Thomas possessed all the moral virtues to a very high degree and so closely bound together that, as he himself insists should be the case, they formed one whole in charity "which informs the acts of all the virtues" (II-II, xxiii, 8: I-II, lxv). If, however, we seek to discover the peculiar and specific characteristics of his sanctity, there occurs to Us in the first place that virtue which gives Thomas a certain likeness to the angelic natures, and that is chastity; he preserved it unsullied in a crisis of the most pressing danger and was therefore considered worthy to be surrounded by the angels with a mystic girdle. This perfect regard for purity was accompanied at the same time by an equal aversion for fleeting possessions and a contempt for honours; it is recorded that his firmness of purpose overcame the obstinate persistence of relatives who strove their utmost to induce him to accept a lucrative situation in the world and that later, when the Supreme Pontiff would have offered him a mitre, his prayers were successful in securing that such a dread burden should not be laid upon him. The most distinctive feature, however, of the sanctity of Thomas is what St. Paul describes as the "word of wisdom" (1 *Cor.* xii, 8) and that combination of the two forms of wisdom, the acquired and the infused, as they are termed, with which nothing accords so well as humility, devotion to prayer, and the love of God.

That humility was the foundation upon which the other virtues of Thomas were based is clear to anyone who considers how submissively he obeyed a lay brother in the course of their communal life; and it is no less patent to anyone reading his writings which manifest such respect for the Fathers of the Church that "because he had the utmost reverence for the doctors of antiquity, he seems to have inherited in a way the intellect of all" (Leo XIII, *ex Card. Caietano, litt. Encycl. Aeterni Patris,* 4th August, 1879); but the most magnificent illustration of it is to be found in the fact that he devoted the faculties of his divine intellect not in the least to gain glory for himself, but to the advancement of truth. Most philosophers as a rule are eager to establish their own reputations, but Thomas strove to efface himself completely in the teaching of his philosophy so that the light of heavenly truth might shine with its own effulgence.

This humility, therefore, combined with the purity of heart We have mentioned, and sedulous devotion to prayer, disposed the mind of Thomas to docility in receiving the inspirations of the Holy Ghost and following His illuminations, which are the first principles of contemplation. To obtain them from above, he would frequently fast, spend whole nights in prayer, lean his head in the fervour of his unaffected piety against the tabernacle containing the august Sacrament, constantly turn his eyes and mind in sorrow to the image of the crucified Jesus; and he confessed to his intimate friend St. Bonaventura that it was from that Book especially that he derived all his learning. It may, therefore, be truly said of Thomas what is commonly reported of St. Dominic, Father and Lawgiver, that in his conversation he never spoke but about God or with God.

But as he was accustomed to contemplate all things in God, the first Cause and ultimate End of all things, it was easy for him to follow in his *Summa Theologica* no less than in his life the two kinds of wisdom before referred to. He himself describes them as follows: "The wisdom which is acquired by human effort . . . gives a man a sound judgement with regard to divine things according as he makes a perfect use of reason. . . . But there is another kind of wisdom which comes down from above . . . and judges divine things in virtue of a certain connaturality with them. This wisdom is the gift of the Holy Ghost . . . and through it a man becomes perfect in divine things, not only by learning but also by experiencing divine things" (II-II xlv, 1, ad 2; 2).

This wisdom, therefore, which comes down from, or is infused by, God, accompanied by the other gifts of the Holy Ghost, continually grew and increased in Thomas, along with charity, the mistress and queen of all the virtues. Indeed it was an absolutely certain doctrine of his that the love of God should ever continually increase "in accordance with the very words of the commandment: 'Thou shalt love the Lord, thy God, with thy whole heart'; for the whole and the perfect are one same thing. . . . Now the end of the commandment is charity from a pure heart, and a good conscience and an unfeigned faith, as the Apostle says (*I Tim.* i, 5), but no standard of measure is applicable to the end, but only to such things as conduce to the end (II-II, clxxxiv, 3)." This is the very reason why the perfection of charity falls under the commandment as the end to which we ought all to strive, each according to his degree. Moreover, as "it is the characteristic of charity to make man tend to God by uniting the affections of man to God in such a way that man ceases to live for himself and lives only for God" (II-II, xvii, 6, ad 3), so the love of God, continually increasing in Thomas along with that double wisdom, induced in him in the end such absolute forgetfulness of self that when Jesus spoke to him from the cross, saying: "Thomas, thou hast written well about me," and asked him: "What reward shall I give thee for all thy labour?" the saint made answer: "None but Thyself, O Lord!" Instinct with charity, therefore, he unceasingly continued to serve the convenience of others, not counting the cost, by writing admirable books, helping his brethren in their labours, depriving himself of his own garments to give them to the poor, even restoring the sick to health as, for example, when preaching in the Vatican Basilica on the occasion of the Easter celebrations, he suddenly cured a woman who had touched the hem of his habit of a chronic haemorrhage.

In what other Doctor was this "word of wisdom" mentioned by St. Paul more remarkable and abundant than in the Angelic Doctor? He was not satisfied with enlightening the minds of men by his teaching: he exerted himself strenuously to rouse their hearts to make a return of His love to God, the Creator of all things. "The love of God is the source and origin of goodness in things" he magnificently declares (I, xx, 2), and he ceaselessly illustrates this diffusion of the divine goodness in his discussion of every several mystery. "Hence it is of the nature of perfect good to communicate itself in a perfect way and this is done in a supreme degree by God . . . in the Incarnation" (III, i, 1). Nothing, however, shows the force of his genius and charity so clearly as the Office which he himself composed for the august Sacrament. The words he uttered on his death-bed, as he was about to receive the holy Viaticum, are the measure of his devotion to that Sacrament throughout his life: "I receive Thee, Price of the redemption of my soul, for the love of Whom I have studied, kept vigil and toiled."

After this slight sketch of the great virtues of Thomas, it is easy to understand the pre-eminence of his doctrine and the marvellous authority it enjoys in the Church. Our Predecessors, indeed, have always unanimously extolled it. Even during the lifetime of the saint, Alexander IV had no hesitation in addressing him in these terms: "To Our beloved son, Thomas Aquinas, distinguished alike for nobility of blood and integrity of character, who has acquired by the grace of God the treasure of divine and human learning." After his death, again, John XXII seemed to consecrate both his virtues and his doctrine when, addressing the Cardinals, he uttered in full Consistory the memorable sentence: "He alone enlightened the Church more than all other doctors; a man can derive more profit in a year from his books than from pondering all his life the teaching of others."

He enjoyed a more than human reputation for intellect and learning and Pius V was therefore moved to enroll him officially among the holy Doctors with the title of *Angelic*. Again, could there be any more manifest indication of the very high esteem in which this Doctor is held by the Church than the fact that the Fathers of Trent resolved that two volumes only, Holy Scripture and the *Summa Theologica*, should be reverently laid open on the altar during their deliberations? And in this order of ideas, to avoid recapitulating the innumerable testimonies of the Apostolic See, We are happy to recall that the philosophy of Aquinas was revived by the authority and at the instance of Leo XIII; the merit of Our illustrious Predecessor in so doing is such, as We have said elsewhere, that if he had not been the author of many acts and decrees of surpassing wisdom, this alone would be sufficient to establish his undying glory. Pope Pius X of saintly memory followed shortly afterwards in his footsteps, more particularly in his Motu Proprio *Doctoris Angelici*, in which this memorable phrase occurs: "For ever since the happy death of the holy Doctor, the Church has not held a single Council but he has been present at it with all the wealth of his doctrine." Closer to Us, Our greatly regretted Predecessor Benedict XV repeatedly declared that he was entirely of the same opinion and he is to be praised for having promulgated the Code of Canon Law in which "the system, philosophy and principles of the Angelic Doctor" are unreservedly sanctioned. We so heartily approve the magnificent tribute of praise bestowed upon this most divine genius that We consider that Thomas should be called not only the Angelic, but also the *Common* or Universal Doctor of the Church; for the Church has adopted his philosophy for her own, as innumerable documents of every kind attest. It would be an endless task to explain here all the reasons which moved Our Predecessors in this respect, and it will be sufficient perhaps to point out that Thomas wrote under the inspiration of the supernatural spirit which animated his life and that his writings, which contain the principles of, and the laws governing, all sacred studies, must be said to possess a universal character.

In dealing orally or in writing with divine things, he provides theologians with a striking example of the intimate connexion which should exist between the spiritual and the intellectual life. For just as a man cannot really be said to know some distant country, if his acquaintance is confined merely to a description of it, however accurate, but must have dwelt in it for some little time; so nobody can attain to an intimate knowledge of God by mere scientific investigation, unless he also dwells in the most intimate association with God. The aim of the whole theology of St. Thomas is to bring us into close living intimacy with God. For even as in his childhood at Monte Cassino he unceasingly put the question: "What is God?"; so all the books he wrote concerning the creation of the world, the nature of man, laws, the virtues, and the Sacraments, are all concerned with God, the Author of eternal salvation.

Again, discussing the causes of the sterility of such studies, namely curiosity, that is to say the unbridled desire for knowledge, indolence of mind, aversion from effort and lack of perseverance, he insists that there is no other remedy than zeal in work with the fervour of piety which derives from the life of the spirit. Sacred studies, therefore, being directed by a triple light, undeviating reason, infused faith and the gifts of the Holy Ghost, by which the mind is brought to perfection, no one ever was more generously endowed with these than Our Saint. After spending all the riches of his intellect on some matter of exceptional difficulty, he would seek the solution of his problem from God by the most humble prayer and fasting; and God was wont to listen to His suppliant so kindly that He dispatched the Princes of the Apostles at times to instruct him. It is not therefore surprising that toward the end of his life he had risen to such a degree of contemplation as to declare that all he had written seemed to him mere chaff and that he was incapable of dictating another word; his eyes even then were fixed on eternity alone, his one desire was to see God. For, according to Thomas, by far the most important benefit to be derived from sacred studies, is that they inspire a man with a great love for God and a great longing for eternal things.

He not only instructs us by his example how to pursue such a diversity of studies, but also teaches us firm and enduring principles of each single science. For, in the first place, who has provided a better explanation than he of the nature and character of philosophy, its various divisions and the relative importance of each? Consider how clearly he demonstrates the congruence and harmony between all the various sections which go to make up the body as it were of this science. "It is the function of the wise man," he declares, "to put things in order, because wisdom is primarily the perfection of reason and it is the characteristic of reason to know order; for although the sensitive faculties know some things absolutely, only the intellect or reason can know the relation one thing bears to another. The sciences, therefore, vary according to the various forms of order which reason perceives to be peculiar to each. The order which the consideration of reason establishes in its own peculiar activity pertains to rational philosophy or logic, whose function is to consider the order of the parts of speech in their mutual relations and in relation to the conclusions which may be drawn from them. It is for natural philosophy or physics to consider the order in things which human reason considers but does not itself institute, so that under natural philosophy we include also metaphysics. But the order of voluntary acts is for the consideration of moral philosophy which is divided into three sections: the first considers the activities of the individual man in relation to their end and is called 'monastics'; the second considers the activities of the family group or community and is called economics; the third considers the activities of the State and is called politics" (*Ethics,* I, 1). Thomas dealt thoroughly with all these several divisions of philosophy, each according to its appropriate method, and, beginning with things nearest to our human reason, rose step by step to things more remote until he stood in the end on "the topmost peak of all things" (*Contra Gentes,* II, lvi: IV, i).

His teaching with regard to the power or value of the human mind is irrefragable. "The human mind has a natural knowledge of being and the things which are in themselves part of being as such, and this knowledge is the foundation of our knowledge of first principles" (*Contra Gentes,* II, lxxxiii). Such a doctrine goes to the root of the errors and opinions of these modern philosophers who maintain that it is not being itself which is perceived in the act of intellection, but some modification of the percipient; the logical consequence of such errors is *agnosticism,* which was so vigorously condemned in the Encyclical *Pascendi.*

The arguments adduced by St. Thomas to prove the existence of God and that God alone is subsisting Being Itself are still to-day, as they were in the Middle Ages, the most cogent of all arguments and clearly confirm that dogma of the Church which was solemnly proclaimed at the Vatican Council and succinctly expressed by Pius X as follows: "The certain knowledge of God as the first principle of creation and its end and demonstrable proof of His existence can be inferred, like the knowledge of a cause from its effect, by the light of the natural reason, from creation, that is to say the visible works of creation" (Motu Proprio *Sacrorum Antistitum* of the 1st September, 1910). The metaphysical philosophy of St. Thomas, although exposed to this day to the bitter onslaughts of prejudiced critics, yet still retains, like gold which no acid can dissolve, its full force and splendour unimpaired. Our Predecessor therefore rightly observed: "To deviate from Aquinas, in metaphysics especially, is to run grave risk" (Encycl. *Pascendi* of the 8th September, 1907).

Philosophy is undoubtedly a most noble science, but as things are now constituted by divine Providence, it must not be said to excel all others, because it does not embrace the whole universality of things. Indeed, in the introduction to his *Summa Contra Gentes,* as also to his *Summa Theologica,* the saintly Doctor describes another order of things set above nature and eluding the grasp of reason, an order which man would never have suspected unless the divine goodness had revealed it to him. This is the region in which faith is supreme, and the science of faith is called Theology. Science of this kind will be all the more perfect in a man in proportion as he is the better acquainted with the evidence for faith and has at the same time a more fully developed and trained faculty of philosophizing. There can be no doubt that Aquinas raised Theology to the highest eminence, for his knowledge of divine things was absolutely perfect and the power of his mind made him a marvellously capable philosopher. Thomas is therefore considered the Prince of teachers in our schools, not so much on account of his philosophical system as because of his theological studies. There is no branch of theology in which he did not exercise the incredible fecundity of his genius.

For in the first place he established apologetics on a sound and genuine basis by defining exactly the difference between the province of reason and the province of faith and carefully distinguishing the

natural and the supernatural orders. When the sacred
Vatican Council, therefore, in determining what natural knowledge of religion was possible, affirmed the
relative necessity of some divine revelation for sure
and certain knowledge and the absolute necessity of
divine revelation for knowledge of the mysteries, it
employed arguments which were borrowed precisely
from St. Thomas. He insists that all who undertake to
defend the Christian faith shall hold sacrosanct the
principle that: "It is not mere folly to assent to the
things of faith although they are beyond reason"
(*Contra Gentes,* I, vi). He shows that, although the
articles of belief are mysterious and obscure, the
reasons which persuade us to believe are nevertheless
clear and perspicuous, for, says he, "a man would not
believe unless he saw that there were things to be
believed" (II-II, i, 4); and he adds that, so far from
being considered a hindrance or a servile yoke imposed
upon man, faith should, on the contrary, be reckoned
a very great blessing, because "faith in us is a sort of
beginning of eternal life" (*Qq. disp, de Veritate,* xiv,
2).

The other branch of Theology, which is concerned
with the interpretation of dogmas, also found in St.
Thomas by far the richest of all commentators; for
nobody ever more profoundly penetrated or expounded with greater subtlety all the august mysteries,
as, for example, the intimate life of God, the obscurity
of eternal predestination, the supernatural government of the world, the faculty granted to rational
creatures of attaining their end, the redemption of
the human race achieved by Jesus Christ, and continued by the Church and the sacraments, both of
which the Angelic Doctor describes as "relics, so to
speak, of the divine Incarnation."

He also composed a substantial moral theology, capable of directing all human acts in accordance with the supernatural last end of man. And as he is, as We have said, the perfect theologian, so he gives infallible rules and precepts of life not only for individuals, but also for civil and domestic society which is the object also of moral science, both economic and politic. Hence those superb chapters in the second part of the *Summa Theologica* on paternal or domestic government, the lawful power of the State or the nation, natural and international law, peace and war, justice and property, laws and the obedience they command, the duty of helping individual citizens in their need and co-operating with all to secure the prosperity of the State, both in the natural and the supernatural order. If these precepts were religiously and inviolably observed in private life and public affairs, and in the duties of mutual obligation between nations, nothing else would be required to secure mankind that "peace of Christ in the Kingdom of Christ" which the world so ardently longs for. It is therefore to be wished that the teaching of Aquinas, more particularly his exposition of international law and the laws governing the mutual relations of peoples, become more and more studied, for it contains the foundations of a genuine 'League of Nations.'

His eminence in the learning of asceticism and mysticism is no less remarkable; for he brought the whole science of morals back to the theory of the virtues and gifts, and marvellously defined both the science and the theory in relation to the various conditions of men, both those who desire to live the common everyday life and those who strive to attain Christian perfection and fullness of spirit, in the active no less than in the contemplative life. If anyone, therefore, desires to understand fully all the implications of the commandment to love God, the growth of charity and the conjoined gifts of the Holy Ghost, the differences between the various states of life, such as the state of perfection, the religious life and the apostolate, and the nature and value of each, all these and other articles of ascetical and mystical theology, he must have recourse in the first place to the Angelic Doctor.

Everything he wrote was securely based upon Holy Scripture and that was the foundation upon which he built. For as he was convinced that Scripture was entirely and in every particular the true word of God, he carefully submitted the interpretation of it to those very rules which Our recent Predecessors have sanctioned, Leo XIII in his Encyclical *Providentissimus Deus* and Benedict XV in his Encyclical *Spiritus Paraclitus*. He laid down the principle "The chief Author of Sacred Scripture is the Holy Ghost. . . . But man was the instrumental author" (*Quodlib.*, vii, 14, ad 5), and would not allow the absolute historicity of the Bible to be doubted; but on the basis of the meaning of the words or literal sense he established the fecundity and riches of the spiritual sense, the triple nature of which, allegorical, tropological and anagogical, he expounded with the most ingenius commentary.

Lastly, our Doctor possessed the exceptional and highly privileged gift of being able to convert his precepts into liturgical prayers and hymns and so became the poet and panegyrist of the Divine Eucharist. For wherever the Catholic Church is to be found in the world among whatsoever nations, there she zealously uses and ever will continue to use in her sacred services the hymns composed by St. Thomas. They are the expression of the ardent supplications of a soul in prayer and at the same time a perfect statement of the doctrine of the august Sacrament transmitted by the Apostles, which is pre-eminently described as the Mystery of Faith. If these considerations are borne in mind as well as the praise bestowed by Christ Himself to which We have already referred, nobody will be surprised that St. Thomas should also have received the title of the Doctor of the Eucharist.

The following very relevant conclusions may be drawn from all that has gone before. Let our young men especially consider the example of St. Thomas and strive dilligently to imitate the eminent virtues which adorn his character, his humility above all, which is the foundation of the spiritual life, and his chastity. Let them learn from this man of supreme intellect and consummate learning to abhor all pride of mind and to obtain by humble prayer a flood of divine light upon their studies; let them learn from his teaching to shun nothing so sedulously as the blandishments of sensual pleasure, so that they may bring the eyes of the mind undimmed to the contemplation of wisdom. For he confirmed by his precept, as We have said, his own practice of life: "To abstain from the pleasures of the body so as to be certain of greater leisure and liberty for the contemplation of truth is to act in conformity with the dictates of reason" (II-II, clvii, 2). Wherefore we are warned in Holy Scripture: ". . . wisdom will not enter into a malicious soul, nor dwell in a body subject to sins" (*Wisdom,* i, 4). If the purity of Thomas therefore had failed in the extreme peril into which, as we have seen, it had fallen, it is very probable that the Church would never have had her Angelic Doctor.

Inasmuch, therefore, as We see the majority of young men, caught in the quicksands of passion, rapidly jettisoning holy purity and abandoning themselves to sensual pleasures, We instantly exhort you, Venerable Brethren, to propagate everywhere, and particularly among seminarians, the society of the *Angelic Militia* founded under the patronage of Thomas for the preservation and maintenance of holy chastity and We confirm the privileges of pontifical indulgences heaped upon it by Benedict XIII and others of Our Predecessors. And that the Faithful may be persuaded the more eagerly to enrol in this Militia, We grant members of it the privilege of wearing instead of a cord a medal round the neck impressed on the obverse with a picture of St. Thomas and the Angels surrounding him with a girdle and on the reverse a picture of Our Lady, Queen of the Most Holy Rosary.

But inasmuch as St. Thomas has been duly proclaimed patron of all Catholic schools because he marvellously combined both forms of wisdom, the rational and the divinely inspired, because he had recourse to prayer and fasting to solve the more difficult problems, because he used the image of Christ crucified in place of all books, let him be a model also for seminarians, so that they may learn how to pursue their studies to the best advantage and with the greatest profit to themselves. Members of religious communities should look upon the life of St. Thomas as upon a mirror; he refused even the highest dignities offered to him in order to live in the practice of the most perfect obedience and to die in the sanctity of his profession. Let all the Faithful of Christ take the Angelic Doctor as a model of devotion to the august Queen of Heaven, for it was his custom often to repeat the "Hail Mary" and to inscribe the sweet Name upon his pages, and let them ask the Doctor of the Eucharist himself to inspire them with love for the divine Sacrament. Priests above all will be zealous in so doing, as is only proper. "For Thomas was accustomed, unless prevented by illness, to say Mass daily and heard another Mass said by his *socius* or some other friar which he very often served," declares the careful historian of his life. But could anyone find words to express the spiritual fervour with which he said Mass himself, the anxious care with which he made his preparation, the thanksgivings he offered to the divine Majesty after he had said it?

Again, if we are to avoid the errors which are the source and fountain-head of all the miseries of our time, the teaching of Aquinas must be adhered to more religiously than ever. For Thomas refutes the theories propounded by Modernists in every sphere, in philosophy, by protecting, as We have reminded you, the force and power of the human mind and by demonstrating the existence of God by the most cogent arguments; in dogmatic theology, by distinguishing the supernatural from the natural order and explaining the reasons for belief and the dogmas themselves; in theology, by showing that the articles of faith are not based upon mere opinion but upon truth and therefore cannot possibly change; in exegesis, by transmitting the true conception of divine inspiration; in the science of morals, in sociology and law, by laying down sound principles of legal and social, communicative and distributive, justice, and explaining the relations between justice and charity; in the theory of asceticism, by his precepts concerning the perfection of the Christian life and his confutation of the enemies of the religious orders in his own day. Lastly, against the much vaunted liberty of the human reason and its independence in regard to God he asserts the rights of primary

Truth and the authority over us of the Supreme Master. It is therefore clear why Modernists are so amply justified in fearing no Doctor of the Church so much as Thomas Aquinas.

Accordingly, just as it was said to the Egyptians of old in time of famine: 'Go to Joseph,' so that they should receive a supply of wheat from him to nourish their bodies, so We now say to all such as are desirous of the truth: 'Go to Thomas,' and ask him to give you from his ample store the food of substantial doctrine wherewith to nourish your souls unto eternal life. Evidence that such food is ready to hand and accessible to all men was given on oath at the hearing of the case for the canonization of Thomas himself, in the following words: "Innumerable secular and religious masters flourished under the lucid and limpid teaching of this Doctor, because his method was concise, clear and easily followed . . . even laymen and persons of little instruction are eager to possess his writings."

We desire those especially who are engaged in teaching the higher studies in seminaries sedulously to observe and inviolably to maintain the decrees of Our Predecessors, more particularly those of Leo XIII (the Encyclical *Aeterni Patris*), and Pius X (the Motu Proprio *Doctoris Angelici*) and the instructions We Ourselves issued last year. Let them be persuaded that they will discharge their duty and fulfil Our expectation when, after long and diligent perusal of his writings, they begin to feel an intense devotion for the Doctor Aquinas and by their exposition of him succeed in inspiring their pupils with a like fervour and train them to kindle a similar zeal in others.

We desire that lovers of St. Thomas—and all sons

of the Church who devote themselves to higher studies should be so—be incited by an honourable rivalry in a just and proper freedom which is the lifeblood of studies, but let no spirit of malevolent disparagement prevail among them, for any such, so far from helping truth, serves only to loosen the bonds of charity. Let everyone therefore inviolably observe the prescription contained in the Code of Canon Law that "teachers shall deal with the studies of mental philosophy and theology and the education of their pupils in such sciences according to the method, doctrine and principles of the Angelic Doctor and religiously adhere thereto"; and may they conform to this rule so faithfully as to be able to describe him in very truth as their master. Let none require from another more than the Church, the mistress and mother of all, requires from each: and in questions, which in Catholic schools are matter of controversy between the most reputable authorities, let none be prevented from adhering to whatever opinion seems to him the more probable.

Therefore, as it behoves the whole of Christendom worthily to celebrate this centenary—because in honouring St. Thomas something greater is involved than the reputation of St. Thomas and that is the authority of the teaching Church—We desire that such celebration shall take place throughout the world from the 18th July until the end of next year wherever seminarians are in regular course of instruction, that is to say not only among the Preaching Friars, an Order which, in the words of Benedict XV, "must be praised, not so much for having been the family of the Angelic Doctor, as for never having afterwards departed so much as a hair's breadth from his teaching" (*Acta Ap. Sedis*, viii, 1916, p. 397), but among other religious communities also, and in all seminaries and Catholic colleges and schools to which he has been appointed for heavenly patron. It is only proper that this Eternal City in which Aquinas was once master of the Sacred Palace should take the lead in holding such celebrations and that the Pontifical Angelical College, where St. Thomas may be said to be at home, and the other academies in Rome for the education of priests set the example in these holy rejoicings.

In virtue of Our Apostolic power and for the purpose of increasing the splendour and profit to be derived from this celebration, We grant the following privileges:

1) That in all churches belonging to the Order of Preachers and in all other churches or chapels to which the public has or may have access, more particularly in seminaries, colleges or other institutions for the education of priests, prayers may be said for three or eight or nine days with the pontifical indulgences attaching to them which customarily attach to prayers said in honour of the saints and the blessed;

2) That in the churches of the Friars and the Sisters of St. Dominic the faithful may once on any day they choose in the course of the centenary celebrations, after duly confessing their sins and receiving Holy Communion, obtain a plenary indulgence *toties quoties* if they pray before the altar of St. Thomas;

3) That in churches of the Order of St. Dominic, priests, members of the Order or tertiaries, may, in the course of the centenary year on any Wednesday or the first free day of the week, celebrate Mass in honour of St. Thomas, as on his feastday, with or without the Gloria and the Credo, according to the ritual of the

day, and obtain a plenary remission of sins; those present at any such Mass may also obtain a like indulgence on the usual conditions.

In addition, a disputation shall be held in seminaries and other institutions for the education of priests on some point of philosophy or other important branch of learning in honour of the Angelic Doctor. And that the festival of St. Thomas may be kept in future in a manner worthy of the patron of all Catholic schools, We order it to be kept as a holiday and celebrated not only with a High Mass, but also, at any rate in seminaries and among religious communities, by the holding of a disputation as aforesaid.

Finally, that the studies to which Our young people devote themselves may, under the patronage of Aquinas, daily yield more and more fruit for the glory of God and the Church, We append to this Letter the form of prayer which the Saint himself was accustomed to use and exhort you to see that it be widely published. Let any person duly reciting it know that by Our authority an indulgence of seven years and seven quarantines is granted him.

As an augury of divine favour and in testimony of Our paternal benevolence, We most affectionately grant you, Venerable Brethren, and the clergy and people committed to your care the Apostolic Blessing.

Given at Rome at St. Peter's on the 29th day of June, the feast of the Princes of the Apostles, in the year 1923, the second year of Our Pontificate.

PIUS PP. XI.

PRAYER OF ST. THOMAS

Ineffable Creator, Who out of the treasures of Thy wisdom has appointed three hierarchies of Angels and set them in admirable order high above the heavens and hast disposed the divers portions of the universe in such marvellous array, Thou Who art called the True Source of Light and supereminent Principle of Wisdom, be pleased to cast a beam of Thy radiance upon the darkness of my mind and dispel from me the double darkness of sin and ignorance in which I have been born.

Thou Who makest eloquent the tongues of little children, fashion my words and pour upon my lips the grace of Thy benediction. Grant me penetration to understand, capacity to retain, method and facility in study, subtlety in interpretation and abundant grace of expression.

Order the beginning, direct the progress and perfect the achievement of my work, Thou Who art true God and true Man and livest and reignest for ever and ever. Amen.

HUMANI GENERIS

ENCYCLICAL LETTER
OF
HIS HOLINESS POPE PIUS XII

To Our Venerable Brethren, Patriarchs,
Primates, Archbishops, Bishops and
other local Ordinaries enjoying peace
and communion with the Holy See

concerning some false opinions which
threaten to undermine the foundations of Catholic Doctrine.

Venerable Brethren,
Greetings and Apostolic Benediction!

1) Disagreement and error among men on moral and
religious matters have always been a cause of profound sorrow to all good men, but above all to the
true and loyal sons of the Church, especially today,
when we see the principles of Christian culture being
attacked on all sides.

2) It is not surprising that such discord and error
should always have existed outside the fold of Christ.
For though, absolutely speaking, human reason by its
own natural force and light can arrive at a true and
certain knowledge of the one personal God, Who by
His providence watches over and governs the world,

and also of the natural law, which the Creator has written in our hearts, still there are not a few obstacles to prevent reason from making efficient and fruitful use of its natural ability. The truths that have to do with God and the relations between God and men, completely surpass the sensible order and demand self-surrender and self-abnegation in order to be put into practice and to influence practical life. Now the human intellect, in gaining the knowledge of such truths is hampered both by the activity of the senses and the imagination, and by evil passions arising from original sin. Hence men easily persuade themselves in such matters that what they do not wish to believe is false or at least doubtful.

3) It is for this reason that divine revelation must be considered morally necessary so that those religious and moral truths which are not of their nature beyond the reach of reason in the present condition of the human race, may be known by all men readily with a firm certainty and with freedom from all error.[1]

4) Furthermore the human intelligence sometimes experiences difficulties in forming a judgment about the credibility of the Catholic faith, notwithstanding the many wonderful external signs God has given, which are sufficient to prove with certitude by the natural light of reason alone the divine origin of the Christian religion. For man can, whether from prejudice or passion or bad faith, refuse and resist not only the evidence of the external proofs that are available, but also the impulses of actual grace.

5) If anyone examines the state of affairs outside the Christian fold, he will easily discover the principal trends that not a few learned men are following. Some imprudently and indiscreetly hold that evolution, which has not been fully proved even in the domain

of natural sciences, explains the origin of all things, and audaciously support the monistic and pantheistic opinion that the world is in continual evolution. Communists gladly subscribe to this opinion so that, when the souls of men have been deprived of every idea of a personal God, they may the more efficaciously defend and propagate their dialectical materialism.

6) Such fictitious tenets of evolution which repudiate all that is absolute, firm and immutable, have paved the way for the new erroneous philosophy which, rivaling idealism, immanentism and pragmatism, has assumed the name of existentialism, since it concerns itself only with existence of individual things and neglects all consideration of their immutable essences.

7) There is also a certain historicism, which attributing value only to the events of man's life, overthrows the foundation of all truth and absolute law both on the level of philosophical speculations and especially to Christian dogmas.

8) In all this confusion of opinion it is some consolation to Us to see former adherents of rationalism today frequently desiring to return to the fountain of divinely communicated truth, and to acknowledge and profess the word of God as contained in Sacred Scripture as the foundation of religious teaching. But at the same time it is a matter of regret that not a few of these, the more firmly they accept the word of God, so much the more do they diminish the value of human reason, and the more they exalt the authority of God the Revealer, the more severely do they spurn the teaching office of the Church, which has been instituted by Christ, Our Lord, to preserve and interpret divine revelation. This attitude is not only plainly at variance with Holy Scripture, but is shown to be

false by experience also. For often those who disagree with the true Church complain openly of their disagreement in matters of dogma and thus unwillingly bear witness to the necessity of a living Teaching Authority.

9) Now Catholic theologians and philosophers, whose grave duty it is to defend natural and supernatural truth and instill it in the hearts of men, cannot afford to ignore or neglect these more or less erroneous opinions. Rather they must come to understand these same theories well, both because diseases are not properly treated unless they are rightly diagnosed, and because sometimes even in these false theories a certain amount of truth is contained, and, finally because these theories provoke more subtle discussion and evaluation of philosophical and theological truths.

10) If philosophers and theologians strive only to derive such profit from the careful examination of these doctrines, there would be no reason for any intervention by the Teaching Authority of the Church. However, although We know that Catholic Teachers generally avoid these errors, it is apparent, however, that some today, as in apostolic times, desirous of novelty, and fearing to be considered ignorant of recent scientific findings try to withdraw themselves from the sacred Teaching Authority and are accordingly in danger of gradually departing from revealed truth and of drawing others along with them into error.

11) Another danger is perceived which is all the more serious because it is more concealed beneath the mask of virtue. There are many who, deploring disagreement among men and intellectual confusion, through an imprudent zeal for souls, are urged by a great and ardent desire to do away with the barrier

that divides good and honest men; these advocate an "eirenism" according to which, by setting aside the questions which divide men, they aim not only at joining forces to repel the attacks of atheism, but also at reconciling things opposed to one another in the field of dogma. And as in former times some questioned whether the traditional apologetics of the Church did not constitute an obstacle rather than a help to the winning of souls for Christ, so today some are presumptive enough to question seriously whether theology and theological methods, such as with the approval of ecclesiastical authority are found in our schools, should not only be perfected, but also completely reformed, in order to promote the more efficacious propagation of the kingdom of Christ everywhere throughout the world among men of every culture and religious opinion.

12) Now if these only aimed at adapting ecclesiastical teaching and methods to modern conditions and requirements, through the introduction of some new explanations, there would be scarcely any reason for alarm. But some through enthusiasm for an imprudent "eirenism" seem to consider as an obstacle to the restoration of fraternal union, things founded on the laws and principles given by Christ and likewise on institutions founded by Him, or which are the defense and support of the integrity of the faith, and the removal of which would bring about the union of all, but only to their destruction.

13) These new opinions, whether they originate from a reprehensible desire of novelty or from a laudable motive, are not always advanced in the same degree, with equal clarity nor in the same terms, nor always with unanimous agreement of their authors. Theories that today are put forward rather covertly by some,

not without cautions and distinctions, tomorrow are openly and without moderation proclaimed by others more audacious, causing scandal to many, especially among the young clergy and to the detriment of ecclesiastical authority. Though they are usually more cautious in their published works, they express themselves more openly in their writings intended for private circulation and in conferences and lectures. Moreover, these opinions are disseminated not only among members of the clergy and in seminaries and religious institutions, but also among the laity, and especially among those who are engaged in teaching youth.

14) In theology some want to reduce to a minimum the meaning of dogmas; and to free dogma itself from terminology long established in the Church and from philosophical concepts held by Catholic teachers, to bring about a return in the explanation of Catholic doctrine to the way of speaking used in Holy Scripture and by the Fathers of the Church. They cherish the hope that when dogma is stripped of the elements which they hold to be extrinsic to divine revelation, it will compare advantageously with the dogmatic opinions of those who are separated from the unity of the Church and that in this way they will gradually arrive at a mutual assimilation of Catholic dogma with the tenets of the dissidents.

15) Moreover they assert that when Catholic doctrine has been reduced to this condition, a way will be found to satisfy modern needs, that will permit of dogma being expressed also by the concepts of modern philosophy, whether of immanentism or idealism or existentialism or any other system. Some more audacious affirm that this can and must be done, because they hold that the mysteries of faith are never expressed by truly adequate concepts but only by ap-

proximate and ever changeable notions, in which the truth is to some extent expressed, but is necessarily distorted. Wherefore they do not consider it absurd, but altogether necessary, that theology should substitute new concepts in place of the old ones in keeping with the various philosophies which in the course of time it uses as its instruments, so that it should give human expression to divine truths in various ways which are even somewhat opposed, but still equivalent, as they say. They add that the history of dogmas consists in the reporting of the various forms in which revealed truth has been clothed, forms that have succeeded one another in accordance with the different teachings and opinions that have arisen over the course of the centuries.

16) It is evident from what We have already said, that such tentatives not only lead to what they call dogmatic relativism, but that they actually contain it. The comtempt of doctrine commonly taught and of the terms in which it is expressed strongly favor it. Everyone is aware that the terminology employed in the schools and even that used by the Teaching Authority of the Church itself is capable of being perfected and polished; and we know also that the Church itself has not always used the same terms in the same way. It is also manifest that the Church cannot be bound to every system of philosophy that has existed for a short space of time. Nevertheless, the things that have been composed through common effort by Catholic teachers over the course of the centuries to bring about some understanding of dogma are certainly not based on any such weak foundation. These things are based on principles and notions deduced from a true knowledge of created things. In the process of deducing, this knowledge, like a star, gave enlightenment to the

human mind through the Church. Hence it is not astonishing that some of these notions have not only been used by the Oecumenical Councils, but even sanctioned by them, so that it is wrong to depart from them.

17) Hence to neglect, or to reject, or to devalue so many and such great resources which have been conceived, expressed and perfected so often by the age-old work of men endowed with no common talent and holiness, working under the vigilant supervision of the holy magisterium and with the light and leadership of the Holy Ghost in order to state the truths of the faith ever more accurately, to do this so that these things may be replaced by conjectural notions and by some formless and unstable tenets of a new philosophy, tenets which, like the flowers of the field, are in existence today and die tomorrow; this is supreme imprudence and something that would make dogma itself a reed shaken by the wind. The contempt for terms and notions habitually used by scholastic theologians leads of itself to the weakening of what they call speculative theology, a discipline which these men consider devoid of true certitude because it is based on theological reasoning.

18) Unfortunately these advocates of novelty easily pass from despising scholastic theology to the neglect of and even contempt for the Teaching Authority of the Church itself, which gives such authoritative approval to scholastic theology. This Teaching Authority is represented by them as a hindrance to progress and an obstacle in the way of science. Some non-Catholics consider it as an unjust restraint preventing some more qualified theologians from reforming their subject. And although this sacred Office of Teacher in matters of faith and morals must be the proximate and uni-

versal criterion of truth for all theologians, since to it has been entrusted by Christ Our Lord the whole deposit of faith—Sacred Scripture and divine Tradition—to be preserved, guarded and interpreted, still the duty that is incumbent on the faithful to flee also those errors which more or less approach heresy, and accordingly "to keep also the constitutions and decrees by which such evil opinions are proscribed and forbidden by the Holy see," [2] is sometimes as little known as if it did not exist. What is expounded in the Encyclical Letters of the Roman Pontiffs concerning the nature and constitution of the Church, is deliberately and habitually neglected by some with the idea of giving force to a certain vague notion which they profess to have found in the ancient Fathers, especially the Greeks. The Popes, they assert, do not wish to pass judgment on what is a matter of dispute among theologians, so recourse must be had to the early sources, and the recent constitutions and decrees of the Teaching Church must be explained from the writings of the ancients.

19) Although these things seem well said, still they are not free from error. It is true that Popes generally leave theologians free in those matters which are disputed in various ways by men of very high authority in this field; but history teaches that many matters that formerly were open to discussion, no longer now admit of discussion.

20) Nor must it be thought that what is expounded in Encyclical Letters does not of itself demand consent, since in writing such Letters the Popes do not exercise the supreme power of their Teaching Authority. For these matters are taught with the ordinary teaching authority, of which it is true to say: "He who heareth you, heareth me"; [3] and generally what is ex-

pounded and inculcated in Encyclical Letters already
for other reasons appertains to Catholic doctrine. But if
the Supreme Pontiffs in their official documents pur-
posely pass judgment on a matter up to that time
under dispute, it is obvious that that matter, according to the mind and will of the same Pontiffs, cannot
be any longer considered a question open to discussion among theologians.

21) It is also true that theologians must always return to the sources of divine revelation: for it belongs
to them to point out how the doctrine of the living
Teaching Authority is to be found either explicitly or
implicitly in the Scriptures and in Tradition.[4] Besides,
each source of divinely revealed doctrine contains so
many rich treasures of truth, that they can really
never be exhausted. Hence it is that theology through
the study of its sacred sources remains ever fresh; on
the other hand, speculation which neglects a deeper
search into the deposit of faith, proves sterile, as we
know from experience. But for this reason even positive theology cannot be on a par with merely historical
science. For, together with the sources of positive
theology God has given to His Church a living Teaching Authority to elucidate and explain what is contained in the deposit of faith only obscurely and implicitly. This deposit of faith our Divine Redeemer
has given for authentic interpretation not to each of
the faithful, not even to theologians, but only to the
Teaching Authority of the Church. But if the Church
does exercise this function of teaching, as she often
has through the centuries, either in the ordinary or
extraordinary way, it is clear how false is a procedure
which would attempt to explain what is clear by means
of what is obscure. Indeed the very opposite procedure
must be used. Hence Our Predecessor of immortal

memory, Pius IX, teaching that the most noble office of theology is to show how a doctrine defined by the Church is contained in the sources of revelation, added these words, and with very good reason: "in that sense in which it has been defined by the Church."

22) To return, however, to the new opinions mentioned above, a number of things are proposed or suggested by some even against the divine authorship of Sacred Scripture. For some go so far as to pervert the sense of the Vatican Council's definition that God is the author of Holy Scripture, and they put forward again the opinion, already often condemned, which asserts that immunity from error extends only to those parts of the Bible that treat of God or of moral and religious matters. They even wrongly speak of a human sense of the Scriptures, beneath which a divine sense, which they say is the only infallible meaning, lies hidden. In interpreting Scripture, they will take no account of the analogy of faith and the Tradition of the Church. Thus they judge the doctrine of the Fathers and of the Teaching Church by the norm of Holy Scripture, interpreted by the purely human reason of exegetes, instead of explaining Holy Scripture according to the mind of the Church which Christ Our Lord has appointed guardian and interpreter of the whole deposit of divinely revealed truth.

23) Further, according to their fictitious opinions, the literal sense of Holy Scripture and its explanation, carefully worked out under the Church's vigilance by so many great exegetes, should yield now to a new exegesis, which they are pleased to call symbolic or spiritual. By means of this new exegesis the Old Testament, which today in the Church is a sealed book, would finally be thrown open to all the faithful. By this method, they say, all difficulties vanish, difficulties

which hinder only those who adhere to the literal meaning of the Scriptures.

24) Everyone sees how foreign all this is to the principles and norms of interpretation rightly fixed by our predecessors of happy memory, Leo XIII in his Encyclical "Providentissimus," and Benedict XV in the Encyclical "Spiritus Paraclitus," as also by Ourselves in the Encyclical "Divino Afflante Spiritu."

25) It is not surprising that novelties of this kind have already borne their deadly fruit in almost all branches of theology. It is now doubted that human reason, without divine revelation and the help of divine grace, can, by arguments drawn from the created universe, prove the existence of a personal God; it is denied that the world had a beginning; it is argued that the creation of the world is necessary, since it proceeds from the necessary liberality of divine love; it is denied that God has eternal and infallible foreknowledge of the free actions of men—all this in contradiction to the decrees of the Vatican Council.[5]

26) Some also question whether angels are personal beings, and whether matter and spirit differ essentially. Others destroy the gratuity of the supernatural order, since God, they say, cannot create intellectual beings without ordering and calling them to the beatific vision. Nor is this all. Disregarding the Council of Trent, some pervert the very concept of original sin, along with the concept of sin in general as an offense against God, as well as the idea of satisfaction performed for us by Christ. Some even say that the doctrine of transubstantiation, based on an antiquated philosophic notion of substance, should be so modified that the real presence of Christ in the Holy Eucharist be reduced to a kind of symbolism, whereby the consecrated species would be merely efficacious signs of the spiritual pres-

ence of Christ and of His intimate union with the faithful members of His Mystical Body.

27) Some say they are not bound by the doctrine, explained in Our Encyclical Letter of a few years ago, and based on the sources of revelation, which teaches that the Mystical Body of Christ and the Roman Catholic Church are one and the same thing.[6] Some reduce to a meaningless formula the necessity of belonging to the true Church in order to gain eternal salvation. Others finally belittle the reasonable character of the credibility of Christian faith.

28) These and like errors, it is clear, have crept in among certain of Our sons who are deceived by imprudent zeal for souls or by false science. To them We are compelled with grief to repeat once again truths already well known, and to point out with solicitude clear errors and dangers of error.

29) It is well known how highly the Church regards human reason, for it falls to reason to demonstrate with certainty the existence of God, personal and one; to prove beyond doubt from divine signs the very foundations of the Christian faith; to express properly the law which the Creator has imprinted in the hearts of men; and finally to attain to some notion, indeed a very fruitful notion, of mysteries.[7] But reason can perform these functions safely and well, only when properly trained, that is, when imbued with that sound philosophy which has long been, as it were, a patrimony handed down by earlier Christian ages, and which moreover possesses an authority of even higher order, since the Teaching Authority of the Church, in the light of divine revelation itself, has weighed its fundamental tenets, which have been elaborated and defined little by little by men of great genius. For this philosophy, acknowledged and accepted by the

Church, safeguards the genuine validity of human knowledge, the unshakable metaphysical principles of sufficient reason, causality, and finality, and finally the mind's ability to attain certain and unchangeable truth.

30) Of course this philosophy deals with much that neither directly nor indirectly touches faith or morals, and which consequently the Church leaves to the free discussion of experts. But this does not hold for many other things, especially those principles and fundamental tenets to which We have just referred. However, even in these fundamental questions, we may clothe our philosophy in a more convenient and richer dress, make it more vigorous with a more effective terminology, divest it of certain scholastic aids found less useful, prudently enrich it with the fruits of progress of the human mind. But never may we overthrow it, or contaminate it with false principles, or regard it as a great, but obsolete, relic. For truth and its philosophic expression cannot change from day to day, least of all where there is question of self-evident principles of the human mind or of those propositions which are supported by the wisdom of the ages and by divine revelation. Whatever new truth the sincere human mind is able to find, certainly cannot be opposed to truth already acquired, since God, the highest Truth, has created and guides the human intellect, not that it may daily oppose new truths to rightly established ones, but rather that, having eliminated errors which may have crept in, it may build truth upon truth in the same order and structure that exist in reality, the source of truth. Let no Christian therefore, whether philosopher or theologian, embrace eagerly and lightly whatever novelty happens to be thought up from day to day, but

rather let him weigh it with painstaking care and a balanced judgment, lest he lose or corrupt the truth he already has, with grave danger and damage to his faith.

31) If one considers all this well, he will easily see why the Church demands that future priests be instructed in philosophy "according to the method, doctrine, and principles of the Angelic Doctor," [8] since, as we well know from the experience of centuries, the method of Aquinas is singularly preeminent both for teaching students and for bringing truth to light; his doctrine is in harmony with divine revelation, and is most effective both for safeguarding the foundation of faith, and for reaping, safely and usefully, the fruits of sound progress.[9]

32) How deplorable it is then that this philosophy, received and honored by the Church, is scorned by some, who shamelessly call it outmoded in form and rationalistic, as they say, in its method of thought. They say that this philosophy upholds the erroneous notion that there can be a metaphysic that is absolutely true; whereas in fact, they say, reality, especially transcendent reality, cannot better be expressed than by disparate teachings, which mutually complete each other, although they are in a way mutually opposed. Our traditional philosophy, then, with its clear exposition and solution of questions, its accurate definition of terms, its clear-cut distinctions, can be, they concede, useful as a preparation for scholastic theology, a preparation quite in accord with medieval mentality; but this philosophy hardly offers a method of philosophizing suited to the needs of our modern culture. They allege, finally, that our perennial philosophy is only a philosophy of immutable essences, while the contemporary mind must look to the existence of things

and to life, which is ever in flux. While scorning our philosophy, they extol other philosophies of all kinds, ancient and modern, oriental and occidental, by which they seem to imply that any kind of philosophy or theory, with a few additions and corrections if need be, can be reconciled with Catholic dogma. No Catholic can doubt how false this is, especially where there is question of those fictitious theories they call immanentism, or idealism, or materialism, whether historic or dialectic, or even existentialism, whether atheistic or simply the type that denies the validity of the reason in the field of metaphysics.

33) Finally, they reproach this philosophy taught in our schools for regarding only the intellect in the process of cognition, while neglecting the function of the will and the emotions. This is simply not true. Never has Christian philosophy denied the usefulness and efficacy of good dispositions of soul for perceiving and embracing moral and religious truths. In fact, it has always taught that the lack of these dispositions of good will can be the reason why the intellect, influenced by the passions and evil inclinations, can be so obscured that it cannot see clearly. Indeed St. Thomas holds that the intellect can in some way perceive higher goods of the moral order, whether natural or supernatural, inasmuch as it experiences a certain "connaturality" with these goods, whether this "connaturality" be purely natural, or the result of graces;[10] and it is clear how much even this somewhat obscure perception can help the reason in its investigations. However it is one thing to admit the power of the dispositions of the will in helping reason to gain a more certain and firm knowledge of moral truths; it is quite another thing to say, as these innovators do, indiscriminately mingling cognition and

act of will, that the appetitive and affective faculties have a certain power of understanding, and that man, since he cannot by using his reason decide with certainty what is true and is to be accepted, turns to his will, by which he freely chooses among opposite opinions.

34) It is not surprising that these new opinions endanger the two philosophical sciences which by their very nature are closely connected with the doctrine of faith, that is, theodicy and ethics; they hold that the function of these two sciences is not to prove with certitude anything about God or any other transcendental being, but rather to show that the truths which faith teaches about a personal God and about His precepts, are perfectly consistent with the necessities of life and are therefore to be accepted by all, in order to avoid despair and to attain eternal salvation. All these opinions and affirmations are openly contrary to the documents of Our Predecessors Leo XIII and Pius X, and cannot be reconciled with the decrees of the Vatican Council. It would indeed be unnecessary to deplore these aberrations from the truth, if all, even in the field of philosophy, directed their attention with the proper reverence to the Teaching Authority of the Church, which by divine institution has the mission not only to guard and interpret the deposit of divinely revealed truth, but also to keep watch over the philosophical sciences themselves, in order that Catholic dogmas may suffer no harm because of erroneous opinions.

35) It remains for Us now so speak about those questions which, although they pertain to the positive sciences, are nevertheless more or less connected with the truths of the Christian faith. In fact, not a few insistently demand that the Catholic religion take these

sciences into account as much as possible. This certainly would be praiseworthy in the case of clearly proved facts; but caution must be used when there is rather question of hypotheses, having some sort of scientific foundation, in which the doctrine contained in Sacred Scripture or in Tradition is involved. If such conjectural opinions are directly or indirectly opposed to the doctrine revealed by God, then the demand that they be recognized can in no way be admitted.

36) For these reasons the Teaching Authority of the Church does not forbid that, in conformity with the present state of human sciences and sacred theology, research and discussions, on the part of men experienced in both fields, take place with regard to the doctrine of evolution, in as far as it inquires into the origin of the human body as coming from pre-existent and living matter—for the Catholic faith obliges us to hold that souls are immediately created by God. However this must be done in such a way that the reasons for both opinions, that is, those favorable and those unfavorable to evolution, be weighed and judged with the necessary seriousness, moderation and measure, and provided that all are prepared to submit to the judgment of the Church, to whom Christ has given the mission of interpreting authentically the Sacred Scriptures and of defending the dogmas of faith.[11] Some however rashly transgress this liberty of discussion, when they act as if the origin of the human body from pre-existing and living matter were already completely certain and proved by the facts which have been discovered up to now and by reasoning on those facts, and as if there were nothing in the sources of divine revelation which

demands the greatest moderation and caution in this question.

37) When, however, there is question of another conjectural opinion, namely polygenism, the children of the Church by no means enjoy such liberty. For the faithful cannot embrace that opinion which maintains either that after Adam there existed on this earth true men who did not take their origin through natural generation from him as from the first parent of all, or that Adam represents a certain number of first parents. Now it is in no way apparent how such an opinion can be reconciled with that which the sources of revealed truth and the documents of the Teaching Authority of the Church propose with regard to original sin, which proceeds from a sin actually committed by an individual Adam and which through generation is passed on to all and is in everyone as his own.[12]

38) Just as in the biological and anthropological sciences, so also in the historical sciences there are those who boldly transgress the limits and safeguards established by the Church. In a particular way must be deplored a certain too free interpretation of the historical books of the Old Testament. Those who favor this system, in order to defend their cause, wrongly refer to the Letter which was sent not long ago the Archbishop of Paris by the Pontifical Commission on Biblical Studies.[13] This Letter, in fact, clearly points out that the first eleven chapters of Genesis, although properly speaking not conforming to the historical method used by the best Greek and Latin writers or by competent authors of our time, do nevertheless pertain to history in a true sense, which however must be further studied and deter-

mined by exegetes; the same chapters (the Letter points out), in simple and metaphorical language adapted to the mentality of a people but little cultured, both state the principal truths which are fundamental for our salvation, and also give a popular description of the origin of the human race and the chosen people. If, however, the ancient sacred writers have taken anything from popular narrations (and this may be conceded), it must never be forgotten that they did so with the help of divine inspiration, through which they were rendered immune from any error in selecting and evaluating those documents.

39) Therefore, whatever of the popular narrations have been inserted into the Sacred Scriptures must in no way be considered on a par with myths or other such things, which are more the product of an extravagant imagination than of that striving for truth and simplicity which in the Sacred Books, also of the Old Testament, is so apparent that our ancient sacred writers must be admitted to be clearly superior to the ancient profane writers.

40) Truly, we are aware that the majority of Catholic doctors, the fruit of whose studies is being gathered in universities, in seminaries and in the colleges of religious, are far removed from those errors which today, whether through a desire of novelty or through a certain immoderate zeal for the apostolate, are being spread either openly or covertly. But we know also that such new opinions can entice the incautious; and therefore we prefer to withstand the very beginnings rather than to administer the medicine after the disease has grown inveterate.

41) For this reason, after mature reflexion and consideration before God, that We may not be wanting in Our sacred duty, We charge the Bishops

and the Superiors General of Religious Orders, binding them most seriously in conscience, to take most diligent care that such opinions be not advanced in schools, in conferences or in writings of any kind, and that they be not taught in any manner whatsoever to the clergy or the faithful.

42) Let the teachers in ecclesiastical institutions be aware that they cannot with tranquil conscience exercise the office of teaching entrusted to them, unless in the instruction of their students they religiously accept and exactly observe the norms which We have ordained. That due reverence and submission which in their unceasing labor they must profess towards the Teaching Authority of the Church, let them instill also into the minds and hearts of their students.

43) Let them strive with every force and effort to further the progress of the sciences which they teach; but let them also be careful not to transgress the limits which We have established for the protection of the truth of Catholic faith and doctrine. With regard to new questions, which modern culture and progress have brought to the foreground, let them engage in most careful research, but with the necessary prudence and caution; finally, let them not think, indulging in a false "eirenism," that the dissident and erring can happily be brought back to the bosom of the Church, if the whole truth found in the Church is not sincerely taught to all without corruption or diminution.

44) Relying on this hope, which will be increased by your pastoral care, as a pledge of celestial gifts and a sign of Our paternal benevolence, We impart with all Our heart to each and all of you, Venerable Brethren, and to your clergy and people the Apostolic Benediction.

45) Given at Rome, at St. Peter's, August 12, 1950, the twelfth year of Our Pontificate.

PIUS PP. XII.

NOTES TO *Humani Generis*

[1] Conc. Vatic. D.B., 1876, Const. *De Fide cath.*, cap. 2, *De revelatione.*

[2] C.I.C., can. 1324; cfr. Conc. Vat., D.B., 1820, Const. *De Fide cath.*, cap. 4, *De Fide et ratione,* post canones.

[3] Luke, X, 16.

[4] Pius IX, *Inter gravissimas,* 28 oct., 1870, *Acta,* vol. I, p. 260.

[5] Cfr. Conc. Vat., Const. *De Fide cath.*, cap. 1, *De Deo rerum omnium creatore.*

[6] Cfr. Litt. Enc. *Mystici Corporis Christi,* A.A.S., vol. XXXV, p. 193 sq.

[7] Cfr. Conc. Vat., D.B., 1796.

[8] C.I.C., can. 1366, 2.

[9] A.A.S., vol. XXXVIII, 1946, p. 387.

[10] Cfr. S. Thom., *Summa Theol.*, II-II, quaest. 1, art. 4 ad 3 et quaest. 45, art. 2, in c.

[11] Cfr. Allocut. Pont. to the members of the Academy of Science, November 30, 1941: A.A.S., vol. XXXIII, p. 506.

[12] Cfr. *Rom.*, V, 12-19; Conc. Trid., sess. V, can. 1-4.

[13] January 16, 1948: A.A.S., vol. XL, pp. 45-48.

SOME WORKS ABOUT SAINT THOMAS AND HIS TEACHINGS.[1]

Malachy G. Carroll, *Time Cannot Dim,* Chicago (Regnery), 1955.

M.D. Chenu, O.P., *Introduction à l'étude de saint Thomas d'Aquin,* Paris (Vrin) 2nd ed., 1954.

G. K. Chesterton, *St. Thomas Aquinas,* New York (S & W), 1933; reprinted in the Doubleday *Image Books,* D36.

Reginald M. Coffey, O.P., *The Man from Rocca Sicca,* Milwaukee (Bruce), 1944.

F. C. Copleston, *Aquinas,* in the Penguin *Pelican Books,* A349.

M. C. D'Arcy, S.J., *Thomas Aquinas,* Westminster (Newman), 1944.

Etienne Gilson, *The Christian Philosophy of St. Thomas Aquinas,* with *A Catalogue of St. Thomas's Works* by I. T. Eschmann, O.P., New York (Random House), 1956.

Etienne Gilson, *The Spirit of Mediaeval Philosophy,* New York (Scribner), 1940.

Martin Grabmann, *Thomas Aquinas, His Personality and Thought,* New York (Longmans), 1928.

Martin Grabman, *The Interior Life of St. Thomas Aquinas,* Presented from His Works and the Acts of His Canonization Process, Milwaukee (Bruce), 1951.

Raïssa Maritain, *Saint Thomas Aquinas, The Angel of the Schools,* New York (Longmans), 2nd ed., 1955.

[1] For an excellent bibliographical start in this extremely large field, see Etienne Gilson, *History of Christian Philosophy in the Middle Ages,* New York (Random House), 1955, Part 8, note 95, pp. 709-711.

Josef Pieper, *The Silence of St. Thomas,* New York (Pantheon), 1957.

Santiago Ramirez, O.P., *The Authority of St. Thomas Aquinas,* reprinted from *The Thomist,* XV, 1 (January, 1952).

A. D. Sertillanges, *Saint Thomas Aquinas and His Work,* London (B.O. & W.), 1932.

Gerald Vann, O.P., *Saint Thomas Aquinas,* London (Dent), 1940.

R. B. Vaughan, O.S.B., *The Life and Labours of S. Thomas of Aquin,* 2 vols., London (Longmans), 1871-1872.

Angelus Walz, O.P., *St. Thomas Aquinas, A Biographical Study,* Westminster (Newman), 1951.

Louis de Wohl, *The Quiet Light,* Philadelphia (Lippincott), 1950.

PREFACE

[1] "There too will the eagles be gathered." Matt. 24/28; Luke 17/37.

[2] "Woe to me, if I do not Thomistize." (Cf. I Cor. 9/16).

[3] I tried in *Art and Scholasticism* to show how a dialogue between the enduring philosophy and the art of our day could be engaged in. Years later the same effort was resumed, on a larger scale, in *Creative Intuition in Art and Poetry* (Note to the second edition).

[4] Ezech. III, 27.

CHAPTER I

[1] This date has been established by Father Mandonnet in his invaluable critical studies to which it will always be necessary to refer on matters concerning the life of Saint Thomas. One may also consult Father Petitot's *Saint Thomas d'Aquin;* Monsignor M. Grabmann's *Thomas von Aquin;* as well as the Pègues-Maquart translation of William of Tocco and of the testimonies presented at the process of canonization.

[2] Some of Thomas' brothers having taken part in the uprising of 1246 against Frederick II, his family was forced into exile in the papal Campagna. It was at that time that Raynaldo of Aquino was tortured and put to death by order of the Emperor. Saint Thomas no doubt remembered these events when he wrote the article of the *Summa* in which he affirmed, in conformity with the Church's teaching, her right to depose prince or emperor—a striking instance of her power of intervention in politics for the safeguarding of the spiritual. (*Sum. theol.*, II-II, 12, 2.)

[3] *Sum. theol.*, II-II, 189, 6.

[4] As Father Mandonnet has established, this event, like the imprisonment at Roccasecca, has been a bit embellished by the first historians. If they have added some-

thing of the picturesque to the capture of Thomas by his
brothers, the reality which they thus embroider, that is,
the reality of the constraint undergone, remains nevertheless incontestable, and it is in vain that one would try
to remove from these incidents every trace of brutality.
That Thomas, who had lived in Naples according to the
state of a young noble of his time, knew very well how to
mount a horse, we have no doubt. In the circumstances,
and after the fight he had to put up to prevent being
stripped of his habit, it is very likely that he carried on the
resistance up to the very end, and that they had, as the
old accounts report it, to set him on the horse by force.

⁵ He composed at that time, for his old fellow-students
in the Faculty of Arts, the two *opuscula*, *De Propositionibus Modalibus* and *De Fallaciis*.

⁶ According to Mandonnet, the commentary on the
Divine Names would have been composed later (about
1261). It seems, according to some very serious arguments
which Father Théry has been kind enough to share with
me, that this work dated from the youth of Saint Thomas
and would have to have been written before 1256, perhaps
even at Cologne, about 1248-1250. It is to this work that
Tocco would be alluding when he says that Thomas, the
dumb ox, began to *legere* when he was at Cologne.

⁷ Sermon *De vetula*.

⁸ *Ps.* 103, 13.

⁹ On the team of secretaries who worked for Saint
Thomas, see the excellent book by Antoine Dondaine, O.P.,
Secrétaires de Saint Thomas, Commissio leonina, Rome,
Sainte-Sabine, 1956 (Note to the second edition).

¹⁰ According to Grabmann (*Mittelalterliches Geistesle-
ben*, 1926, ch. VIII), the commentaries on the Physics, the
Metaphysics, the Ethics and the Politics were composed
after the year 1268.

¹¹ According to the latest works of Father Mandonnet
(cf. *Revue Thomiste*, 1927, p. 157, and the Introduction
to the latest edition of the *Opuscula* [Lethielleux]), the
Compendium was composed in the years 1272-1273. The
Sermons to students are also of this period.

¹² "In the middle of the Church the Lord opened his
mouth." *Introit* of the Common of Doctors (cf. Eccl. 15/5).

¹³ This sentence is borrowed from a line of the French

poet Mallarmé: "tel qu'en lui-même enfin l'éternité le change" (such as into himself at last eternity changes him). [Translator's note.]

[14] A saying of Cajetan taken up by Leo XIII and Pius XI.

[15] H. Woroniecki.

[16] According to Dom Baudot (*Dict. d'Hagiographie*, p. 387), Julienne du Mont-Cornillon died the 5th of April, 1255.

[17] Such is at least the opinion of Father Mandonnet in his work on *Siger de Brabant*. According to Father Chossat (*Revue de Philosophie*, 1914, XXIV and XXV), it is the *De anima intellectiva* of Siger which was an answer to Saint Thomas' *De unitate intellectus*, itself written against another work of Siger, *Super III° de Anima*.

[18] The divine touch had been too profound to permit him to give himself thenceforth to his ordinary works. Nevertheless, he forced himself to compose, on his way to the Council of Lyons, his brief *Responsio ad Bernardum abbatem;* and on his deathbed he did for the monks of Fossanova his second commentary (now lost) on the *Canticle of Canticles*. (I say his *second* commentary, not his *third*, for of the two commentaries attributed to Saint Thomas only one is authentic.)

[19] *Ps.* 131, 14.

[20] My book appeared before the pontificate of Pius XII. I am happy to be offered by this new edition an opportunity to mention his important statements on the matter (see Appendix II and Appendix III). (Note to the second edition.)

CHAPTER II

[1] The same remarks and the same doubts about the metaphysical authenticity of the doctrines in question are clearly valid for the existentialist movement which later developed in Germany and in France as an offshoot of phenomenology (Note to the second edition).

[2] Cf. *Primauté du spirituel*, p. 8.

[3] I do not mean by this that regional and linguistic particularism does not correspond to conditions which the

statesman is bound to take into account. I mean that this particularism cannot constitute a political *end* or circumscribe the proper object of politics.

⁴ As to the idea of a "primitive mentality" essentially different from civilized mentality, Lucien Lévy-Bruhl himself explicitly rejected it. Cf. my book *Quatre essais sur l'esprit dans sa condition charnelle,* 2nd ed., Paris, Alsatia, 1956, pp. 10-11 (Note to the second edition).

⁵ *Primauté du spirituel,* pp. 145-147.

⁶ *Ibid.,* p. 164.

⁷ The exact title was *The Light of the East* (published from 30 Park Street, Calcutta).

⁸ *Bulletins de la Classe des Lettres et des Sciences morales et politiques de l'Académie Royale de Belgique* (*"Indianisme": Discours de M. Louis de la Vallée Poussin,* 9th May, 1928). We recall that Father de Nobili, in his various treatises in Tamil or Sanskrit, also propounded Christian wisdom—and the arguments of Saint Thomas— under Hindu modes of thought. For example, criticizing in his treatise on the soul, *Attumanirunayam,* the doctrine of transmigration, "he opposes with perfect ease the Aristotelian concept of form, of the *principium vitae,* to the Brahminical idea of the soul imprisoned in the body like a bird in a cage: 'When a man dwells in a house, does the house grow with him? When he is not at home, does the house fall to bits?' All through the book we find Brahminical allegories and legends woven into the woof of the argument" (Pierre Dahmen, *Un jésuite brahme, Robert de Nobili,* Brussels, 1925).

⁹ More recent examples could be cited: I am thinking of the remarkable works of Olivier Lacombe on Hindu philosophy and of Louis Gardet on Islam, and of their studies of comparative mysticism. The book *Introduction à la Théologie Musulmane* (Paris, Vrin, 1948), by Louis Gardet and M. M. Anawati, was given a very favorable reception in Musulman circles (Note to the second edition).

¹⁰ To the order of the *spiritual* par excellence, that is to say, of the supernatural spiritual.

¹¹ In the vocabulary of French philosophers these two words are almost synonymous, whereas many German and Russian thinkers distinguish *civilization* from *culture,* understanding by the first term, taken in a pejorative sense,

a development above all *material* of social life. In the sense in which we understand it, a civilization merits this name only if it is a culture, a development truly human and therefore principally intellectual, moral and spiritual (taking the word "spiritual" in its widest acceptation).

[12] Charles Journet.

[13] Cf. "Le Thomisme et la civilisation" in *Revue de Philosophie,* March-April, 1928, pp. 138-139.

[14] *Primauté du spirituel,* p. 124. In Father Allo's book on the *Apocalypse,* we find the following remarks, which seem to me very deserving of our attention: "If this is so [if the figure 42, equal to 3 x 14, is a Messianic figure], there follows from this a consequence of great importance for exegesis: *in the Apocalypse, the duration of the power of evil on earth is represented by a Messianic figure.* In other words, the terrestrial phase of the Kingdom of God, that of the conquests of the Gospel, entirely coincides with the last and the most violent efforts of Satan to oppose this Kingdom. What we had already dimly perceived in regard to 3½—the time of the persecutions and of the ministry of Christ—is singularly confirmed by 42.

". . . This fusion of the most sinister prospects with the most glowing aspects of the present and the future is in no way inadmissible *a priori.* It was not inadmissible in Jewish circles, to judge from the statements of various rabbis, that the days of the Messiah were to know more than one calamity. Khiya ben Nehemia depicts the days of the Messiah as so sad in one respect that it would be impossible to distinguish guilt from innocence. (Koheleth rabba, XII, I; but similar ideas are already to be found in the Talmud. Cf. Volz, pp. 62-63; Lagrange, *Le Messianisme chez les Juifs,* pp. 99-115.) The idea was to be just as familiar to Christians who referred to the Gospel.

". . . Besides, in our Apocalypse itself, we have already seen the two aspects continually mingled: the beneficent Horseman of VI, 2 goes forth to conquer spiritually *at the same time* as the other horsemen will be spreading disaster; the elect of God, in VII, will be preserved *at the same time* as the great tribulation, etc. (Cf. infra, Ch. XII.) It is the quite simple transposition of the *sufferings of the Messiah* to the preparation for the Second Coming." E. B. Allo, *L'Apocalypse de saint Jean* (Paris, Gabalda, 1921), pp. 145-146.

CHAPTER III

[1] This chapter is taken from a conference (the text, to avoid repetitions, has been somewhat revised and compressed) given at Avignon, October 20, 1923, during the course of a triduum arranged by the Archbishop of Avignon to celebrate the sixth centenary of the canonization of Saint Thomas.

[2] "If your eye is worthless, your whole body will be in darkness." Matt. 6/23; Luke 11/34.

[3] "And the truth shall make you free." John 8/32.

[4] Pius XI, Encyclical *Studiorum Ducem*.

[5] As Father Petitot rightly observes, Saint Thomas, who had a passage from the *Collationes* of Cassian read to him daily, may be said to have remained deeply imbued with Benedictine spirituality, so little introverted, so little preoccupied with "psychology."

[6] "This is a hard saying." John, 6/61.

[7] Cf. Father Garrigou-Lagrange, "La première donnée de l'intelligence" in *Mélanges thomistes, 1923.*

[8] "Wisdom preaches in the open spaces, she cries in the streets." Prov. 1/20.

[9] "Unless you become as little children." Matt. 18/3.

CHAPTER IV

[1] *Sum. theol.*, I, 1, 8, ad 2.

[2] Cf. Denzinger-Bannwart, 1797, 1799, 1674, 1682, 1714; 1681, 1786 (Cf. Vacant, *Etudes théologiques sur le Concile du Vatican,* I, p. 347; St. Thomas Aquinas, *Sum. theol.*, I, 1, 1; *Sum. contra Gent.*, I, 4; Garrigou-Lagrange, *De Revelatione,* I, pp. 411-415); 1798, 1674; 1683-1684.

[3] "Even during Thomas' lifetime, he received from Alexander IV a letter in which the Pope did not hesitate to write: 'To Our Beloved son, Thomas Aquinas, distinguished alike for nobility of blood and for the radiance of his virtues, to whom the grace of God has accorded the treasure of the science of the Scriptures'." Pius XI, Encyclical *Studiorum Ducem*.

⁴ J. J. Berthier, *Sanctus Thomas Aquinas "Doctor Communis" Ecclesiae,* vol. I, *Testimonia Ecclesiae,* Romae, 1914.

⁵ Motu Proprio *Doctoris Angelici.* The words are taken up by Pius XI in the Encyclical *Studiorum Ducem.*

⁶ "The Franciscan school, at the instigation of Scotus and with the enthusiastic support of the faithful, asserted with all its strength that the Mother of God had to be and was in fact immaculate. It was a matter of reaching by any course this port which their ardent love for the Most Holy Virgin made them desire so intensely: hence they were more concerned with speeding up the ship and quickening the journey than with plotting the exact course.

"St. Thomas and his school, accustomed to applying the brake of reason to the emotions and to not risking an advance over the mysterious terrain of dogma without first drawing light from the beacon of already defined dogmas, asserted no less strenuously that the Mother of God, like every child of Adam, had to be really and personally redeemed by the Blood of Calvary, and that they were ready to block the way of the Mother of God even, so long as they would not consider her as unreservedly involved in the way of *personal debt,* the only one which motivates redemption by the blood of Jesus Christ.

"Exposed to this dual influence—the Scotist fervor and the Thomist rudder—the barque of the Immaculate made slow but steady progress for centuries. Without Scotus and his school it would never have moved at all, or at any rate would have made but little progress; without the intervention of St. Thomas and his disciples it would certainly have lost its way. After God and His Church, it is to Scotus and his school that we are indebted for the definition of the *Immaculate* Conception, but it is to St. Thomas and his disciples that we owe the definition of the *true* Immaculate Conception." F. Marin-Sola, *L'Evolution homogène du dogme catholique,* Fribourg, 1924, vol. I, pp. 327-328.

See above all, on this question, Father del Prado's *Divus Thomas et Bulla Dogmatica "Ineffabilis Deus"* (Fribourg, 1919). What St. Thomas teaches (against certain erroneous ways of arguing for the Immaculate Conception) is that the Mother of the Savior was *redeemed,* she too, by the merits of her Son, and that we must recognize in her *all* degrees of purity, *provided they be compatible* with her redemption by Jesus Christ. All that is then required is a more explicit statement, together with the addition that this redemption was a *preserving* redemption (presupposing not sin, but the *debitum,* the personal and proximate debt remitted by the foreseen merits of Christ at the very moment of creation and infusion of the soul), for us to have the notion of the Immaculate Conception such as the Church has defined it, a notion expressed very precisely in the Oration of the Mass for the feast of December 8: *"Deus . . . qui ex morte ejusdem Filii tui praevisa, eam ab omni labe praeservasti . . ."* ("God, Who by the foreseen death of Thy son, preserved her from all stain.")

[7] See the Appendices, p. 183.

[8] Letter of December 12, 1884, to M. Pidal.

[9] November 25, 1898.

[10] December 30, 1892.

[11] From Father Janvier's essay, *Action intellectuelle et politique de Léon XIII en France.*

[12] Col. 2/8.

[13] *Thomas von Aquino und Kant, ein Kampf zweier Welten, Kantstudien,* VI, 1901.

[14] Pius XII's encyclical *Humani Generis*—published many years after the writing of this book—appears in Appendix III of the present edition. (Note to the second edition.)

[15] Leo XIII, Encyclical *Aeterni Patris.*

[16] See the Appendices (III, p. 215) for the full text of this *Motu Proprio.*

[17] Can. 1366, par. 2.—To make exception for the customs and traditions peculiar to the Oriental Church, the first canon of the Code of Canon Law states that the Code applies only to the Latin Church. The juridical obligation to make St. Thomas the basis of studies does not therefore extend, by the letter of the Code, to the Eastern Church. But what is here important to consider above all is the thought and the desire of the Church, of which its laws are the expression adapted to time and place. And there is no doubt but that in the mind of the Church it is in the light of the principles of St. Thomas that the wisdom of the Greek Fathers and of the Oriental traditions must also be understood and systematized. The teachings and exhorta-

tions of the Popes on this subject have an absolutely universal bearing.

[18] Encyclical *Fausto appetente die,* for the seventh centenary of the death of St. Dominic (June 29, 1921).—See also the testimony given to St. Thomas, whose philosophy is *according to Christ,* in the Motu Proprio *Non Multo* on the Roman Academy of St. Thomas: "But since We, in common with Our Predecessors, are perfectly convinced that We should be concerned only with that philosophy which is *according to Christ (Col.,* II, 8), and that consequently We are bound to insist altogether on the study of philosophy itself according to the principles and method of Aquinas . . ."

[19] August 1, 1922.

[20] Encyclical *Aeterni Patris.*

[21] Let us quote also the following lines, concerning theology: "What We say of philosophy must likewise be said of theology. This follows from these words of Sixtus V: 'This most salutary science flows from the most fertile fountains of the Divine Scriptures, the acts of the Popes, the works of the Fathers, and the decisions of the Councils; the knowledge and the use of theology have always been a powerful aid for the Church, either to understand and to interpret with exactitude and fidelity the Scriptures themselves, or to read and explain the Fathers with more surety and more fruit, or to discover and refute the different errors and heresies. But it is especially in our day, when we live in those times full of perils described by the Apostle, when blasphemous, arrogant and seductive men unceasingly progress in evil, plunged in error and dragging others into it, that this science is supremely necessary for confirming the dogmas of the Catholic Faith and refuting the heresies.' (Bull *Triumphantis,* 1588.)

"Now what is it that makes theology a discipline possessing the force of a science truly worthy of the name, capable of providing, in the admirable words of Our lamented Predecessor Pope Benedict XV (Motu Proprio *De Romana Sancti Thomae Academia,* 1914), 'an explanation as complete as human reason permits and a victorious defense of the truth revealed by God'? It is the Scholastic philosophy, and it alone, employed under the guidance and leadership of St. Thomas Aquinas and put at the service of theology. It is it that furnishes 'that exact and solid connection of things with each other and with their principles, that order and disposition which make one think of an army drawn up in battle array, those luminous definitions and distinctions, that solidity in argument and that subtlety in controversy, all that ensemble which separates light from darkness and truth from error, and which denounces and lays bare the falsehoods of the heretics by ripping off the mask of illusions and sophisms with which they cover themselves' (Sixtus V, *loc. cit.*).

"They, consequently, understand wrongly the education of young clerics, who, setting aside the Scholastic method, think that one ought to give the whole theological teaching according to what is known as the *positive* method; and those teachers fail still more in their duty who have their whole course in theology consist of going over, in learned disquisitions, the list of dogmas and heresies. The positive method is the necessary complement of the Scholastic method, but it does not suffice by itself alone. Our clergy must be armed not only for establishing the truth of the Faith but also for explaining and defending it. But to review, in chronological order, the dogmas of the Faith and the opposed errors, is to teach ecclesiastical history, not theology." (*Ibid.*, August 1, 1922.)

[22] Encyclical *Studiorum Ducem*. See the Appendices (III, pp. 222) for the full text of the encyclical.

One may consult with profit the remarkable commentary on this encyclical by Father Benoït Lavaud: *Saint Thomas guide des études*, Paris, Téqui, 1925.

[23] As regards theology, let us note these remarkable lines which show how this science asks of itself to be completed in contemplation:

"A man is not said to know a country thoroughly if he just knows some description, even a detailed description, of it, but only if he has lived in that country for some time; so also no one acquires an intimate knowledge of God by scientific investigation alone, if he does not live likewise in an intimate union with Him."

And on the theological work of St. Thomas:

"First of all, he established apologetics on its true bases, determining clearly the distinction between the truths of reason and those of faith, between the natural order and the supernatural order. Also, when the Vatican Council defines the possibility of knowing some truths of religion by the lights of reason, the moral necessity of a divine revelation with certitude and without error, and finally the absolute necessity of a revelation if we are to know the mysteries, it employs arguments borrowed from St. Thomas only. Thomas expects that all the apologists of Catholic dogma hold as sacred this principle: 'to give assent to the truths of faith is not arbitrariness, even though they are above reason' (*Contra Gent.* I, 6). He shows indeed that however mysterious and obscure the truths of faith may be, the reasons at least which impel man to believe are clear and manifest, so that 'he would not believe if he did not see that it is necessary to believe' (I-II, 1, 4). He adds that, far from considering faith as an impediment or a yoke of burden imposed on humanity, we must look upon it as a most precious gift, since 'faith is in us as a kind of beginning of eternal life' (*De Verit.*, XIV, 2).

"The second part of theology, which has to do with the explanation of dogma, is also examined by St. Thomas with exceptional richness. No one has penetrated more deeply or expounded more wisely all the sacred mysteries, especially the intimate life of God, the abyss of eternal predestination, the supernatural government of the world, the power afforded rational natures of attaining their end, the redemption of the human race effected by Jesus Christ and continued by the Church and the Sacraments, those two 'relics of the divine Incarnation,' as the holy Doctor put it.

"In morals, too, Thomas established a solid theological doctrine, aimed at directing all our acts in a manner appropriate to our supernatural end. And because he is, as We have said, the perfect theologian, he assigns the steady purposes and the rules of life which must guide not only the individual in his personal life, but also the family and civil society, which latter are the objects, respectively, of those divisions of moral science that are 'economics' and politics."

[We may observe that these few lines, affirming so unmistakably the principle of the subordination of politics to morals and to the theological light, pointed out beforehand in the doctrine of St. Thomas the remedy for the *political naturalism* since condemned by the Supreme Pontiff.]

"And We have then, in the second part of the *Summa Theologiae*, those admirable teachings on paternal or domestic government, lawful power in bodies politic or nations, natural law and the law of nations, peace and war, justice and property, laws and their observance, the duty of helping individuals in their needs and of co-operating for the well-being of the political community, and this in the natural order and in the supernatural order.

"The day when, in private life, in public life and in the relationships between nations and nations, these rules would be religiously and inviolably observed, nothing else would be required for men to be assured of that 'peace in Christ through the reign of Christ' for which the whole world longs so ardently."

Thus does the Encyclical *Studiorum Ducem* itself describe the office of *wise architect* incumbent upon the Angelic Doctor in regard to the restoration of Christian culture in the modern world.

[24] Cf. the anti-Modernist oath prescribed by Pius X (Motu Proprio *Sacrorum Antistitum,* September 1, 1910).

[25] By common sense I mean here the understanding of first principles, and the first rational certitudes which follow, as an endowment of nature, upon the spontaneous exercise of reason. From this common sense as natural *intellection* must carefully be distinguished common sense as primitive *imagery,* which pictures the earth as flat, the sun as revolving around the earth, the upper and the lower as absolute properties of space, etc., and which has no philosophical value.

[26] Cf. Garrigou-Lagrange, *Le Sens commun, la philosophie de l'être et les formules dogmatiques,* 3rd ed., Paris, Desclée de Brouwer.

[27] Cf. A. D. Sertillanges, *Revue des Jeunes,* August 25, 1921.

[28] Cf. note 18 above.

[29] Cf. above, p. 136.

[30] See above, p. 137.

[31] These twenty-four theses have been explained and commented on in a work by Father Mattiussi: *Le XXIV tesi della filosofia di S. Tommaso d'Aquino*, 2 ed., Roma, 1925; translated into French by Father Levillain under the title: *Les points fondamentaux de la philosophie thomiste*, Torino (Marietti), 1926. See also Father Hugon's *Les vingt-quatre thèses thomistes*, 7e éd., Paris (Téqui), 1937.

[32] Pius XI, Encyclical *Studiorum Ducem*.

MERIDIAN BOOKS

17 Union Square West, New York 3, New York

Titles listed here are not necessarily available in the British Empire.

Titles listed here are not necessarily available in the British Empire.

LIVING AGE BOOKS

Published by MERIDIAN BOOKS INC.
17 Union Square West, New York 3, New York

LIVING AGE BOOKS, an inexpensive paperbound series, contains works of proven merit on history, art, literature, theology and Biblical studies, as they illuminate the development of Christian tradition in the West.

Titles listed here are not necessarily available in the British Empire.

MERIDIAN BOOKS

17 Union Square West, New York 3, New York

Titles listed here are not necessarily available in the British Empire.